D0436555

The Beacon Book of

Essays by Contemporary American Women

The Beacon Book of

Essays by Contemporary American Women

NATIONAL UNIVERSITY
LIBRARY   SACRAMENTO

THE BEACON BOOK OF

Essays by
Contemporary American Women

Edited by Wendy Martin

with the editorial assistance of

Thomas Allen, Kimberly Cortner,

Rochelle Johnson, and Jamie Marchant

BEACON PRESS

BOSTON

Beacon Press
25 Beacon Street
Boston, Massachusetts 02108-2892

Beacon Press books
are published under the auspices of
the Unitarian Universalist Association of Congregations.

© 1996 by Wendy Martin
All rights reserved
Printed in the United States of America

99 98 97 96   8 7 6 5 4 3 2 1

Text design by Janis Owens
Composition by Wilsted & Taylor

Library of Congress Cataloging-in-Publication Data

The Beacon book of essays by contemporary American women / edited by
    Wendy Martin.
        p.   cm.
    Includes bibliographical references (p.   ) and index.
    ISBN 0-8070-6346-0
        1. American essays—Women authors.   2. Women—United States.
    I. Martin, Wendy, 1940–
    PS683.W65B43   1996
    814'.540809287—dc20   95-21117
                                                                        CIP

To

my daughter, Laurel Martin Harris,

my husband, Jed Harris,

and

my students at the Claremont Graduate School

CONTENTS

Contents

III. BREAKING THE SILENCE: WOMEN CONFRONT OPPRESSION AND VIOLENCE

IV. WOMEN'S BODIES, WOMEN'S CHOICES

V. WHAT THE LOVER KNOWS: ESSAYS ON NATURE

ACKNOWLEDGMENTS

I would like to thank the following students in the Department of English at the Claremont Graduate School for their help with this project: Laura Behling, Michael Ernest, Aracelly Friedman, and Trudy Kennedy. Kimberly Cortner, Rochelle Johnson, and Jamie Marchant collaborated in every phase of this project, and I am grateful for their hard work and good judgment. Special thanks go to Thomas Allen, who worked on this collection from the beginning and who understood the importance of capturing the scope and complexity of the lives of American women.

INTRODUCTION

An essay is a trial effort, an attempt at a proof which is imperfect and is partial, experimental, and subject to change. It presents a point of view, an individual perspective. By its nature, the essay form is suited to capturing the openness, complexity, and flux of the American experience. Whether expressing the depths of personal feeling or presenting a carefully analyzed political argument, the essay has proved to be a robust and flexible form. Its provisional, change-oriented approach has made the essay particularly suitable to the articulation of women's lives.

The essay has served American women writers especially well. Certainly, the essay has been crucial to women gaining a voice in democratic discourse and the process of social change. The essay has been the means by which women in the United States—Judith Sargent Murray, Margaret Fuller, and Charlotte Perkins Gilman, to name a few of the earliest—made their personal feelings and political commitments known to the widest possible audience. It has been instrumental in helping women to transcend the stigma of participating in public life. Even when it was considered unfeminine for women to speak or write for a public audience, American women often published essays using pseudonyms or under the category "Anonymous." The periodical literature just before and after the American Revolution is filled with essays by women using pen-names on the subject of freedom and the meaning of liberty, especially in the context of women's rights.

Questions about the nature of womanhood and the rights of women have been asked since the founding of the new nation, and these questions have usually been framed in the essay. Using the pseudonym "Constantia," Judith Sargent Murray, one of the most outstanding women essayists of the early years of the new Republic, wrote on a wide range of subjects including women's right to vote, to hold property whether married or single, to divorce, and to have lives that paralleled those of men.

The early widespread use of pseudonyms reflects the bias against women speaking out in the public sphere. This prejudice against women who presented their ideas and opinions from the lecture podium or in print is rooted in the notion that woman was a private creature whose place was in the home. It was widely believed in Victorian America that women were inherently more delicate than men and therefore were unfit for the rigors of public life and public discourse. It was also believed that the womb and brain were inversely related; that is, energy required by the mental activity of reading and writing impaired the reproductive capacity of women. A thinking woman—that is, a woman who wrote or spoke in public about political or personal issues—was an aberration of nature.

Defying customs that held that women should not move beyond the private sphere of the home, nineteenth-century American suffragettes including Lucy Stone, Amelia Bloomer, Susan B. Anthony, and Elizabeth Cady Stanton wrote essays about the importance of the enfranchisement of women. They had to fight extraordinary opposition. Listen, for example, to Orestes Brownson, who argued in "The Woman Question," published in 1873, that women are best suited to be the comforters of men and that they are not "fit to have their own head," that a man commits a grievous error when he abdicates control by allowing himself to be "governed, we might say, deprived of his reason, by woman, herself seduced by the serpent that man fell, and brought sin and woe into the world":

> She has all the qualities that fit her to be a help-meet of man, to be the mother of his children, to be their nurse, their early guardian, their life-long friend; to be his companion, his comforter, his consoler in sorrow, his friend in trouble, his ministering angel in sickness; but as an independent existence, free to follow her own fancies and vague longings, her own ambition and natural love of power, without masculine direction or control, she is out of her element, and a

social anomaly, sometimes a hideous monster, which men seldom are, excepting through a woman's influence. This is no excuse for men, but it proves that women need a head, and the restraint of father, husband, or priest of God.

In spite of the widespread disapproval of the public display of opinion by women, American women persisted in writing essays. Perhaps the most celebrated female essayist after Judith Sargent Murray was Margaret Fuller, whose treatises on the nature of masculinity and femininity are still read with much interest today. Fuller's essays were first published in the *Dial* magazine and then expanded and published as *The Great Lawsuit* in 1843 and as *Woman in the Nineteenth Century* in 1845. Like her predecessors, Fuller asks that women be granted the wider life enjoyed by men. In the twentieth century, Crystal Eastman, Margaret Sanger, Betty Friedan, Kate Millet, Adrienne Rich, and Gloria Steinem, among others, have extended these arguments using the essay form.

The essays in this collection celebrate the diversity of American women's experiences while affirming the individuality of each writer. The writers are old and young, rich and poor, healthy and sick, reclusive and politically active, adventurous and timid, lesbian and heterosexual. Written from the perspective of women who are single, married, divorced, widowed, grandmothers, mothers, daughters, aunts, sisters, these essays also represent a wide range of ethnic and racial perspectives—Asian-American, Afro-American, Hispanic, and native American.

Some essays such as Nancy Mairs's "Here: Grace" capture the immediacy of a particular woman's experience in a local context; others such as Betty Friedan's "Thoughts on Becoming a Grandmother" or Alice Walker's "Brothers and Sisters" or Sandra Cisneros's "Only Daughter" express broader familial concerns. Margaret Mead's "On Having a Baby" is grounded in intergenerational maternal experience. Anne Taylor Fleming's "Sperm in a Jar" addresses previously unknown reproductive choices created by technology. Mary McCarthy's "Names," Joan Didion's "On Going Home," and Mary Gordon's "A Moral Choice" are written in a formal and elegant style; other essays such as Barbara Mor's "Amazing Rage" are informal, even conversational. And some, as in the case of Felicita Garcia's "I Just Came Out Pregnant," broaden the definition of how we speak and write about our experiences, challenging the boundaries of traditional literacy itself.

Several of the pieces in this collection are not essays in the classic sense in that they do not make an argument or attempt a proof; they are efforts, sometimes tentative efforts, to provide insights into experiences that are rarely or never given voice. It is in this *process* of being articulated that women's experiences often gain a recognizable form and substance; in other words, through the process of writing, women's lives take shape and find direction. The confessional mode of many of these essays is characteristic of much contemporary writing by both women and men; this emphasis on subjective experience serves women well by providing an opportunity for women to recover and revision their lives.

Representing a range of women's experiences since 1945, this collection offers an extraordinary diversity of perspectives; at the same time, by writing these essays, these women are defining our lives in all their complexity, multiplicity, contradictions, and commonalities. Through the collective effort of women writers in general, and women essayists in particular, we probe the realities and anticipate the possibilities of female experience. Not only do the essays in this collection provide a chronicle of women's experiences in the second half of the twentieth century, they also indicate potential future directions for women's lives. In this sense, this writing provides a map of the territory we have already explored and a guide for the lives we have yet to live.

The Beacon Book of

Essays by Contemporary American Women

PART ONE

Generations

Essays on the Family

> *Fortunately, I happen to be rebellious in nature,*
>
> *and enjoy the challenge of disproving*
>
> *assumptions made about me.*
>
> AMY TAN

JOAN DIDION

On Going Home

I am home for my daughter's first birthday. By "home" I do not mean the house in Los Angeles where my husband and I and the baby live, but the place where my family is, in the Central Valley of California. It is a vital although troublesome distinction. My husband likes my family but is uneasy in their house, because once there I fall into their ways, which are difficult, oblique, deliberately inarticulate, not my husband's ways. We live in dusty houses ("D-U-S-T," he once wrote with his finger on surfaces all over the house, but no one noticed it) filled with mementos quite without value to him (what could the Canton dessert plates mean to him? how could he have known about the assay scales, why should he care if he did know?), and we appear to talk exclusively about people we know who have been committed to mental hospitals, about people we know who have been booked on drunk-driving charges, and about property, particularly about property, land, price per acre and C-2 zoning and assessments and freeway access. My brother does not understand my husband's inability to perceive the advantage in the rather common real-estate transaction known as "sale-leaseback," and my husband in turn does not understand why so many of the people he hears about in my father's house have recently been committed to mental hospitals or booked on drunk-driving charges. Nor does he understand that when we talk about

3

sale-leasebacks and right-of-way condemnations we are talking in code about the things we like best, the yellow fields and the cottonwoods and the rivers rising and falling and the mountain roads closing when the heavy snow comes in. We miss each other's points, have another drink, and regard the fire. My brother refers to my husband, in his presence, as "Joan's husband." Marriage is the classic betrayal.

Or perhaps it is not anymore. Sometimes I think that those of us who are now in our thirties were born into the last generation to carry the burden of "home," to find in family life the source of all tension and drama. I had by all objective accounts a "normal" and a "happy" family situation, and yet I was almost thirty years old before I could talk to my family on the telephone without crying after I had hung up. We did not fight. Nothing was wrong. And yet some nameless anxiety colored the emotional charges between me and the place that I came from. The question of whether or not you could go home again was a very real part of the sentimental and largely literary baggage with which we left home in the fifties; I suspect that it is irrelevant to the children born of the fragmentation after World War II. A few weeks ago in a San Francisco bar I saw a pretty young girl on crystal take off her clothes and dance for the cash prize in an "amateur-topless" contest. There was no particular sense of moment about this, none of the effect of romantic degradation, of "dark journey," for which my generation strived so assiduously. What sense could that girl possibly make of, say, *Long Day's Journey into Night*? Who is beside the point?

That I am trapped in this particular irrelevancy is never more apparent to me than when I am home. Paralyzed by the neurotic lassitude engendered by meeting one's past at every turn, around every corner, inside every cupboard, I go aimlessly from room to room. I decide to meet it head-on and clean out a drawer, and I spread the contents on the bed. A bathing suit I wore the summer I was seventeen. A letter of rejection from *The Nation*, an aerial photograph of the site for a shopping center my father did not build in 1954. Three teacups hand-painted with cabbage roses and signed "E.M.," my grandmother's initials. There is no final solution for letters of rejection from *The Nation* and teacups hand-painted in 1900. Nor is there any answer to snapshots of one's grandfather as a young man on skis, surveying around Donner Pass in the year 1910. I smooth out the snapshot and look into his face, and do and do not see my own. I close the drawer, and have another cup of coffee with my mother. We get along very well, veterans of a guerrilla war we never understood.

Days pass. I see no one. I come to dread my husband's evening call, not only because he is full of news of what by now seems to me our remote life in Los Angeles, people he has seen, letters which require attention, but because he asks what I have been doing, suggests uneasily that I get out, drive to San Francisco or Berkeley. Instead I drive across the river to a family graveyard. It has been vandalized since my last visit and the monuments are broken, overturned in the dry grass. Because I once saw a rattlesnake in the grass I stay in the car and listen to a country-and-Western station. Later I drive with my father to a ranch he has in the foothills. The man who runs his cattle on it asks us to the roundup, a week from Sunday, and although I know that I will be in Los Angeles I say, in the oblique way my family talks, that I will come. Once home I mention the broken monuments in the graveyard. My mother shrugs.

I go to visit my great-aunts. A few of them think now that I am my cousin, or their daughter who died young. We recall an anecdote about a relative last seen in 1948, and they ask if I still like living in New York City. I have lived in Los Angeles for three years, but I say that I do. The baby is offered a horehound drop, and I am slipped a dollar bill "to buy a treat." Questions trail off, answers are abandoned, the baby plays with the dust motes in a shaft of afternoon sun.

It is time for the baby's birthday party: a white cake, strawberry-marshmallow ice cream, a bottle of champagne saved from another party. In the evening, after she has gone to sleep, I kneel beside the crib and touch her face, where it is pressed against the slats, with mine. She is an open and trusting child, unprepared for and unaccustomed to the ambushes of family life, and perhaps it is just as well that I can offer her little of that life. I would like to give her more. I would like to promise her that she will grow up with a sense of her cousins and of rivers and of her great-grandmother's teacups, would like to pledge her a picnic on a river with fried chicken and her hair uncombed, would like to give her *home* for her birthday, but we live differently now and I can promise her nothing like that. I give her a xylophone and a sundress from Madeira, and promise to tell her a funny story.

1968

ALICE WALKER

Brothers and Sisters

We lived on a farm in the South in the fifties, and my brothers, the four of them I knew (the fifth had left home when I was three years old), were allowed to watch animals being mated. This was not unusual; nor was it considered unusual that my older sister and I were frowned upon if we even asked, innocently, what was going on. One of my brothers explained the mating one day, using words my father had given him: "The bull is getting a little something on his stick," he said. And he laughed. "What stick?" I wanted to know. "Where did he get it? How did he pick it up? Where did he put it?" All my brothers laughed.

I believe my mother's theory about raising a large family of five boys and three girls was that the father should teach the boys and the mother teach the girls the facts, as one says, of life. So my father went around talking about bulls getting something on their sticks and she went around saying girls did not need to know about such things. They were "womanish" (a very bad way to be in those days) if they asked.

The thing was, watching the matings filled my brothers with an aimless sort of lust, as dangerous as it was unintentional. They knew enough to know that cows, months after mating, produced calves, but they were not bright enough to make the same connection between women and their offspring.

6

Sometimes, when I think of my childhood, it seems to me a particularly hard one. But in reality, everything awful that happened to me didn't seem to happen to *me* at all, but to my older sister. Through some incredible power to negate my presence around people I did not like, which produced invisibility (as well as an ability to appear mentally vacant when I was nothing of the kind), I was spared the humiliation she was subjected to, though at the same time, I felt every bit of it. It was as if she suffered for my benefit, and I vowed early in my life that none of the things that made existence so miserable for her would happen to me.

The fact that she was not allowed at official matings did not mean she never saw any. While my brothers followed my father to the mating pens on the other side of the road near the barn, she stationed herself near the pigpen, or followed our many dogs until they were in a mating mood, or, failing to witness something there, she watched the chickens. On a farm it is impossible *not* to be conscious of sex, to wonder about it, to dream . . . but to whom was she to speak of her feelings? Not to my father, who thought all young women perverse. Not to my mother, who pretended all her children grew out of stumps she magically found in the forest. Not to me, who never found anything wrong with this lie.

When my sister menstruated she wore a thick packet of clean rags between her legs. It stuck out in front like a penis. The boys laughed at her as she served them at the table. Not knowing any better, and because our parents did not dream of actually *discussing* what was going on, she would giggle nervously at herself. I hated her for giggling, and it was at those times I would think of her as dim-witted. She never complained, but she began to have strange fainting fits whenever she had her period. Her head felt as if it were splitting, she said, and everything she ate came up again. And her cramps were so severe she could not stand. She was forced to spend several days of each month in bed.

My father expected all of his sons to have sex with women. "Like bulls," he said, "a man *needs* to get a little something on his stick." And so, on Saturday nights, into town they went, chasing the girls. My sister was rarely allowed into town alone, and if the dress she wore fit too snugly at the waist, or if her cleavage dipped too far below her collarbone, she was made to stay home.

"But why can't I go too," she would cry, her face screwed up with the effort not to wail.

7

"They're boys, your brothers, *that's* why they can go."

Naturally, when she got the chance, she responded eagerly to boys. But when this was discovered she was whipped and locked up in her room.

I would go in to visit her.

"Straight Pine," she would say, "you don't know what it *feels* like to want to be loved by a man."

"And if this is what you get for feeling like it I never will," I said, with—I hoped—the right combination of sympathy and disgust.

"Men smell so good," she would whisper ecstatically. "And when they look into your eyes, you just melt."

Since they were so hard to catch, naturally she thought almost any of them terrific.

"Oh, that Alfred!" she would moon over some mediocre, square-headed boy, "he's so *sweet!*" And she would take his ugly picture out of her bosom and kiss it.

My father was always warning her not to come home if she ever found herself pregnant. My mother constantly reminded her that abortion was a sin. Later, although she never became pregnant, her period would not come for months at a time. The painful symptoms, however, never varied or ceased. She fell for the first man who loved her enough to beat her for looking at someone else, and when I was still in high school, she married him.

My fifth brother, the one I never knew, was said to be different from the rest. He had not liked matings. He would not watch them. He thought the cows should be given a choice. My father had disliked him because he was soft. My mother took up for him. "Jason is just tender-hearted," she would say in a way that made me know he was her favorite; "he takes after me." It was true that my mother cried about almost anything.

Who was this oldest brother? I wondered.

"Well," said my mother, "he was someone who always loved you. Of course he was a great big boy when you were born and out working on his own. He worked on a road gang building roads. Every morning before he left he would come in the room where you were and pick you up and give you the biggest kisses. He used to look at you and just smile. It's a pity you don't remember him."

I agreed.

At my father's funeral I finally "met" my oldest brother. He is tall and black with thick gray hair above a young-looking face. I watched my sister cry over my father until she blacked out from grief. I saw my brothers sobbing, reminding each other of what a great father he had been. My oldest brother and I did not shed a tear between us. When I left my father's grave he came up and introduced himself. "You don't ever have to walk alone," he said, and put his arms around me.

One out of five ain't *too* bad, I thought, snuggling up.

But I didn't discover until recently his true uniqueness: He is the only one of my brothers who assumes responsibility for all his children. The other four all fathered children during those Saturday-night chases of twenty years ago. Children—my nieces and nephews whom I will probably never know—they neither acknowledge as their own, provide for, or even see.

It was not until I became a student of women's liberation ideology that I could understand and forgive my father. I needed an ideology that would define his behavior in context. The black movement had given me an ideology that helped explain his colorism (he *did* fall in love with my mother partly because she was so light; he never denied it). Feminism helped explain his sexism. I was relieved to know his sexist behavior was not something uniquely his own, but, rather, an imitation of the behavior of the society around us.

All partisan movements add to the fullness of our understanding of society as a whole. They never detract; or, in any case, one must not allow them to do so. Experience adds to experience. "The more things the better," as O'Connor and Welty both have said, speaking, one of marriage, the other of Catholicism.

I desperately needed my father and brothers to give me male models I could respect, because white men (for example; being particularly handy in this sort of comparison)—whether in films or in person—offered man as dominator, as killer, and always as hypocrite.

My father failed because he copied the hypocrisy. And my brothers—except for one—never understood they must represent half the world to me, as I must represent the other half to them.

1975

SANDRA CISNEROS

Only Daughter

Once, several years ago, when I was just starting out my writing career, I was asked to write my own contributor's note for an anthology I was part of. I wrote: "I am the only daughter in a family of six sons. *That* explains everything."

Well, I've thought about that ever since, and yes, it explains a lot to me, but for the reader's sake I should have written: "I am the only daughter in a *Mexican* family of six sons." Or even: "I am the only daughter of a Mexican father and a Mexican-American mother." Or: "I am the only daughter of a working-class family of nine." All of these had everything to do with who I am today.

I was/am the only daughter and *only* a daughter. Being an only daughter in a family of six sons forced me by circumstance to spend a lot of time by myself because my brothers felt it beneath them to play with a *girl* in public. But that aloneness, that loneliness, was good for a would-be writer—it allowed me time to think and think, to imagine, to read and prepare myself.

Being only a daughter for my father meant my destiny would lead me to become someone's wife. That's what he believed. But when I was in fifth grade and shared my plans for college with him, I was sure he understood. I remember my father saying, "*Que bueno, mi'ja*, that's good." That meant a lot to me, especially since my brothers thought the idea hilarious. What I didn't realize was that my father thought college was good for girls—for finding a husband. After four years in college and two more in graduate school, and still no husband, my father shakes his head even now and says I wasted all that education.

In retrospect, I'm lucky my father believed daughters were meant for husbands. It meant it didn't matter if I majored in something silly like English. After all, I'd find a nice professional eventually, right? This allowed me the liberty to putter about embroidering my little poems and stories without my father interrupting with so much as a "What's that you're writing?"

But the truth is, I wanted him to interrupt. I wanted my father to understand what it was I was scribbling, to introduce me as "My only daughter, the writer." Not as "This is my only daughter. She teaches." *El maestra*—teacher. Not even *profesora*.

In a sense, everything I have ever written has been for him, to win his approval even though I know my father can't read English words, even though my father's only reading includes the brown-ink *Esto* sports magazines from Mexico City and the bloody *¡Alarma!* magazines that feature yet another sighting of *La Virgen de Guadalupe* on a tortilla or a wife's revenge on her philandering husband by bashing his skull in with a *molcajete* (a kitchen mortar made of volcanic rock). Or the *fotonovelas*, the little picture paperbacks with tragedy and trauma erupting from the characters' mouths in bubbles.

My father represents, then, the public majority. A public who is disinterested in reading, and yet one whom I am writing about and for, and privately trying to woo.

When we were growing up in Chicago, we moved a lot because of my father. He suffered periodic bouts of nostalgia. Then we'd have to let go our flat, store the furniture with mother's relatives, load the station wagon with baggage and bologna sandwiches, and head south. To Mexico City.

We came back, of course. To yet another Chicago flat, another Chicago neighborhood, another Catholic school. Each time, my father would seek out the parish priest in order to get a tuition break, and complain or boast: "I have seven sons."

He meant *siete hijos*, seven children, but he translated it as "sons." "I have seven sons." To anyone who would listen. The Sears Roebuck employee who sold us the washing machine. The short-order cook where my father ate his ham-and-eggs breakfasts. "I have seven sons." As if he deserved a medal from the state.

My papa. He didn't mean anything by that mistranslation, I'm sure. But somehow I could feel myself being erased. I'd tug my father's sleeve and whisper: "Not seven sons. Six! and *one daughter.*"

When my oldest brother graduated from medical school, he fulfilled my father's dream that we study hard and use this—our heads, instead of this—our hands. Even now my father's hands are thick and yellow, stubbed by a history of hammer and nails and twine and coils and springs. "Use this," my father said, tapping his head, "and not this," showing us those hands. He always looked tired when he said it.

Wasn't college an investment? And hadn't I spent all those years in college? And if I didn't marry, what was it all for? Why would anyone go to college and then choose to be poor? Especially someone who had always been poor.

Last year, after ten years of writing professionally, the financial rewards started to trickle in. My second National Endowment for the Arts Fellowship. A guest professorship at the University of California, Berkeley. My book, which sold to a major New York publishing house.

At Christmas, I flew home to Chicago. The house was throbbing, same as always; hot *tamales* and sweet *tamales* hissing in my mother's pressure cooker, and everybody—my mother, six brothers, wives, babies, aunts, cousins—talking too loud and at the same time, like in a Fellini film, because that's just how we are.

I went upstairs to my father's room. One of my stories had just been translated into Spanish and published in an anthology of Chicano writing, and I wanted to show it to him. Ever since he recovered from a stroke two years ago, my father likes to spend his leisure hours horizontally. And that's how I found him, watching a Pedro Infante movie on Galavision and eating rice pudding.

There was a glass filmed with milk on the bedside table. There were several vials of pills and balled Kleenex. And on the floor, one black sock and a plastic urinal that I didn't want to look at but looked at anyway. Pedro Infante was about to burst into song, and my father was laughing.

I'm not sure if it was because my story was translated into Spanish, or because it was published in Mexico, or perhaps because the story dealt with

Tepeyac, the *colonia* my father was raised in, but at any rate, my father punched the mute button on his remote control and read my story.

I sat on the bed next to my father and waited. He read it very slowly. As if he were reading each line over and over. He laughed at all the right places and read lines he liked out loud. He pointed and asked questions: "Is this So-and-so?" "Yes," I said. He kept reading.

When he was finally finished, after what seemed like hours, my father looked up and asked: "Where can we get more copies of this for the relatives?"

Of all the wonderful things that happened to me last year, that was the most wonderful.

1990

Ruth's Song

(Because She Could Not Sing It)

Happy or unhappy, families are all mysterious. We have only to imagine how differently we would be described—and will be, after our deaths—by each of the family members who believe they know us. The only question is, Why are some mysteries more important than others?

The fate of my Uncle Ed was a mystery of importance in our family. We lavished years of speculation on his transformation from a brilliant young electrical engineer to the town handyman. What could have changed this elegant, Lincolnesque student voted "Best Dressed" by his classmates to the gaunt, unshaven man I remember? Why did he leave a young son and a first wife of the "proper" class and religion, marry a much less educated woman of the "wrong" religion, and raise a second family in a house near an abandoned airstrip; a house whose walls were patched with metal signs to stop the wind? Why did he never talk about his transformation?

For years, I assumed that some secret and dramatic events of a year he spent in Alaska had made the difference. Then I discovered that the trip had come after his change and probably had been made because of it. Strangers he worked for as a much-loved handyman talked about him as one more tragedy of the Depression, and it was true that Uncle Ed's father, my paternal grandfather, had lost his money in the stockmarket Crash and died of (depending on who was telling the story) pneumonia or a broken heart. But the Crash of 1929 also had come long after Uncle Ed's transformation. Another theory was that he was afflicted with a mental problem that lasted most of his life, yet he was supremely competent at his work, led an independent life, and asked for help from no one.

Perhaps he had fallen under the spell of a radical professor in the early days of the century, the height of this country's romance with socialism and anarchism. That was the theory of an uncle on my mother's side. I do remember that no matter how much Uncle Ed needed money, he would charge no more for his work than materials plus 10 percent, and I never saw him in anything other than ancient boots and overalls held up with strategic safety pins. Was he really trying to replace socialism-in-one-country with socialism-in-one-man? If so, why did my grandmother, a woman who herself had run for the school board in coalition with anarchists and socialists, mistrust his judgment so much that she left his share of her estate in trust, even though he was over fifty when she died? And why did Uncle Ed seem uninterested in all other political words and acts? Was it true instead that, as another relative insisted, Uncle Ed had chosen poverty to disprove the myths of Jews and money?

Years after my uncle's death, I asked a son in his second family if he had the key to this family mystery. No, he said. He had never known his father any other way. For that cousin, there had been no question. For the rest of us, there was to be no answer.

For many years I also never imagined my mother any other way than the person she had become before I was born. She was just a fact of life when I was growing up, someone to be worried about and cared for; an invalid who lay in bed with eyes closed and lips moving in occasional response to voices only she could hear; a woman to whom I brought an endless stream of toast and coffee, bologna sandwiches and dime pies, in a child's version of what meals should be. She was a loving, intelligent, terrorized woman who tried hard to clean our littered house whenever she emerged from her private world, but who could rarely be counted on to finish one task. In many ways, our roles were reversed: I was the mother and she was the child. Yet that didn't help her, for she still worried about me with all the intensity of a frightened mother, plus the special fears of her own world full of threats and hostile voices.

Even then I suppose I must have known that, years before she was thirty-five and I was born, she had been a spirited, adventurous young woman who struggled out of a working-class family and into college, who found work she loved and continued to do, even after she was married and my older sister was there to be cared for. Certainly, our immediate family and nearby relatives, of whom I was by far the youngest, must have remembered her life as a whole and functioning person. She was thirty before she gave up her own career to help my father run the Michigan summer resort that was the most practical of his many dreams, and she worked hard there as everything from bookkeeper to bar manager. The family must have watched this energetic, fun-loving, book-loving woman turn into someone who was afraid to be alone, who could not hang on to reality long enough to hold a job, and who could rarely concentrate enough to read a book.

Yet I don't remember any family speculation about the mystery of my mother's transformation. To the kind ones and those who liked her, this new Ruth was simply a sad event, perhaps a mental case, a family problem to be accepted and cared for until some natural process made her better. To the less kind, or those who had resented her earlier independence, she was a willful failure, someone who lived in a filthy house, a woman who simply would not pull herself together.

Unlike the case of my Uncle Ed, exterior events were never suggested as reason enough for her problems. Giving up her own career was never cited as her personal parallel of the Depression. (Nor was there discussion of the Depression itself, though my mother, like millions of others, had made potato soup and cut up blankets to make my sister's winter clothes.) Her fears of dependence and poverty were no match for my uncle's possible political beliefs. The real influence of newspaper editors who had praised her reporting was not taken as seriously as the possible influence of one radical professor.

Even the explanation of mental illness seemed to contain more personal fault when applied to my mother. She had suffered her first "nervous breakdown," as she and everyone else called it, before I was born and when my sister was about five. It followed years of trying to take care of a baby, be the wife of a kind but financially irresponsible man with show-business dreams, and still keep her much-loved, exhausting job at the newspaper. After many months in a sanitarium, she was pronounced recovered. That is, she was able to take care of my sister again, to move away from the city and the job she loved, and to work with my father at the isolated rural lake in Michigan he was trying to transform into a resort worthy of the big dance bands of the 1930s.

But she was never again completely without the spells of depression, anxiety, and visions into some other world that eventually were to turn her into the nonperson I remember. And she was never again without a bottle of dark, acrid-smelling liquid she called "Doc Howard's medicine": a solution of chloral hydrate that I later learned was the main ingredient in "Mickey Finns" or "knockout drops," and that probably made my mother and her doctor the pioneers of modern tranquilizers. Though friends and relatives saw this medicine as one more evidence of weakness and indulgence, to me it always seemed an embarrassing but necessary evil. It slurred her speech and slowed her coordination, making our neighbors and my school friends believe she was a drunk. But without it, she would not sleep for days, even a week at a time, and her feverish eyes began to see only that private world in which wars and hostile voices threatened the people she loved.

Because my parents had divorced and my sister was working in a faraway city, my mother and I were alone together then, living off the meager fixed income that my mother got from leasing her share of the remaining land in Michigan. I remember a long Thanksgiving weekend spent hanging on to her with one hand and holding my eighth-grade assignment of *A Tale of Two Cities* in the other hand, because the war outside our house was so real to my mother that she had plunged her hand through a window, badly cutting her arm in an effort to help us escape. Only when she finally agreed to swallow the medicine could she sleep, and only then could I end the terrible calm that comes with crisis and admit to myself how afraid I had been.

No wonder that no relative in my memory challenged the doctor who prescribed this medicine, or asked if some of her suffering and hallucinating might be due to overdose or withdrawal, or even consulted another doctor about its use. It was our relief as well as hers.

But why was she never returned even to that first sanitarium? Or to help that might come from other doctors? It's hard to say. Partly, it was her own fear of returning. Partly, it was too little money, and a family's not-unusual assumption that mental illness is an inevitable part of someone's personality. Or perhaps other family members had feared something like my experience when, one hot and desperate summer between the sixth and seventh grade, I finally persuaded her to let me take her to the only doctor from those sanitarium days whom she remembered without fear.

Yes, this brusque old man told me after talking to my abstracted, timid mother for twenty minutes: she definitely belongs in a state hospital. She should be put there right away. But even at that age, *Life* magazine and newspaper exposés had told me what horrors went on inside those hospitals. Assuming there to be no alternative, I took her home and never tried again.

In retrospect, perhaps the biggest reason my mother was cared for but not helped for twenty years was the simplest: her functioning was not that necessary to the world. Like women alcoholics who drink in their kitchens while costly programs are constructed for executives who drink, or like the homemakers subdued with tranquilizers while male patients get therapy and personal attention instead, my mother was not an important worker. She was not even the caretaker of a very young child, as she had been when she was hospitalized the first time. My father had patiently brought home the groceries and kept our odd household going until I was eight or so and my sister went away to college. Two years later when wartime gas rationing closed his summer resort and he had to travel to buy and sell in summer as well as winter, he said: How can I travel and take care of your mother? How can I make a living? He was right. It was impossible to do both. I did not blame him for leaving once I was old enough to be the bringer of meals and answerer of my mother's questions. ("Has your sister been killed in a car crash?" "Are there German soldiers outside?") I replaced my father; my mother was left with one more person to maintain a sad status quo, and the world went on undisturbed.

That's why our lives, my mother's from forty-six to fifty-three, and my own from ten to seventeen, were spent alone together. There was one sane winter in a house we rented to be near my sister's college in Massachusetts, then one bad summer we spent house-sitting in suburbia while my mother hallucinated and my sister struggled to hold down a summer job in New York. But the rest of those years were lived in Toledo where both my mother and father had been born, and on whose city newspapers an earlier Ruth had worked.

First we moved into a basement apartment in a good neighborhood. In those rooms behind a furnace, I made one last stab at being a child. By pretending to be much sicker with a cold than I really was, I hoped my mother would suddenly turn into a sane and cheerful woman bringing me chicken soup a la Hollywood. Of course, she could not. It only made her feel worse that she could not. I stopped pretending.

But for most of those years, we lived in the upstairs of the house my mother had grown up in and that her parents left her—a deteriorating farmhouse engulfed by the city, with poor but newer houses stacked against it and a major highway a few feet from its sagging porch. For a while, we could rent the two downstairs apartments to a newlywed factory-working couple and a local butcher's family. Later, the health department condemned our ancient furnace for the final time, sealing it so tight that even my resourceful Uncle Ed couldn't produce illegal heat.

In that house, I remember:

. . . lying in the bed my mother and I shared for warmth, listening on the early morning radio to the royal wedding of Princess Elizabeth and Prince Philip being broadcast live, while we tried to ignore and thus protect each other from the unmistakable sounds of the factory worker downstairs beating up and locking out his pregnant wife.

. . . hanging paper drapes I had bought in the dime store; stacking books and papers in the shape of two armchairs and covering them with blankets; evolving my own dishwashing system (I waited until all the dishes were dirty, then put them in the bathtub); and listening to my mother's high praise for these housekeeping efforts to bring order from chaos, though in retrospect I think they probably depressed her further.

. . . coming back from one of the Eagles' Club shows where I and other veterans of a local tap-dancing school made ten dollars a night for two shows, and finding my mother waiting with a flashlight and no coat in the dark cold of the bus stop, worried about my safety walking home.

. . . in a good period, when my mother's native adventurousness came through, answering a classified ad together for an amateur acting troupe that performed biblical dramas in churches, and doing several very corny performances of *Noah's Ark* while my proud mother shook metal sheets backstage to make thunder.

. . . on a hot summer night, being bitten by one of the rats that shared our house and its back alley. It was a terrifying night that turned into a touching one when my mother, summoning courage from some unknown reservoir of love, became a calm, comforting parent who took me to a hospital emergency room despite her terror at leaving home.

. . . coming home from a local library with the three books a week into which I regularly escaped, and discovering for once that there was no need to escape. My mother was calmly planting hollyhocks in the vacant lot next door.

But there were also times when she woke in the early winter dark, too frightened and disoriented to remember that I was at my usual after-school job, and so called the police to find me. Humiliated in front of my friends by sirens and policemen, I would yell at her—and she would bow her head in fear and say, "I'm sorry, I'm sorry, I'm sorry," just as she had done so often when my otherwise-kindhearted father had yelled at her in frustration. Perhaps the worst thing about suffering is that it finally hardens the hearts of those around it.

And there were many, many times when I badgered her until her shaking hands had written a small check to cash at the corner grocery and I could leave her alone while I escaped to the winter comfort of well-heated dime stores that smelled of fresh doughnuts, or to summer air-conditioned movies that were windows on a very different world.

But my ultimate protection was this: I was just passing through, a guest in the house; perhaps this wasn't my mother at all. Though I knew very well that I was her daughter, I sometimes imagined that I had been adopted and that my real parents would find me, a fantasy I've since discovered is common. (If children wrote more and grown-ups less, being adopted might be seen not only as a fear but also as a hope.) Certainly, I didn't mourn the wasted life of this woman who was scarcely older than I am now. I worried only about the times when she got worse.

Pity takes distance and a certainty of surviving. It was only after our house was bought for demolition by the church next door, and after my sister had performed the miracle of persuading my father to give me a care-free time before college by taking my mother with him to California for a year, that I could afford to think about the sadness of her life. Suddenly, I was far away in Washington, living with my sister and sharing a house with several of her friends. While I finished high school and discovered to my surprise that my classmates felt sorry for me because my mother *wasn't* there, I also realized that my sister, at least in her early childhood, had known a very different person who lived inside our mother, an earlier Ruth.

She was a woman I met for the first time in a mental hospital near

Baltimore, a humane place with gardens and trees where I visited her each weekend of the summer after my first year away at college. Fortuantely, my sister hadn't been able to work and be our mother's caretaker, too. After my father's year was up, my sister had carefully researched hospitals and found the courage to break the family chain.

At first, this Ruth was the same abstracted, frightened woman I had lived with all those years; though now all the sadder for being approached through long hospital corridors and many locked doors. But gradually she began to talk about her past life, memories that doctors there must have been awakening. I began to meet a Ruth I had never known.

A tall, spirited, auburn-haired high school girl who loved basketball and reading; who tried to drive her uncle's Stanley Steamer when it was the first car in the neighborhood; who had a gift for gardening and who sometimes, in defiance of convention, wore her father's overalls; a girl with the courage to go to dances even though her church told her that music itself was sinful, and whose sense of adventure almost made up for feeling gawky and unpretty next to her daintier, dark-haired sister.

. . . A very little girl, just learning to walk, discovering the body places where touching was pleasurable, and being punished by her mother who slapped her hard across the kitchen floor.

. . . A daughter of a handsome railroad engineer and a schoolteacher who felt she had married "beneath her"; the mother who took her daughters on Christmas trips to faraway New York on an engineer's railroad pass and showed them the restaurants and theaters they should aspire to—even though they could only stand outside them in the snow.

. . . A good student at Oberlin College, whose freethinking traditions she loved, where friends nicknamed her "Billy"; a student with a talent for both mathematics and poetry, who was not above putting an invisible film of Karo syrup on all the john seats in her dormitory the night of a big prom; a daughter who had to return to Toledo, live with her family, and go to a local university when her ambitious mother—who had scrimped and saved, ghostwritten a minister's sermons, and made her daughters' clothes in order to get them to college at all—ran out of money. At home, this Ruth became a part-time bookkeeper in a lingerie shop for the very rich, commuting to classes and listening to her mother's harsh lectures on the security of becoming a teacher; but also a young woman who was still rebellious enough to fall in love with my father, the editor of her university newspaper, a funny and charming young man who was a terrible student, had no intention of graduating, put on all the dances, and was unacceptably Jewish.

I knew from family lore that my mother had married my father twice: once secretly, after he invited her to become the literary editor of his campus newspaper, and once a year later in a public ceremony, which some members of both families refused to attend as the "mixed marriage" of its day.

And I knew that my mother had gone on to earn a teaching certificate. She had used it to scare away truant officers during the winters when, after my father closed the summer resort for the season, we lived in a house trailer and worked our way to Florida or California and back by buying and selling antiques.

But only during those increasingly ambitious weekend outings from the hospital—going shopping, to lunch, to the movies—did I realize that she had taught college calculus for a year in deference to her mother's insistence that she have teaching to "fall back on." And only then did I realize she had fallen in love with newspapers along with my father. After graduating from the university paper, she wrote a gossip column for a local tabloid, under the name "Duncan MacKenzie," since women weren't supposed to do such things, and soon had earned a job as society reporter on one of Toledo's two big dailies. By the time my sister was four or so, she had worked her way up to the unusual position of Sunday editor.

It was a strange experience to look into those brown eyes I had seen so often and realize suddenly how much they were like my own. For the first time, I realized that I might really be her daughter.

I began to think of the many pressures that might have led up to that first nervous breakdown: leaving my sister whom she loved very much with a grandmother whose values she didn't share; trying to hold on to a job she loved but was being asked to leave by her husband; wanting very much to go with a woman friend to pursue their own dreams in New York; falling in love with a co-worker at the newspaper who frightened her by being more sexually attractive, more supportive of her work than my father, and perhaps a man she should have married; and finally, nearly bleeding to death with a miscarriage because her own mother had little faith in doctors and refused to get help.

Did those months in the sanitarium brainwash her in some Freudian or very traditional way into making what were, for her, probably the wrong choices? I don't know. It almost doesn't matter. Without extraordinary support to the contrary, she was already convinced that divorce was unthinkable. A husband could not be left for another man, and certainly not for a reason as selfish as a career. A daughter could not be deprived of her father and certainly not be uprooted and taken off to an uncertain future in New York. A bride was supposed to be virginal (not "shopworn" as my euphemistic mother used to say), and if your husband turned out to be kind, but innocent of the possibility of a woman's pleasure, then just be thankful for the kindness.

Of course, other women have torn themselves away from work and love and still survived. But a story my mother told me years later has symbolized for me the formidable forces arrayed against her:

"It was early spring, nothing was open yet. There was nobody for miles around. We had stayed at the lake that winter, so I was alone a lot while your father took the car and traveled around on business. You were a baby. Your sister was in school, and there was no phone. The last straw was that the radio broke. Suddenly it seemed like forever since I'd been able to talk with anyone—or even hear the sound of another voice.

"I bundled you up, took the dog, and walked out to the Brooklyn road. I thought I'd walk the four or five miles to the grocery store, talk to some people, and find somebody to drive me back. I was walking along with Fritzie running up ahead in the empty road—when suddenly a car came out of nowhere and down the hill. It hit Fritzie on the head and threw him over to the side of the road. I yelled and screamed at the driver, but he never slowed down. He never looked at us. He never even turned his head.

"Poor Fritzie was all broken and bleeding, but he was still alive. I carried him and sat down in the middle of the road, with his head cradled in my arms. I was going to *make* the next car stop and help.

"But no car ever came. I sat there for hours, I don't know how long, with you in my lap and holding Fritzie, who was whimpering and looking up at me for help. It was dark by the time he finally died. I pulled him over to the side of the road and walked back home with you and washed the blood out of my clothes.

"I don't know what it was about that one day—it was like a breaking point. When your father came home, I said: 'From now on, I'm going with you. I won't bother you. I'll just sit in the car. But I can't bear to be alone again.'"

I think she told me that story to show she had tried to save herself, or perhaps she wanted to exorcise the painful memory by saying it out loud. But hearing it made me understand what could have turned her into the woman I remember even while my parents were married: a solitary figure sitting in the car, perspiring through the summer, bundled up in winter, waiting for my father to come out of this or that antique shop, grateful just not to be alone. I was there, too, because I was too young to be left at home, and I loved helping my father wrap and unwrap the newpaper around the china and small objects he had bought at auctions and was selling to dealers. It made me feel necessary and grown-up. But sometimes it was hours before we came back to the car again and to my mother who was always patiently, silently waiting.

At the hospital and later when Ruth told me stories of her past, I used to say, "But why didn't you leave? Why didn't you take the job? Why didn't you marry the other man?" She would always insist it didn't matter, she was lucky to have my sister and me. If I pressed her hard enough, she would add, "If I'd left, you never would have been born."

I always thought but never had the courage to say: *But you might have been born instead.*

I'd like to tell you that this story has a happy ending. The best I can do is one that is happier than its beginning.

After many months in that Baltimore hospital, my mother lived on her own in a small apartment for two years while I was in college and my sister married and lived nearby. When she felt the old terrors coming back, she returned to the hospital at her own request. She was approaching sixty by the time she emerged from there and from a Quaker farm that served as a halfway house, but she confounded her psychiatrists' predictions that she would be able to live outside for shorter and shorter periods. In fact, she never returned. She lived more than another twenty years, and for six of them, she was well enough to stay in a rooming house that provided both privacy and company. Even after my sister and her husband moved to a larger house and generously made two rooms into an apartment for her, she continued to have some independent life and many friends. She worked part-time as a "salesgirl" in a china shop; went away with me on yearly vacations and took one trip to Europe with relatives; went to women's club meetings; found a multiracial church that she loved; took meditation courses; and enjoyed many books. Still, she could not bear to see a sad movie, to stay alone with any of her six grandchildren when they were babies, to live without many tranquilizers, or to talk about those bad years in Toledo. The old terrors were still in the back of her mind, and each day was a fight to keep them down.

It was the length of her illness that had made doctors pessimistic. In fact, they could not identify any serious mental problem and diagnosed her only as having "an anxiety neurosis": low self-esteem, a fear of being dependent, a terror of being alone, a constant worry about money. She also had spells of what would now be called agoraphobia, a problem almost entirely confined to dependent women: fear of going outside the house, and incapacitating anxiety attacks in unfamiliar or public places.

Would you say, I asked one of her doctors, that her spirit had been broken? "I guess that's as good a diagnosis as any," he said. "And it's hard to mend anything that's been broken for twenty years."

But once out of the hospital for good, she continued to show flashes of the different woman inside; one with a wry kind of humor, a sense of adventure, and a love of learning. Books on math, physics, and mysticism occupied a lot of her time. ("Religion," she used to say firmly, "begins in the laboratory.") When she visited me in New York during her sixties and seventies, she always told taxi drivers that she was eighty years old ("so they will tell me how young I look") and convinced theater ticket sellers that she was deaf long before she really was ("so they'll give us seats in the front row"). She made friends easily, with the vulnerability and charm of a person who feels entirely dependent on the approval of others. After one of her visits, every shopkeeper within blocks of my apartment would say, "Oh yes, I know your mother!" At home, she complained that people her own age were too old and stodgy for her. Many of her friends were far younger than she. It was as if she were making up for her own lost years.

She was also overly appreciative of any presents given to her—and that made giving them irresistible. I loved to send her clothes, jewelry, exotic soaps, and additions to her collection of tarot cards. She loved receiving them, though we both knew they would end up stored in boxes and drawers. She carried on a correspondence in German with our European relatives, and exchanges with many other friends, all written in her painfully slow, shaky handwriting. She also loved giving gifts. Even as she worried about money and figured out how to save pennies, she would buy or make carefully chosen presents for grandchildren and friends.

Part of the price she paid for this much health was forgetting. A single reminder of those bad years in Toledo was enough to plunge her into days of depression. There were times when this fact created a loneliness for me, too. Only two of us had lived most of my childhood. Now, only one of us remembered. But there were also times in later years when, no matter how much I pleaded with reporters *not* to interview our friends and neighbors in Toledo, *not* to say that my mother had been hospitalized, they published things that hurt her very much and sent her into a downhill slide.

On the other hand, she was also her mother's daughter, a person with a certain amount of social pride and pretension, and some of her objections had less to do with depression than false pride. She complained bitterly about one report that we had lived in a house trailer. She finally asked angrily: "Couldn't they at least say 'vacation mobile home'?" Divorce was still a shame to her. She might cheerfully tell friends, "I don't know *why* Gloria says her father and I were divorced—we never were." I think she justified this to herself with the idea that they had gone through two marriage ceremonies, one in secret and one in public, but had been divorced only once. In fact, they were definitely divorced, and my father briefly had been married to someone else.

She was very proud of my being a published writer, and we generally shared the same values. After her death, I found a mother-daughter morals quiz I once had written for a women's magazine. In her unmistakably shaky handwriting, she had recorded her own answers, her entirely accurate imagination of what my answers would be, and a score that concluded our differences were less than those "normal for women separated by twenty-odd years." Nonetheless, she was quite capable of putting a made-up name on her name tag when going to a conservative women's club where she feared our shared identity would bring up controversy or even just questions. When I finally got up the nerve to tell her I was signing a 1972 petition of women who publicly said we had had abortions and were demanding the repeal of laws that made them illegal and dangerous, her only reply was sharp and aimed to hurt back. "Every starlet says she's had an abortion," she said. "It's just a way of getting publicity." I knew she agreed that abortion should be a legal choice, but I also knew she would never forgive me for being honest in public.

In fact, her anger and a fairly imaginative ability to wound with words increased in her last years when she was most dependent, most focused on herself, and most likely to need the total attention of others. When my sister made a courageous decision to go to law school at the age of fifty, leaving my mother in a house that not only had many loving teenage grandchildren in it but a kindly older woman as a paid companion besides, my mother reduced my sister to frequent tears by insisting that this was a family with no love in it, no home-cooked food in the refrigerator; not a real family at all. Since arguments about home cooking wouldn't work on me, my punishment was creative and different. She was going to call up the *New York Times*, she said, and tell them that this was what feminism did: it left old sick women all alone.

Some of this bitterness brought on by failing faculties was eventually solved by a nursing home near my sister's house where my mother not only got the twenty-four-hour help her weakening body demanded, but the attention of affectionate nurses besides. She charmed them, they loved her, and she could still get out for an occasional family wedding. If I ever had any doubts about the debt we owe to nurses, those last months laid them to rest.

When my mother died just before her eighty-second birthday in a hospital room where my sister and I were alternating the hours in which her heart wound slowly down to its last sounds, we were alone together for a few hours. My mother seemed bewildered by her surroundings and the tubes that invaded her body, but her consciousness cleared long enough for her to say: "I want to go home. Please take me home." Lying to her one last time, I said I would. "Okay, honey," she said. "I trust you." Those were her last understandable words.

The nurses let my sister and me stay in the room long after there was no more breath in her body. She had asked us to do that. One of her many fears came from a story she had been told as a child about a man whose coma was mistaken for death. She had made out a living will requesting that no extraordinary measures be used to keep her alive, and that her ashes be sprinkled in the same stream as my father's.

Her memorial service was in the Episcopalian church that she loved because it fed the poor, let the homeless sleep in its pews, had members of every race, and had been sued by the Episcopalian hierarchy for having a woman priest. Most of all, she loved the affection with which its members had welcomed her, visited her at home, and driven her to services. I think she would have liked the Quaker-style informality with which people rose to tell their memories of her. I know she would have loved the presence of many friends. It was to this church that she had donated some of her remaining Michigan property in the hope that it could be used as a multiracial camp, thus getting even with those people in the tiny nearby town who had snubbed my father for being Jewish.

I think she also would have been pleased with her obituary. It emphasized her brief career as one of the early women journalists and asked for donations to Oberlin's scholarship fund so others could go to this college she loved so much but had to leave.

I know I will spend the next years figuring out what her life has left in me.

I realize that I've always been more touched by old people than by children. It's the talent and hopes locked in a failing body that gets to me; a poignant contrast that reminds me of my mother, even before she was old.

I've always been drawn to any story of a mother and daughter on their own in the world. I saw A *Taste of Honey* several times both as a play and a film, and never stopped feeling it. Even *Gypsy* I saw over and over again, sneaking in backstage for the musical and going to the movie as well. I told myself that I was learning the tap-dance routines, but actually my eyes were full of tears.

I once fell in love with a man only because we both belonged to that large and secret club of children who had "crazy mothers." We traded stories of the shameful houses to which we could never invite our friends. Before he was born, his mother had gone to jail for her pacifist convictions. Then she married the politically ambitious young lawyer who had defended her, stayed home and raised many sons. I fell out of love when he confessed that he wished I wouldn't smoke or swear, and he hoped I wouldn't go on working. His mother's plight had taught him self-pity—and nothing else.

I'm no longer obsessed, as I was for many years, with the fear that I would end up in a house like that one in Toledo. Now, I'm obsessed instead with the things I could have done for my mother while she was alive, or the things I should have said.

I still don't understand why so many, many years passed before I saw my mother as a person and before I understood that many of the forces in her life are patterns women share. Like a lot of daughters, I suppose I couldn't afford to admit that what had happened to my mother was not all personal or accidental, and therefore could happen to me.

One mystery has finally cleared. I could never understand why my mother hadn't been helped by Pauline, her mother-in-law; a woman she seemed to love more than her own mother. This paternal grandmother had died when I was five, before my mother's real problems began but long after that "nervous breakdown," and I knew Pauline was once a suffragist who addressed Congress, marched for the vote, and was the first woman elected to a school board in Ohio. She must have been a courageous and independent woman, yet I could find no evidence in my mother's reminiscences that Pauline had helped my mother toward a life of her own.

I finally realized that my grandmother never changed the politics of her own life, either. She was a feminist who kept a neat house for a husband and four antifeminist sons, a vegetarian among five male meat eaters, and a woman who felt so strongly about the dangers of alcohol that she used only paste vanilla; yet she served both meat and wine to the men of the house and made sure their lives and comforts were continued undisturbed. After the vote was won, Pauline seems to have stopped all feminist activity. My mother greatly admired the fact that her mother-in-law kept a spotless house and prepared a week's meals at a time. Whatever her own internal torments, Pauline was to my mother a woman who seemed able to "do it all." "Whither thou goest, I shall go," my mother used to say to Pauline, quoting the Ruth of the Bible. In the end, her mother-in-law may have added to my mother's burdens of guilt.

Perhaps like many later suffragists, my grandmother was a public feminist and a private isolationist. That may have been heroic in itself, the most she could be expected to do, but the vote and a legal right to work were not the only kind of help my mother needed.

The world still missed a unique person named Ruth. Though she had longed to live in New York and Europe, she became a woman who was afraid to take a bus across town. Though she drove the first Stanley Steamer, she married a man who never let her drive at all.

I can only guess what she might have become. The clues are in moments of spirit or humor.

After all the years of fear, she still went to Oberlin with me when I was giving a speech there. She remembered everything about its history as the first college to admit blacks and the first to admit women, and responded to students with the dignity of a professor, the accuracy of a journalist, and a charm that was all her own.

When she could still make trips to Washington's wealth of libraries, she became an expert genealogist, delighting especially in finding the rogues and rebels in our family tree.

Just before I was born, when she had cooked one more enormous meal for all the members of some famous dance band at my father's resort and they failed to clean their plates, she had taken a shotgun down from the kitchen wall and held it over their frightened heads until they had finished the last crumb of strawberry shortcake. Only then did she tell them the gun wasn't loaded. It was a story she told with great satisfaction.

Though sex was a subject she couldn't discuss directly, she had a great appreciation of sensuous men. When a friend I brought home tried to talk to her about cooking, she was furious. ("He came out in the kitchen and talked to me about *stew!*") But she forgave him when we went swimming. She whispered, "He has wonderful legs!"

On her seventy-fifth birthday, she played softball with her grandsons on the beach, and took pride in hitting home runs into the ocean.

Even in the last year of her life, when my sister took her to visit a neighbor's new and expensive house, she looked at the vertical stripes of a very abstract painting in the hallway, and asked, tartly, "Is that the price code?"

She worried terribly about being socially accepted herself, but she never withheld her own approval for the wrong reasons. Poverty or style or lack of education couldn't stand between her and a new friend. Though she lived in a mostly white society and worried if I went out with a man of the "wrong" race, just as she had married a man of the "wrong" religion, she always accepted each person as an individual.

"Is he *very* dark?" she once asked worriedly about a friend. But when she met this very dark person, she only said afterward, "What a kind and nice man!"

My father was the Jewish half of the family, yet it was my mother who taught me to have pride in that tradition. It was she who encouraged me to listen to a radio play about a concentration camp when I was little. "You should know that this can happen," she said. Yet she did it just enough to teach, not to frighten.

It was she who introduced me to books and a respect for them, to poetry that she knew by heart, and to the idea that you could never criticize someone unless you "walked miles in their shoes."

It was she who sold that Toledo house, the only home she had, with the determination that the money be used to start me in college. She gave both her daughters the encouragement to leave home for four years of independence that she herself had never had.

After her death, my sister and I found a journal she had kept of her one cherished and belated trip to Europe. It was a trip she had described very little when she came home: she always deplored people who talked boringly about their personal travels and showed slides. Nonetheless, she had written a descriptive essay called "Grandma Goes to Europe." She still must have thought of herself as a writer. Yet she showed this long journal to no one.

I miss her—but perhaps no more in death than I did in life. Dying seems less sad than having lived too little.

But at least we're now asking questions about all the Ruths and all our family mysteries.

If her song inspires that, I think she would be the first to say: It was worth the singing.

1983

Mother Tongue

I am not a scholar of English or literature. I cannot give you much more than personal opinions on the English language and its variations in this country or others.

I am a writer. And by that definition, I am someone who has always loved language. I am fascinated by language in daily life. I spend a great deal of my time thinking about the power of language—the way it can evoke an emotion, a visual image, a complex idea, or a simple truth. Language is the tool of my trade. And I use them all—all the Englishes I grew up with.

Recently, I was made keenly aware of the different Englishes I do use. I was giving a talk to a large group of people, the same talk I had already given to half a dozen other groups. The nature of the talk was about my writing, my life, and my book, *The Joy Luck Club*. The talk was going along well enough, until I remembered one major difference that made the whole talk sound wrong. My mother was in the room. And it was perhaps the first time she had heard me give a lengthy speech—using the kind of English I have never used with her. I was saying things like, "The intersection of memory upon imagination" and "There is an aspect of my fiction that relates to thus-and-thus"—a speech filled with carefully wrought grammatical phrases, burdened, it suddenly seemed to me, with nominalized forms, past perfect tenses, conditional phrases—all the forms of standard English that I had learned in school and through books, the forms of English I did not use at home with my mother.

Just last week, I was walking down the street with my mother, and I again found myself conscious of the English I was using, the English I do use with her. We were talking about the price of new and used furniture and I heard myself saying this: "Not waste money that way." My husband was with us as well, and he didn't notice any switch in my English. And then I realized why. It's because over the twenty years we've been together I've often used that same kind of English with him, and sometimes he even uses it with me. It has become our language of intimacy, a different sort of English that relates to family talk, the language I grew up with.

So you'll have some idea of what this family talk I heard sounds like, I'll quote what my mother said during a recent conversation which I videotaped and then transcribed. During this conversation, my mother was talking about a political gangster in Shanghai who had the same last name as her family's, Du, and how the gangster in his early years wanted to be adopted by her family which was rich by comparison. Later, the gangster became more powerful, far richer than my mother's family, and one day showed up at my mother's wedding to pay his respects. Here's what she said in part:

"Du Yusong having business like fruit stand. Like off the street kind. He is Du like Du Zong—but not Tsung-ming Island people. The local people call putong, the river east side, he belong to that side local people. That man want to ask Du Zong father take him in like become own family. Du Zong father wasn't look down on him, but didn't take seriously, until that man big like become a mafia. Now important person, very hard to inviting him. Chinese way, came only to show respect, don't stay for dinner. Respect for making big celebration, he shows up. Mean gives lots of respect. Chinese custom. Chinese social life that way. If too important won't have to stay too long. He come to my wedding. I didn't see, I heard it. I gone to boys' side, they have YMCA dinner. Chinese age I was nineteen."

You should know that my mother's expressive command of English belies how much she actually understands. She reads the Forbes report, listens to Wall Street Week, converses daily with her stockbroker, reads all of Shirley MacLaine's books with ease—all kinds of things I can't begin to understand. Yet some of my friends tell me they understand 50 percent of what my mother says. Some say they understand 80 to 90 percent. Some say they understand none of it, as if she were speaking pure Chinese. But to me, my mother's English is perfectly clear, perfectly natural. It's my mother tongue. Her language, as I hear it, is vivid, direct, full of observation and imagery. That was the language that helped shape the way I saw things, expressed things, made sense of the world.

Lately, I've been giving more thought to the kind of English my mother speaks. Like others, I have described it to people as "broken" or "fractured" English. But I wince when I say that. It has always bothered me that I can think of no way to describe it other than "broken," as if it were damaged and needed to be fixed, as if it lacked a certain wholeness and soundness. I've heard other terms used, "limited English," for example. But they seem just as bad, as if everything is limited, including people's perception of the limited English speaker.

I know this for a fact, because when I was growing up, my mother's "limited" English limited *my* perception of her. I was ashamed of her English. I believed that her English reflected the quality of what she had to say. That is, because she expressed them imperfectly her thoughts were imperfect. And I had plenty of empirical evidence to support me: the fact that people in department stores, at banks, and at restaurants did not take her seriously, did not give her good service, pretended not to understand her, or even acted as if they did not hear her.

My mother has long realized the limitations of her English as well. When I was fifteen, she used to have me call people on the phone to pretend I was she. In this guise, I was forced to ask for information or even to complain and yell at people who had been rude to her. One time it was a call to her stockbroker in New York. She had cashed out her small portfolio and it just so happened we were going to go to New York the next week, our very first trip outside California. I had to get on the phone and say in an adolescent voice that was not very convincing, "This is Mrs. Tan."

And my mother was standing in the back whispering loudly, "Why he don't send me check, already two weeks late. So mad he lie to me, losing me money."

And then I said in perfect English, "Yes, I'm getting rather concerned. You had agreed to send the check two weeks ago, but it hasn't arrived."

Then she began to talk more loudly, "What he want, I come to New York tell him front of his boss, you cheating me?" And I was trying to calm her down, make her be quiet, while telling the stockbroker, "I can't tolerate any more excuses. If I don't receive the check immediately, I am going to have to speak to your manager when I'm in New York next week." And sure enough, the following week there we were in front of this astonished stock-broker, and I was sitting there red-faced and quiet, and my mother, the real Mrs. Tan, was shouting at his boss in her impeccable broken English.

We used a similar routine just five days ago, for a situation that was far less humorous. My mother had gone to the hospital for an appoint-ment, to find out about a benign brain tumor a CAT scan had revealed a month ago. She said she had spoken very good English, her best English, no mistakes. Still, she said, the hospital did not apologize when they said they had lost the CAT scan and she had come for nothing. She said they did not seem to have any sympathy when she told them she was anxious to know the exact diagnosis since her husband and son had both died of brain tumors. She said they would not give her any more information until the next time and she would have to make another appointment for that. So she said she would not leave until the doctor called her daughter. She wouldn't budge. And when the doctor finally called her daughter, me, who spoke in perfect English—lo and behold—we had assurances the CAT scan would be found, promises that a conference call on Monday would be held, and apologies for any suffering my mother had gone through for a most regrettable mistake.

I think my mother's English almost had an effect on limiting my pos-sibilities in life as well. Sociologists and linguists probably will tell you that a person's developing language skills are more influenced by peers. But I do think that the language spoken in the family, especially in immigrant families which are more insular, plays a large role in shaping the language of the child. And I believe that it affected my results on achievement tests, IQ tests, and the SAT. While my English skills were never judged as poor, compared to math, English could not be considered my strong suit. In grade school, I did moderately well, getting perhaps B's, sometimes B+'s in English, and scoring perhaps in the sixtieth or seventieth percentile on achievement tests. But those scores were not good enough to override the opinion that my true abilities lay in math and science, because in those areas I achieved A's and scored in the ninetieth percentile or higher.

This was understandable. Math is precise; there is only one correct answer. Whereas, for me at least, the answers on English tests were always a judgment call, a matter of opinion and personal experience. Those tests were constructed around items like fill-in-the-blank sentence completion, such as "Even though Tom was ___, Mary thought he was ___." And the correct answer always seemed to be the most bland combinations of thoughts, for example, "Even though Tom was shy, Mary thought he was charming," with the grammatical structure "even though" limiting the correct answer to some sort of semantic opposites, so you wouldn't get answers like "Even though Tom was foolish, Mary thought he was ridiculous." Well, according to my mother, there were very few limitations as to what Tom could have been, and what Mary might have thought of him. So I never did well on tests like that.

The same was true with word analogies, pairs of words, in which you were supposed to find some sort of logical, semantic relationship—for example, " 'sunset' is to 'nightfall' as ___ is to ___." And here, you would be presented with a list of four possible pairs, one of which showed the same kind of relationship: "red" is to "stoplight," "bus" is to "arrival," "chills" is to "fever," "yawn" is to "boring." Well, I could never think that way. I knew what the tests were asking, but I could not block out of my mind the images already created by the first pair, "sunset is to nightfall"—and I would see a burst of colors against a darkening sky, the moon rising, the lowering of a curtain of stars. And all the other pairs of words—red, bus, stoplight, boring—just threw up a mass of confusing images, making it impossible for me to sort out something as logical as saying: "A sunset precedes nightfall" is the same as "a chill precedes a fever." The only way I would have gotten that answer right would have been to imagine an associative situation, for example, my being disobedient and staying out past sunset, catching a chill at night, which turns into feverish pneumonia as punishment, which indeed did happen to me.

I have been thinking about all this lately, about my mother's English, about achievement tests. Because lately I've been asked, as a writer, why there are not more Asian-Americans represented in American literature. Why are there few Asian-Americans enrolled in creative writing programs? Why do so many Chinese students go into engineering? Well, these are broad sociological questions I can't begin to answer. But I have noticed in surveys—in fact, just last week—that Asian students, as a whole, always do significantly better on math achievement tests than in English. And this makes me think that there are other Asian-American students whose English spoken in the home might also be described as "broken" or "limited." And perhaps they also have teachers who are steering them away from writing and into math and science, which is what happened to me.

Fortunately, I happen to be rebellious in nature, and enjoy the challenge of disproving assumptions made about me. I became an English major my first year in college after being enrolled as pre-med. I started writing nonfiction as a freelancer the week after I was told by my former boss that writing was my worst skill and I should hone my talents toward account management.

But it wasn't until 1985 that I finally began to write fiction. And at first I wrote using what I thought to be wittily crafted sentences, sentences that would finally prove I had mastery over the English language. Here's an example from the first draft of a story that later made its way into *The Joy Luck Club*, but without this line: "That was my mental quandary in its nascent state." A terrible line, which I can barely pronounce.

Fortunately, for reasons I won't get into today, I later decided I should envision a reader for the stories I would write. And the reader I decided upon was my mother, because these were stories about mothers. So with this reader in mind—and in fact, she did read my early drafts—I began to write stories using all the Englishes I grew up with: the English I spoke to my mother, which for lack of a better term might be described as "simple"; the English she used with me, which for lack of a better term might be described as "broken"; my translation of her Chinese, which could certainly be described as "watered down"; and what I imagined to be her translation of her Chinese if she could speak in perfect English, her internal language, and for that I sought to preserve the essence, but not either an English or a Chinese structure. I wanted to capture what language ability tests can never reveal: her intent, her passion, her imagery, the rhythms of her speech and the nature of her thoughts.

Apart from what any critic had to say about my writing, I knew I had succeeded where it counted when my mother finished reading my book, and gave me her verdict: "So easy to read."

1989

My Father's Penis

When I was growing up, my father wore what we used to call string pajamas. Actually, I only remember the bottom part of the pajamas, which, as their name might suggest, tied with a string at the waist. (On top he wore a ribbed sleeveless undershirt that tucked into the pajama bottoms.) The pajamas, made of a thin cotton fabric, usually a shade of washed-out blue, but sometimes also striped, were a droopy affair; they tended to bag at the knees and shift position at the waist with every movement. The string, meant to hold the pajamas up, was also meant to keep the fly—just a slit opening in the front—closed. But the fly, we might say modernly, resisted closure and defined itself instead by the meaningful hint of a gap.

As my father wandered through the apartment in the early mornings, performing his domestic rituals (bringing my mother her coffee in bed, making my sister and me breakfast in the kitchen, shaving, watering the plants), this almost gap never failed to catch my eye. It seemed to me as I watched him cheerfully rescue the burning toast and pass from room to room in a slow motion of characteristic aimlessness (memorialized in our family codes by the Yiddish trope of *draying*), that behind the flap lay something important: dark, maybe verging on purple, probably soft and floppy. I also suspected it was hairy in there; I was pretty sure I had glimpsed hair (he had hair everywhere, on his back and shoulders, why not there).

I don't think I wanted to see it—"it" had no name in my ruminations—but there was a peculiar way in which its mysterious daily existence behind the slit in the pajama bottoms loomed large in my prepubescent imagination as somehow connected to the constant tension in our family, especially to my mother's bad moods. Growing up, I had only the vaguest notions of sex; I can still remember my utter astonishment when, sitting on the living room couch and feeling vastly sophisticated, I learned from my mother that a penis had to become "erect" to enter a vagina (I had never really thought about *how* the *man's* penis—in the redundant but always less than instructive language of hygiene classes—gets into the *woman's* vagina). So that several years later when in college I finally had a look at my first penis (this was no small surprise), I realized that I had never visualized the thing to myself at all.

Almost forty years after the scene of these memories, I find myself again, as a middle-aged, therapized intellectual, thinking about my father's penis. Now, living alone after my mother's death in the same apartment, my father, stricken with Parkinson's disease, shuffles through the room *draying*. Boxer shorts have replaced the string pajamas, but the gap remains the same and it's still dark in there. But it's not the same: I have seen his penis. I have even touched it. One day when his fingers had grown so rigid he couldn't, as he puts it, "snare" his penis, he wanted to get up to go to the bathroom. It was late and I wanted to go home, so looking and looking away, I fished his penis out from behind the fly of his shorts and stuck it in the urinal; it felt soft and a little clammy.

Shirley, the nurse's aide who takes care of my father, reported one day that when she arrived at the apartment in the morning, she had found my father in the kitchen "bare-bottomed" and cold. "His — was blue," she said (the cadences of a slight Caribbean accent made the word hard to understand over the phone); "I rubbed it until it turned pink. Then he felt better." Rubbed his *penis*? But what else, in the vicinity of a bare-bottom, of two syllables, could have gone from blue to pink? Did it respond to her rubbing? Become erect? The mystery returns. What do I know? Shirley and I talk about my father, his care. The apartment, despite her efforts, smells of urine. There's no missing this penis-effect. One day, in the middle of eating dinner, his back to me, he demands his urinal from Shirley, which he uses while at table. Shirley buys him new boxer shorts on 14th Street. Six dollars, she says. Apiece? I ask. No, three Fruit of the Loom in a package.

This is the condition of his remaining at home (he gives me a pained look at the mention of going to a "home" that silences me): to get out of bed and make it to the bathroom without falling, or to use the urinal that hangs like a limp penis from the walker he despises (he shows his superiority to his infirmity by carrying the walker in front of him instead of leaning on it). When these solutions fail, Ellen, the neighbor who brings him his daily *New York Times*, says "he peed himself" (my father always talks more elaborately about the "difficulty of urination," of responding in time to the "urgency of its call"). The newspapers now, like the *New Yorkers* to which he maintains his subscription, and which remain unopened in their plastic wrappers, pile up unread in the living room; I throw them away in my weekly sweep through the apartment.

In "Phallus/Penis: Same Difference" (great title) Jane Gallop writes: "The debate over Lacan's and, beyond that, psychoanalysis's value for feminism itself centers on the phallus. Yet the *phallus* is a very complicated notion in Lacan, who distinguishes it from the *penis*. The distinction seems, however, to resist clarification." For a while after touching my father's penis, I went around thinking smugly I would never again confuse penis and phallus, boasting that I had transcended the confusion. Phallus was the way my father could terrify me when I was growing up: throwing me across the room in a blind rage because I had been talking on the phone—endlessly, it's true—when the hospital called to say his mother was dying; knocking me down in the elevator for staying out late one night with my college boyfriend. Phallus was tearing pages out of the typewriter because I hadn't left wide enough margins on my term papers; making me break a date with the cab driver who had picked me up in London on my first visit there (but Daddy, he's *Jewish*, the son of a cantor!).

Penis was that dark-veined, heavy thing lying there against strangely elongated, even darker balls; hanging between emaciated but still elegant thighs. It made problems for me, but they were finally prosaic, unmediated by concepts and the symbolic order. My father doesn't have the phallus; no one does, Lacan said. But, Gallop writes in *The Daughter's Seduction*, "the need, the desire, the wish for the Phallus is great. No matter how oppressive its reign, it is much more comforting than no one in command." So now I decide, say no, and yell; I am responsible for the rest of his life ("it's for your health and welfare," he used to say as his cover for the exercise of an arbitrary authority); maybe I, failing the penis, have my chance at the phallus.

Months after writing this, I come into my father's room. I think I have put an end to all these speculations (penis, phallus, castration, etc.) but when I find him sleeping completely naked, stretched out like an aged Endymion across a hospital bed, I can't resist. His hand is resting in his lap, his penis tucked away out of sight, hidden between his thighs. I move closer.

"So what does it look like?" my sister asks. I don't answer, not only because I want to play big sister one last time, but because I'm not sure I can say what it is that I've seen.

When I wrote "My Father's Penis," I had been thinking more about penises than fathers (or so I thought at the time). Mira Schor, who is a painter and a critic, had done a slide-show lecture on representations of the penis in painting, and I conceived my piece originally as a kind of footnote to her panoply of members—the geriatric extension of her taxonomy. But I was also writing in the aftermath of an intensely charged academic performance in which the status of "experience" in feminist theory had been challenged with a certain phallic—what would a better word be?—insistence. When it then became a matter of publishing "the penis" (it seems impossible to invoke the title or its contents without getting caught in the spiral of catachresis) in *Refiguring the Father*, I felt that I had inadvertently found a destination for it: that the fragmentary essay, because of its mixed origins, born of the troubled intimacies of the autobiographical penis and the theoretical phallus, had unexpectedly come full circle back to feminist revision. But not perhaps back home.

Had my father still been able to read, I would never have written about "the penis." By going public with the details of domestic arrangements on Riverside Drive, I was flying in the face of the parental injunction not to "tell" that had haunted my adolescence and continued well into my adult years; the panic my parents felt that they would be exposed by us; the shame over family secrets. But he was down in his reading to the occasional newspaper headline and, I think, at his end, despite a finely honed personal vanity, beyond caring. He had become no longer himself, and I needed to mourn his disappearance.

My father died before this piece appeared in print. He died, I'm tempted to say, of the penis: at home, as he had wanted, after eating ice cream and watching public television, in the aftermath of a grueling seven-week stay in the hospital that followed a violent urinary tract infection. I dealt with—talked about, looked at, touched, raged at—his penis until the very end. And until the very end, the penis/phallus connection remained alive, impossible to sever. In the hospital, it was war between his penis and the doctors' discourse; or rather my attempt to stand in as phallus for his penis—the rights of his body—against their authority to determine the course of his life; their wish for him to live, against his entire system's disarray (my wish for him?).

When I read one day on my father's chart in the intensive-care unit "Responds only to pain," I found it hard to share the doctor's jubilation over the signs of life dotting the monitor above his respirator. "What do you want me to do," she hissed at me across the network of tubes mapping his body, "kill your father?"

1991

Balancing Act

The oversize cream-colored envelope arrived in the morning mail. I approached it gingerly, circling it at first, then weighing it in my hand as if it might be a letter bomb. Who knew what was inside? The Boston return address stirred my memory the way dreams sometimes break into consciousness, the way once, when I was walking through an unfamiliar city, a rusted gate and blooming garden suddenly reminded me of home.

The Boston postmark reminded me of another home. I saw a stately suburban avenue lined with grand Georgian houses, and one specific house whose inhabitants were preparing for the Sabbath. I heard the clink of silver goblets at the beginning of the Friday night meal, lilting Hebrew melodies after dinner. But most of all I saw a home I had not been welcome in for eight years. Inside the envelope, sent by my aunt, was an engraved invitation to the bas mitzvah of a cousin I had never met.

Eight years earlier, my parents were in a devastating car crash. My mother was in the passenger seat and suffered eighty broken bones; after two weeks, my father died of head injuries. A family feud, which had been brewing beneath the surface for decades, erupted between my father's Orthodox Jewish family and the secularized modern family he had created with my mother. *They* wanted the funeral to be held at Riverside Chapel in New York City. But my mother, her legs in traction, wanted it held at the hospital in New Jersey so she could be wheeled to the services on her gurney. *They* placed an obituary in the newspaper, announcing memorial services to be held at Riverside. But my mother insisted and finally prevailed. Although she had never been inappropriately dressed a day in her life, for her husband's funeral she was wheeled down the center aisle swathed in white—white casts, white sheets.

Soon the family feud that had moved into the open with my father's death gathered steam, and while my mother was recovering, her rage at wrongs both real and imagined knitted into her bones and calcified there. She was unable to hear mention of my father's family without descending into bitterness. *They almost killed me*, she would say. It was impossible for me to maintain a relationship with my father's family. To do so would have meant I was aligned with my mother's enemies. I was equally my mother's daughter as my father's, and my love for her was a deep, nameless thing and had intensified after the car crash. I had watched as she fought, with great dignity, to walk again. I would have held her bones in place for her if I'd thought it would help. Although my aunt called each year on the anniversary of my father's death, I found myself unable to answer the phone.

My response to the invitation was ambivalent. *Why now? Why not eight years ago when I needed you?* Then I was twenty-three and essentially alone. Now I had a busy career, a loving partner. What did I need with the stately house in Boston and all its shadows?

I shocked myself by saying yes, and told my mother I would be away for the weekend, visiting friends in Boston.

By the time I arrived, my family—all sixty of them—had already gathered for dinner. The room was filled with children, strangers to me, born after the beginning of our cold war. My cousins had all married young and stayed married. None had fewer than four children. Yael, Benyamin, Ziporah—it was tough to keep their names straight. They all tried to make me feel at home, the way one might be particularly kind to a guest from another culture.

After dinner, my cousin Mordechai, a rabbi in Vancouver, gave a short talk, the dvar Torah, literally "a word of Torah." I watched as he approached the podium, his thick glasses and long beard reminding me of a weekend nearly twenty years earlier, when I visited my aunt and uncle. I was deeply confused by my parents' religious differences. Although my father had moved far from the culture of his childhood, he had maintained a strictly Orthodox life: a kosher home, devout prayer, observance of all the

Shabbos laws. Meanwhile, in that year of my own bas mitzvah, my mother, who had always kept kosher ("For your father's sake"), had taken me to lunch at a suburban Saks Fifth Avenue and ordered herself a bacon cheeseburger.

Mordechai was a rabbinical student in those days, the ink still damp on his Harvard degree. After Shabbos, we walked through Cambridge and ate hot fudge sundaes in Harvard Square. That night the world felt seamless to me. Mordechai was a cool guy *and* he was going to be a rabbi. To thirteen-year-old eyes, it seemed I could have my bacon cheeseburger and eat it too.

Mordechai's dvar Torah was on the nature of contentment: "A man is rich who is satisfied with what he has." It was so simple, I thought. So uncomplicated, really: the lights that beckon most brightly are the ones illuminating one's own front door. Mordechai paid homage to his parents. He invoked the memory of his grandparents, even his great-grandparents. Everyone in that room understood that each was a link in a generational chain, and when the boys and girls started dancing, in separate circles, I saw that the chain swayed, but was never broken.

My aunt took me by the arm and led me into her study. Leatherbound Hebrew texts shone like artifacts against the softly lit walls. Sabbath had ended. Someone was playing the piano and children's voices sang through the rooms. On her desk was a portrait of her brother, my father. She held it in her hands, her eyes filled with tears. In every generation there is a vault-keeper, one who guards the links fiercely and knows they are more precious than rubies.

My aunt held the portrait out to me, an offering.

"Every day he's in my prayers," she said. "I swore to your father I would never lose track of you."

I stared at my father's face and thought of the woman he had loved most in the world, my mother. Since his death, I'd been having a dialogue with him. *What now, Dad?* I would ask during troubled times. *You'll know what to do,* he would counsel me, an angel perched on my shoulder.

I closed my eyes, the better to hear the whispering voice. *Reach out one hand to your mother,* it said, *the other to your aunt. Now you're in the middle, wings spread, feet planted firmly on the ground.*

1994

45

The Deterioration of My Marriage

The articles in the women's magazines did nothing to help explain the deterioration of my marriage. We had no infidelity; my husband was a good provider and I was a good cook. He encouraged me to resume my dance classes and I listened to him practice the saxophone without interruption. He came directly home from work each afternoon and in the evening after my son was asleep I found as much enjoyment in our marital bed as he.

The form was there, but the spirit had disappeared.

A bizarre sensation pervades a relationship of pretense. No truth seems true. A simple morning's greeting and response appear loaded with innuendo and fraught with implications.

"How are you?" Does he/she really care?

"Fine." I'm not really. I'm miserable, but I'll never tell you.

Each nicety becomes more sterile and each withdrawal more permanent.

Bacon and coffee odors mingled with the aseptic aroma of Lifebuoy soap. Wisps of escaping gas, which were as real a part of a fifty-year-old San Francisco house as the fourteen-foot-high ceilings and the cantankerous plumbing, solidified my reality. Those were natural morning mists. The sense that order was departing my life was refuted by the daily routine.

My family would awaken. I would shower and head for the kitchen to begin making breakfast. Clyde would then take over the shower as Tosh read the newspaper. Tosh would shower while Clyde dressed, collected his crayons and lunch pail for school. We would all sit at breakfast together. I would force unwanted pleasantries into my face. (My mother had taught me: "If you have only one smile in you, give it to the people you love. Don't be surly at home, then go out in the street and start grinning 'Good morning' at total strangers.")

Tosh was usually quiet and amiable. Clyde gabbled about his dreams, which had to do with Roy Rogers as Jesus and Br'er Rabbit as God. We would finish breakfast in a glow of family life and they would both leave me with kisses, off to their separate excitements.

One new morning Tosh screamed from the bathroom, "Where in the hell are the goddamn dry towels?" The outburst caught me as unexpectedly as an upper cut. He knew that I kept the linen closet filled with towels folded as I had seen them photographed in the *Ladies' Home Journal*. More shocking than his forgetfulness, however, was his shouting. Anger generally rendered my husband morose and silent as a stone.

I went to the bathroom and handed him the thickest towel we owned. "What's wrong, Tosh?"

"All the towels in here are wet. You know I hate fucking wet towels."

I didn't know because he had never told me. I went back to the kitchen, not really knowing him, either.

At breakfast, Clyde began a recounting of Roy Rogers on his horse and Red Ryder, riding on clouds up to talk to God about some rustlers in the lower forty.

Tosh turned, looking directly at him, and said, "Shut up, will you. I'd like a little fucking peace and quiet while I eat."

The statement slapped Clyde quiet; he had never been spoken to with such cold anger.

Tosh looked at me. "The eggs are like rocks. Can't you fry a decent goddamn egg? If not, I'll show you."

I was too confounded to speak. I sat, not understanding the contempt. Clyde asked to be excused from the table. I excused him and followed him to the door.

He whispered, "Is Dad mad at me?"

I picked up his belongings, saw him jacketed and told him, "No, not at you. You know grownups have a lot on their minds. Sometimes they're so busy thinking they forget their manners. It's not nice, but it happens."

He said, "I'll go back and tell him 'bye."

"No, I think you should just go on to school. He'll be in a better mood this evening."

I held the front door open.

He shouted, " 'Bye, Dad."

There was no answer as I kissed him and closed the door. Fury quickened my footsteps. How could he scream at my son like that? Who the hell was he? A white-sheeted Grand Dragon of the Ku Klux Klan? I wouldn't have a white man talk to me in that tone of voice and I'd slap him with a coffeepot before he could yell at my child again. The midnight murmuring of soft words was forgotten. His gentle hands and familiar body had become in those seconds the shelter of an enemy.

He was still sitting over coffee, brooding. I went directly to the table.

"What do you mean, screaming at us that way?"

He said nothing.

"You started, first with the towels, then it was Clyde's dream. Then my cooking. Are you going crazy?"

He said, "I don't want to talk about it," still looking down into a half-filled cup of near-cold coffee.

"You sure as hell will talk about it. What have I done to you? What's the matter with you?"

He left the table and headed for the door without looking at me. I followed, raising my protest, hoping to puncture his cloak of withdrawal.

"I deserve and demand an explanation."

He held the door open and turned at last to face me. His voice was soft again and tender. "I think I'm just tired of being married." He pulled the door closed.

There is a shock that comes so quickly and strikes so deep that the blow is internalized even before the skin feels it. The strike must first reach bone marrow, then ascend slowly to the brain where the slowpoke intellect records the deed.

I went about cleaning my kitchen. Wash the dishes, sweep the floor, swipe the sputtered grease from the stove, make fresh coffee, put a fresh starched cloth on the table. Then I sat down. A sense of loss suffused me until I was suffocating within the vapors.

What had I done? I had placed my life within the confines of my marriage. I was everything the magazines said a wife should be. Constant, faithful and clean. I was economical. I was compliant, never offering headaches as excuses for not sharing the marital bed.

I had generously allowed Tosh to share my son, encouraging Clyde to think of him as a permanent life fixture. And now Tosh was "tired of being married."

Experience had made me accustomed to make quick analyses and quick if often bad decisions. So I expected Tosh, having come to the conclusion that marriage was exhausting, to ask me for a divorce when he returned from work. My tears were for myself and my son. We would be thrown again into a maelstrom of rootlessness. I wept for our loss of security and railed at the brutality of fate. Forgotten were my own complaints of the marriage. Unadmitted was the sense of strangulation I had begun to feel, or the insidious quality of guilt for having a white husband, which surrounded me like an evil aura when we were in public.

At my table, immersed in self-pity, I saw my now dying marriage as a union made in heaven, officiated over by St. Peter and sanctioned by God. It wasn't just that my husband was leaving me, I was losing a state of perfection, of grace.

My people would nod knowingly. Again a white man had taken a Black woman's body and left her hopeless, helpless and alone. But I couldn't expect their sympathy. I hadn't been ambushed on a dark country lane or raped by a group of randy white toughs. I had sworn to obey the man and had accepted his name. Anger, first at injustice, then at Tosh, stopped my tears. The same words I had used to voice my anguish I now used to fan the fires of rage. I had been a good wife, kind and compliant. And that wasn't enough for him? It was better than he deserved. More than he could reasonably have expected had he married within his own race. Anyway, had he planned to leave me from the first? Had he intended in the beginning to lure me into trust, then break up our marriage and break my heart? Maybe he was a sadist, scheming to inflict pain on poor, unsuspecting me. Well, he didn't know me. I would show him. I was no helpless biddy to be beckoned, then belittled. He was tired of marriage; all right, then I would leave him.

I got up from the table and cooked dinner, placed the food in the refrigerator and dressed in my best clothes. I left the dinner pots dirty and my bed unmade and hit the streets.

The noontime bar in the popular hotel on Eddy Street was filled with just-awakened petty gamblers and drowsy whores. Pimps not yet clad in their evening air of exquisite brutality spent the whores' earnings on their fellow parasites. I was recognized by a few drinkers, because I was Clydell and Vivian's daughter, because I had worked at the popular record shop or because I was that girl who had married the white man. I knew nothing about strong liquor except the names of some cocktails. I sat down and ordered a Zombie.

I clung to the long, cold drink and examined my predicament. My marriage was over, since I believed the legal bonds were only as good as the emotional desire to make them good. If a person didn't want you, he didn't want you. I could have thrown myself and my son on Tosh's mercy; he was a kind man, and he might have tolerated us in his home and on the edges of his life. But begging had always stuck, resisting, in my throat. I thought women who accepted their husbands' inattention and sacrificed all their sovereignty for a humiliating marriage more unsavory than the prostitutes who were drinking themselves awake in the noisy bar.

A short, thickset man sat down beside me and asked if he could pay for my second Zombie. He was old enough to be my father and reminded me of a kindly old country doctor from sepia-colored B movies. He asked my name and where I lived. I told his soft, near-feminine face that my name was Clara. When I said, "No, I'm not married," he grinned and said, "I don't know what these young men are waiting for. If I was a few years younger, I'd give them a run for they money. Yes siree bob." He made me feel comfortable. His Southern accent was as familiar to me as the smell of baking cornbread and the taste of wild persimmons. He asked if I was "a, uh, a ah a fancy lady?"

I said, "No." Desperate, maybe. Fanciful, maybe. Fancy? No.

He told me he was a merchant marine and was staying in the hotel and asked would I like to come upstairs and have a drink with him.

I would.

I sat on the bed in the close room, sipping the bourbon diluted with tap water. He talked about Newport News and his family as I thought about mine. He had a son and daughter near my age and they were "some kinda good children" and the girl was "some kinda pretty."

He noticed that I was responding to the whiskey, and came near the bed. "Why don't you just stretch out and rest a little while? You'll feel better. I'll rest myself. Just take off your shoes and your clothes. To keep them from wrinkling up on you."

My troubles and memories swam around, then floated out the window when I laid my head on the single pillow.

When I awakened, the dark room didn't smell familiar and my head throbbed. Confusion panicked me. I could have been picked up by an extraterrestrial being and teleported into some funky rocket ship. I jumped out of bed and fumbled along the walls, bumping until I found the light switch. My clothes were folded neatly and my shoes peeked their tidy toes from under the chair. I remembered the room and the merchant marine. I had no idea what had happened since I passed out. I examined myself and found no evidence that the old man had misused my drunkenness.

Dressing slowly, I wondered over the next move. Night had fallen on my affairs, but the sharp edges of rejection were not softened. There was a note on the dresser. I picked it up to read under the naked bulb that dangled from the ceiling; it said in effect:

Dear Clara,

    I tell you like I tell my own daughter. Be careful of strangers. Everybody smile at you don't have to mean you no good. I'll be back in two months from now. You be a good girl, hear? You'll make some boy a good wife.

Abner Green

I walked through the dark streets to Ivonne's house. After I explained what had happened, she suggested I telephone home.

"Hello, Tosh?"

"Marguerite, where are you?" The strain in his voice made me smile.

He asked, "When are you coming home? Clyde hasn't eaten."

I knew that was a lie.

"Nor have I. I can't eat," he said. I wasn't concerned about his appetite.

I said, "You're tired of being married. Yes? Well, I'll be home when I get there." I hung up before he could say more.

Ivonne said, "Maya, you're cold. Aren't you worried about Clyde?"

"No. Tosh loves Clyde. He'll look after him. He loves me too, but I gave up too much and gave in too much. Now we'll see."

The thought of his loneliness in the large apartment made my own less acute. I slept badly on Ivonne's sofa.

I went home the next day and we resumed a sort of marriage, but the center of power had shifted. I was no longer the dutiful wife ready with floors waxed and rugs beaten, with my finger between the pages of a cookbook and my body poised over the stove or spread-eagled on the bed.

One day my back began to hurt with a sullen ache, the kind usually visited only on the arthritic aged. My head pulsed and my side was punished by short, hot stabs of pain. The doctor advised immediate hospitalization. A simple appendectomy developed complications and it was weeks before I was released. The house was weary with failure—I told my husband that I wanted to go to Arkansas. I would stay with my grandmother until I had fully recovered. I meant in mind, as well as body.

He came close and in a hoarse whisper said, "Marguerite. Your grandmother died the day after your operation. You were too sick. I couldn't tell you."

Ah, Momma. I had never looked at death before, peered into its yawning chasm for the face of a beloved. For days my mind staggered out of balance. I reeled on a precipice of knowledge that even if I were rich enough to travel all over the world, I would never find Momma. If I were as good as God's angels and as pure as the Mother of Christ, I could never have Momma's rough slow hands pat my cheek or braid my hair.

Death to the young is more than that undiscovered country; despite its inevitability, it is a place having reality only in song or in other people's grief.

1976

Here: Grace

"You will love me?" my husband asks, and at something in his tone my consciousness rouses like a startled cat, ears pricked, pupils round and onyx-black.

Never voluble, he has been unusually subdued this evening. Thinking him depressed about the mysterious symptoms that have plagued him for months and that we know in our heart of hearts signal a recurrence of cancer, although the tests won't confirm it for several more days, I pressed up against him on the couch and whispered against his neck, "This may be the most troublesome time of our lives, but I'm so happy." This awareness of joy, though it's been growing for several years now, has recently expanded in response to my own failing health. A few weeks ago, pondering the possibility that I might die at any time, I posed myself a new question: *If I died at this very moment, would I die happy?* And the answer burst out without hesitation: *Yes!* Since then, in spite of my fears, I've felt a new contentment. What more could I ever ask than to give an unequivocal response to such a question?

His silence persisted. "Scared?" I asked him after a few moments, thinking of the doctor's appointment that morning, the CAT scan scheduled for later in the week. Head resting on the back of the couch, eyes closed, he nodded. More silence. Finally I said, "George, you know how I love words. I need words!"

And now, words: "You will love me?" Behind his glasses, his eyes have the startled look I associate, incongruously, with the moment of orgasm.

"Yes," I tell him, alert, icy all over. "I can safely promise you that. I will always love you."

"You asked the other day whether my illness could be AIDS," he says unevenly. "I'm pretty sure it isn't, because I had the test for HIV some time ago, after I had an affair for a couple of years with another woman."

The sensation is absolutely nonverbal, but everybody knows it even without words: the stunned breathlessness that follows a jab to the solar plexus. What will astonish me in the days to come is that this sensation can sustain itself long after one would expect to be dead of asphyxiation. I have often wished myself dead. If it were possible to die of grief, I would die at this moment. But it's not, and I don't.

A couple of years. A *couple of years*. This was no fit of passion, no passing fancy, but a sustained commitment. He loved her, loves her still: Their relationship, until he broke it off—for reasons having little to do with me—was a kind of marriage, he says. Time after time after time he went to her, deliberately, telling whatever lies he needed to free himself from me and the children, and later from his mother when she came for a protracted visit after his father's death, throughout at least a couple of years.

More. He'd fallen in love with her six years earlier, I could sense at that time, and they'd had a prolonged flirtation. She was a bitter, brittle woman, and something about her rage inflamed him. Their paths had parted, however, and I had no way of knowing of their later chance encounter, courtship, years-long "marriage." And after that ended—here, in this room, which will ever hereafter be haunted by her tears—four years of silence: too late to tell me, he says, and then too later, and then too later still. Twelve of our twenty-seven years of marriage suddenly called, one way or another, into question. I recall my brother's description of his framing shop after the San Francisco earthquake, how miraculously nothing in it was broken, not even the sheets of glass for covering pictures, but it looked as though some giant gremlin had come in and slid everything a few feet to one side. My past feels similarly shoved out of whack, not shattered but strangely reconfigured, and out of its shadows steps a man I have never seen before: Sandra's lover.

If I were that proverbial virtuous woman, the one whose price is far above rubies, perhaps I would have the right to order George out of my sight, out of my house, out of my life. But I'm not that woman. I'm the other one, the one whose accusers dropped their stones and skulked away. I've desired other men, slept with them, even loved them, although I've never felt married to one. I guess I took my girlhood vow literally: I have always thought of marriage as something one did once and forever. All the same, in brief passionate bursts I've transgressed the sexual taboos that give definition to Christian marriage.

I'm not a virtuous woman, but I am a candid one. Many years ago, George and I pledged that we would not again lie to anyone about anything. I haven't been strictly faithful to the spirit of this promise, either, because I've deliberately withheld information on occasion (although not, according to my mother, often enough, having an unfortunate propensity for spilling the family beans in print); but I have not, when directly challenged, lied. This commitment can have maddening consequences: One night I listened for half an hour or longer to the outpourings of a total stranger in response to an essay in one of my books because I couldn't tell her that I had a pot on the stove about to boil over when I actually didn't. Had Daddy and I meant that vow for *everybody*, my daughter asked after I hung up the telephone, not just for each other? Not even, I can see now, for each other: especially not for each other.

"How can you ever believe me again after this?" George asks, and I shrug: "I've believed you all this time. I'm in the habit of it. Why should I stop now?" And so I go on believing him, but a subtle difference will emerge over time: belief becomes a matter of faith, no longer logically connected to the "truth" of its object, which remains unknowable except insofar as it chooses to reveal itself. I suppose I could hire a private detective to corroborate George's tales, but I'm not going to because George's whereabouts are no less his own business now than they ever were. I can envision some practical difficulties in my being unable to locate him at any given time, but no moral ones, whereas I perceive a serious problem in seeking information that would curb his freedom to lie, a freedom without which he can't freely tell me the truth. I don't want to come by my belief through extortion. Once, I believed George because it never occurred to me not to believe him; now I believe him because I prefer belief, which affirms his goodness, to doubt, which sneers and sniggers at it. No longer a habitual response, belief becomes an act of love.

It does not thereby absolve George of responsibility for the choices he has freely made, however. The years while he was slipping away to sleep with Sandra were among the most wretched of my not conspicuously cheerful life; and by lying to me, he permitted—no, really encouraged—me to believe that my unhappiness was, as always, my own fault, even though, thanks to the wonders of psychopharmacology, I was at last no longer clinically depressed. I remember lying awake, night after night, while he stayed up late grading papers and then dropped into bed, and instantly into sleep, without a word or a touch; as he twitched and snored, I'd prowl through the dark house, sip milk or wine, smoke cigarettes, write in my journal until, shuddering with cold and loneliness, I'd be forced to creep back into bed. Past forty, he must have been conserving his sexual energies, I realize now, but when I expressed concern and sadness, he blamed our chilling relationship on me: I was distracted, too bitchy, not affectionate enough. . . . Ah, he knew my self-doubts thoroughly.

Breakdowns in our relationship, especially sexual ones, had habitually been ascribed to me. "I'm very tired," I wrote in my journal early in this period of misery, twenty years into our marriage, "of his putting me down all the time—telling me that I'm too involved with Anne, that I don't handle Matthew well, that I'm not affectionate (the only signs of affection he recognizes are physical, which I suppose makes sense, since he doesn't communicate verbally). In short, that I'm a bad mother and wife. I just don't know how to feel much affection for someone I feel sorry for, for being married to me." Tired of disparagement I may already have been, but I took over two years more to recognize myself as a collaborator in it: "He survives—thrives—on my culpability. Without it, where would he be today? We've *both* built our lives on it, and if I remove it, our relationship will no longer have any foundation."

This awareness of complicity precipitated out of a homely crisis (the form of most of my crises), in the winter of 1985, involving the proper setting of the thermostat, which George persistently left at sixty degrees even though I couldn't bear the temperature below sixty-five (and, as came out in the course of the dispute, neither could he). When I told him that the coldness of the house represented my growing feelings of neglect and abandonment, he countered that he had to go elsewhere (leaving the thermostat set at sixty) in order to get the touching and affection he needed. It was, I noted, "the same old ploy, trying to trigger my guilt for not being a physically affectionate wife. Only this time I could feel myself not quite biting. Because he wants the physical part to continue regardless of the pain I'm in, even if he causes the pain, and he blames me if I won't put out, come across, what have you. And I'm sick unto death of bearing the blame." He could, I suddenly understood, turn up the heat himself. He chose not to.

Or rather, he chose to turn it up in some other woman's house. In spite of the sexual stresses underlying this controversy, he gave no hint that his longing for "warmth and light" was taking him from the crumbling converted Chinese grocery where the children and I lived to a spacious, immaculate, perfectly appointed home in a tranquil neighborhood miles away; and I didn't guess. Just as he knew how to exploit my self-doubts, he knew how to escape me. Teaching in two programs, he was out of the house from at least eight-thirty in the morning until eight-thirty at night; he devoted his spare time to good works like cooking at Casa María soup kitchen, observing the federal trial of the people who had arranged sanctuary for refugees from El Salvador, and editing ¡Presente!, the local Catholics for Peace and Justice newsletter. With such a schedule, of course he'd have little enough energy left for sex, or even a leisurely family dinner. Another woman (his lover, for instance) might have judged his devotion to illiterate, poor, and oppressed people sanctimonious, even morbid, but I found it natural and necessary.

As a result, he put me in a conscientious bind: I felt abandoned, and I believed that George was neglecting our troubled teenaged son dangerously, but I couldn't make our needs weigh heavily enough against those of five hundred empty bellies at the kitchen door or a Salvadoran woman who'd fled her village in terror when the last of her sons disappeared. Still, I wondered uneasily why the spiritual growth he said he was seeking necessitated his setting out on what appeared to be "a quest—Galahad and the Holy Grail—noble and high-minded and above all out there, beyond the muck and mire of daily living in a decaying house with a crippled wife and a rebellious adolescent son." Forced to let him go, I did so with a bitter blessing: "Feed the poor, my dear. Shelter the refugees. Forget the impoverishment you leave in your wake. It's only Nancy and Matthew and Anne, after all—nothing spiritual there, nothing uplifting, no real needs, just niggling demands that drag at you, cling to you, slow your lofty ascent into the light and life of Christ."

Our approaches to ministry were hopelessly at odds: "I think that the life of Christ is only this life, which one must enter further and further. And I hate the entering. I'd give anything to escape. . . . There's no glamor here, no glory. Only the endless grading of papers. The being present for two difficult children. The making of another meal. The dragging around of an increasingly crippled body, forcing it to one end of the house and back again, out the door, into the classroom, home again, up from the bed, up from the toilet, up from the couch. The extent of my lofty ascent. I want only to do what I must with as much grace as I can." That George, finding these conditions squalid and limiting, sought to minister elsewhere embittered but hardly surprised me. And so, whenever he wanted Sandra, he had only to murmur, "Soup. Sanctuary. *¡Presente!*" in order to be as free of them as he liked.

I have been, it appears, a bit of a fool. "Where did I think you'd gone?" I ask George. "What lies did I believe?" He claims not to remember. He will always claim not to remember such details, which is his prerogative, but the writer in me obsessively scribbles in all the blanks he leaves. I imagine the two of them sitting half-naked beside her pool, sipping cold Coronas and laughing at my naiveté, and then I have to laugh myself: I would have been the last thing on their minds. This sense of my own extinction will prove the most tenacious and terrifying of my responses, the one that keeps me flat on my back in the night, staring into the dark, gasping for breath, as though I've been buried alive. For almost thirty years, except during a couple of severe disintegrative episodes, my presence to George has kept me present to myself. Now, at just the moment when cancer threatens to remove that reassurance of my own reality from my future, it's yanked from my past as well. Throughout his sweet stolen hours with Sandra, George lived where I was not.

"Are you all right?" my daughter asks on the day following George's revelation when she stumbles upon me huddled in my studio, rocking and shivering. I shake my head. "Shall I cut class and stay here with you?"

"No, go to class," I say. "Then come back. We'll talk."

"You're not going to do anything rash while I'm gone?" It's the question of a child seasoned in suicide, and I wish she didn't have to ask it.

"I promise. Scoot."

I hadn't planned to tell Anne, at least not yet; but George is getting sicker by the day, his mother is about to arrive for several weeks, Christmas is coming, and I don't think I can deal with this new complication alone. I have George's permission to tell whomever I wish. "I want you to write about this," he says. "I want you to write about us." For himself, he has never revealed it to anyone except once, early on, the psychotherapist with whom we've worked, together and apart, over the years. But he believes in the value of what I try to do in my work: in reclaiming human experience, insofar as I can find it embodied in my own experience, from the morass of secrecy and shame into which Christian and pre-Christian social taboos have plunged it, to rescue and restore God's good creation. (And if at times the work proves as smelly as pumping a septic tank, well, shit is God's creation, too.) George supports it, but the work itself is mine. If any bad tidings are to be borne, I am the one to bear them.

"But Mom," Anne says when I've finished my tale of woe, "men *do* these things." Transcribed, these words might look like a twenty-five-year-old's cynicism, but in fact her tone rings purely, and characteristically, pragmatic. It's just the tone I need to jerk my attention back from private misery to the human condition. She's right, of course. In the Judaic roots of our culture, as Uta Ranke-Heinemann points out in *Eunuchs for the Kingdom of Heaven*, "a man could never violate his own marriage. The wife belonged to her husband, but the husband did not belong to his wife," and a couple of thousand years of Church teaching on the subject of marital fidelity—not all of it a model of clarity and consistency—has never entirely balanced the expectations placed on the two partners. *People* do these things, Anne means (I know: I have done them myself); but ordinary men, men possessed of healthy sexual appetites, have been tacitly *entitled* to do them. They're just *like* that.

Except for my man. One reviewer of my first book of essays, *Plaintext*, wrote: "The reader will also wish to see more closely some of the people who simply drift through these essays, especially Mairs' husband, who comes across as a saint, staying through extreme mood swings, suicide attempts, severe illness, and a number of love affairs." That's *my* man: a saint. Through my essays I've publicly canonized him. Any man who could stay with a crazy, crippled, unfaithful bitch like me had to be more than humanly patient and loving and long-suffering and self-abnegating and . . . oh, just more than human.

Admittedly, I had help in forming this view, especially from other women; a man whose bearing is as gentle and courtly as George's can seem a true miracle, one my inconstancy plainly didn't merit. "But hasn't he ever slept with another woman?" more than one person has asked, and I've said proudly, gratefully, "No. I've asked him, and he tells me he never has." I often told myself that he "ought to go, get out now, while he's still fairly young, find a healthy woman free from black spells, have some fun. No one could blame him." And occasionally, trying to account for his physical and emotional unavailability, I'd conjecture: "Perhaps another woman— he's so attractive and romantic that that thought always crosses my mind." My guess was dead on, it turns out, formed at the height of his affair with just the sort of healthy woman I'd had in mind, but I took him at his word and felt humbled—humiliated—that he had responded to my infidelities with such steadfastness.

A saint's wife readily falls prey to self-loathing, I discovered, since comparisons are both common and invidious, and recuperation, if it occurs at all, is a protracted and lonely process. One evening a couple of years ago, when I'd been invited to discuss *Plaintext* with a local women's reading group and the conversation turned, as such conversations always seem to, to my infidelity and George's forbearance, I blurted: "Wait a minute! Did it ever occur to you that there might be some advantage to being married to the woman who wrote *Plaintext*?" At last I'd reached the point where I could ask that question. But as I sipped coffee and nibbled a chocolate cookie in the company of these polite and pleasant but plainly distressed strangers, my chances of getting an affirmative answer seemed as remote as ever. In this tale, I was decidedly not the Princess but the Dragon.

George has conspired in his own sanctification. Why wouldn't he? The veneration of others must be seductive. And if, in order to perpetuate it, he had to affirm—to me, and through me to others familiar with my writings—his faithfulness even as he shuttled between Sandra and me, well, what harm was he doing? For her own reasons, Sandra was just as eager as he to keep the affair clandestine. They seldom went out and never got together with friends; he never even encountered her child, who was always, magically, "not there"; she'd even meet him in a parking lot and drive him to her house so that the neighbors wouldn't see his car. He could maintain this oddly hermetic relationship without risk to the sympathy and admiration of friends, family, and book reviewers alike. No one need ever know.

Until, ultimately, me. That is, I don't need to know, not at all, I've done very well indeed without knowing, but he has come to need to tell me. At first, he thought merely breaking with Sandra would calm the dread his father's death and the discovery of melanoma in a lymph node stirred in him, but now he needs a stronger remedy. "I feel this awful blackness inside. I just want to die," he says after confessing, and I shudder, because an awful blackness is precisely what he has inside—a six-centimeter melanoma attached to his small bowel—and I don't want him to die, he can tell me anything, I'll accept whatever he confesses, any number of awful blacknesses, if only please he won't die. He hasn't any control over that, alas, but at least now he has cleared his conscience thoroughly. I think he's after another clarity as well, one that involves putting off sainthood and standing naked—bones jutting under wasted flesh, scars puckering arm and belly, penis too limp now for love—as a man. He wants to be loved as he is, not as we—his mother, my mother, my sisters, our daughter, his students, our friends, maybe even Sandra herself—have dreamed him. I most of all. I look anew at the reviewer's words: "The reader will wish to *see more closely* some of the people who *simply drift* through these essays . . ."

George is accustomed to holding himself slightly aloof. The only child of adoring parents, he grew up believing himself entitled to act on his own desires without regard for the needs of others: There weren't any others. If he wanted the last cookie, it was his. (In fact, even if he didn't want it, his mother probably made him take it.) No noisy wrangles, no division of the coveted cookie followed by wails that "he got the bigger half," no snitching a bite while the other's head was turned or spitting on the other's half to spoil it for both, just complacent munching down to the last sweet crumb. But, by the same token, no whispers and giggles under the covers after Mother has put out the light *for absolutely the last time.* No shared cookies. No shared secrets, either. No entanglements, true. But no intimacy.

Having grown up in an extensive family linked by complicated affections, with a slightly younger sister who still sometimes seems hooked into my flesh, I don't think I ever quite comprehended George's implacable self-sufficiency. Maybe for that reason I allowed, even encouraged, his remoteness. And I did. The reviewer is talking, after all, not about George's nature but about my essays. If the reader wants to "see" George "more closely," then I have not seen him closely enough. George "drifts" through my essays because I permitted him to drift through my life. "I couldn't imagine," he tells me now, "that what I was doing, as long as I kept it in a separate little box, had any effect on the rest of you." Like his indulgent mother, I let him persist in such manly detachment. I'd have served him better as a scrappy sister.

What I might have thought of, in good aging-hippy fashion, as "giving him space," letting him "do his own thing," strikes me now as a failure of love. Respecting another's freedom does not require cutting him loose and letting him drift; the lines of love connecting us one to another are stays, not shackles. I do not want to fail again. After the children and I have each spoken with him separately about the affair, I say to him: "You may have hoped, in confessing to us, that we'd punish you by sending you away, but now you see that we won't do that. If you want to leave, you'll have to go on your own initiative. As far as we're concerned, you're not an only child, you're one of us. We love you. We intend, if you will let us, to keep you."

"You will love me?" George asked at the beginning of this terrible test, and I find, to my relief, that I can keep my promise. "But can you forgive him?" asks our friend Father Ricardo when we seek his counsel, and I reply, without hesitation, "I already have."

I *have*? How can this be? I have never felt more hurt than I do now. I am angry. I am bitter. I try to weep but my eyes feel blasted, although occasionally I shudder and gasp in some stone's version of crying its heart out. I dread going out into the city for fear I'll encounter Sandra. I torment myself with images of George pressing his lips to hers, stroking her hair, slowly unbuttoning her blouse, calling her "sweetheart," too. *She got the sex*, I reflect sardonically as I keep my vigil through surgery and its horrific aftermath, then through chemotherapy, *and I get the death*. I despise her for her willingness to risk my marriage without a thought; and yet in a queer way I pity her because, as it has turned out, she has to live without George and, for the moment, I do not.

Worst of all, ghastly congratulatory cheers ring in my head: *Good-o, George! You've finally given the bitch her comeuppance: tit for tat, an eye for an eye, and not a whit more than she deserves.* "What do you care what people think?" he shrugs when I tell him of this fantastic taunting, but the truth is that, with new comprehension of the suffering my adultery must have caused him, I'm tempted to join the chorus. Still, although our affairs may be connected chronologically (mine all took place before his) and causally (bitterness about mine offered him permission for his), morally they stand separate. I don't merit the pain I'm now in, any more than George ever deserved to be hurt, but we have unquestionably wounded each other horribly and we each bear full moral responsibility for the other's pain. George is right to dismiss my demonic chorus: What matters is not mockery and blame, whether our own or others', but mutual contrition. Over and over when he clings to me and weeps as I cannot and says, "I'm sorry, I'm sorry," I hold him, stroking his back and murmuring reassurances: that I love him, that I'll be all right, that he hasn't "spoiled" us, that through this pain we can grow. Forgiveness is not even in question. It is simply, mysteriously, already accomplished.

Week after week he has stood beside me telling me what I have not wanted to know: *I confess to Almighty God, and to you, my brothers and sisters, that I have sinned, through my own fault, in my thoughts and in my words, in what I have done and in what I have failed to do.* Now that he's divulged the specific contents of his conscience to me, I'm curious what this little ritual of general confession meant during the time he so plainly wasn't sorry for what he was doing. "Did you ever think about Sandra as you said those words?" I ask. "Did you think what you were doing might be wrong?"

"Well, yes, I knew it was. But I also knew I didn't intend to stop. So I just had to hope that God had a sense of humor." Fortunately for George, God has a much better sense of humor than I do. But I've been working on it. Meanwhile, week after week his voice has spoken aloud at my side: *And I ask Blessed Mary ever virgin, all the angels and saints, and you, my brothers and sisters, to pray for me to the Lord our God.* As bidden, I have prayed for him, as for myself and for all the disembodied voices floating up behind me, that God might have mercy on us, forgive us our sins, and lead each one of us to everlasting life. Believing myself forgiven by God, I must believe George equally forgiven. And if forgiven by God, surely no less by me.

One of the elements that drew me into the Catholic Church was the concept of grace, although I've never been able to make more than clumsy sense of it. I am moved by the idea that God always already loves us first, before we love God, wholly and without condition, that God forgives us even before we have done anything to require forgiveness, as we will inevitably do, and that this outpouring of love and forgiveness fortifies us for repentance and reform. I am moved—but not persuaded. I am simply incapable of grasping an abstraction unless I can root it experientially, and nothing in my experience has revealed quite how grace works. Until now. The uncontingent love and forgiveness I feel for George, themselves a gift of grace, unwilled and irresistible, intimate that grace whose nature has eluded me.

For the most theologically unsophisticated of reasons, involving a dead father who went, I was told, to heaven up in the sky, together with continual reiterations, from about the same age on, of "Our Father, who art in heaven . . . ," I always expect spiritual insights to shower like coins of light from on high. When instead they bubble up from the mire like will-o'-the-wisps, I am invariably startled. Grace *here*, among these lies and shattered vows, sleepless nights, remorse, recriminations? Yes, precisely, here: Grace.

But forgiveness does not, whatever the aphorism says, entail forgetfulness. Never mind the sheer impossibility of forgetting that your husband has just told you he's had an affair, a strenuous version of that childhood game in which you try, on a dare, *not* to think about a three-legged green cat licking persimmon marmalade from the tip of its tail. Never mind memory's malarial tenacity, the way that, weeks and months and even years after you think the shock has worn off, as you recall a trip you made to Washington to receive a writing award, it occurs to you that in your absence they may have made love for the first time and all your words, the ones you'd written before and the ones you've written since, shrivel and scatter like ashes. Never mind.

Mind what matters: his presence here, for now. Love is not love, forgiveness is not forgiveness, that effaces the beloved's lineaments by letting him drift, indistinct, through the lives of those who claim him. That way lies lethargy, which is the death of love. I am not married to Saint George, after all. I am married to a man who is, among many other things neither more nor less remarkable, an adulterer. I must remember him: whole.

1993

BETTY FRIEDAN

Thoughts on Becoming a Grandmother

I had been invited to speak at a scientific symposium in Israel on "Mankind, 2000." (He will be eighteen in the year 2000!) Emily had deigned to go with me, on her last spring vacation before finishing medical school. They had been rather cross about that, because the baby was due in three or four weeks, and what if it was born while we were gone? The grandmother's presence was certainly not essential (surely not), but the future aunt, my daughter-the-doctor, was supposed to be on standby, up there at Harvard Medical School, to fly down when labor began and be their personal medical support system at the birthing center. Approaching parenthood with far more confidence than I remember having at that time, Jonathan, my second son, and Helen, the future mother, scorned the sterile, dehumanized, alienating technology of a male-dominated obstetrical-gynecological professional hospital delivery. The future grandmother, ideologically happy at such an expression of second-stage feminism so close to home, and, above all, applauding the zeal and conscientiousness with which the father-to-be shared the birthing preparations, from the first decision about the nurse-midwife to the final breathing exercises, had certain doubts about the absence of sophisticated medical expertise and life-saving equipment if complications arose, but she was not exactly consulted. On the other hand, the future parents seemed to find a certain fortuitous advantage in our making that pilgrimage to Jerusalem, with the birth impending . . .

On the trip things are a bit tense between Emily and me, with currents of unexpressed mother-daughter love and the need to be no longer dependent on that love, for both of us, for we both know that this is probably the last time she will be my giggly roommate, sister-traveler on such a trip, as she has been, off and on, since she was eleven or twelve. Internship, residency, a serious young man, await her return. She turns away from me, our first day in Jerusalem, as we stand in the rain before the Wailing Wall, and I see her slip a little piece of paper out of her purse and put it in a crevice in the wall. When I ask her later, all she will say is that it is a private matter between her and her brother. She has to fly back for the start of medical-school classes again, before my symposium ends.

On my own last day in Jerusalem, those abstract speculations about women and men in the twenty-first century having been delivered, I wander the holy streets of the Old City, not luxuriating as I usually do in the mystery of its past, but impatient, suddenly, to be back where that birth is due. But I have called them that morning in New York, and Jonathan has reported that the baby is in no hurry to get out, the nurse-midwife says not for another week or two. So with no need for me to stop over, I will fly straight back to Boston, where I am doing research at Harvard. Just before sunset, on impulse, I retrace the route to the Wailing Wall. I am not myself formally religious, though lately as I have become interested in the religion of my ancestors, I sometimes suspect I may have inadvertently lived a religious life. (The women's movement, for me, was at times almost a religious experience.) Standing before that wall in Jerusalem, feeling the power of all those centuries of prayer and belief, I say my own silent prayer for a happy, healthy baby. I find myself murmuring the words of the traditional Hebrew prayer that links the generations of our ancestors to whom this wall was holy to that baby who will also say those words, *Shema Yisrael* . . .

All the way back on the plane, in and out of sleep—for I am tired after this hectic week—I'm nagged by a kind of unreasoning apprehension about the birth that for some reason I feel may even now be taking place. The words of the Rilke poem come to me:

> *We are nearing the land that is life.*
> *You will recognize it by its seriousness.*

When we finally land at Logan Airport and I hear my name on the paging system, I am hardly surprised. *Baby born early this morning, a boy, everyone fine, at Lenox Hill Hospital.* But they weren't supposed to be at a hospital! I get the bags through customs, and take the shuttle back to New York. They all are there, at the hospital, my shaken family. A few hours after labor began, there was untoward bleeding. The conscientious birthing-center midwife sent Helen immediately in an ambulance to the nearest hospital. The baby was seen in the X-ray to be positioned wrong, face up. All the preparations for natural childbirth notwithstanding, the doctors now took over. Emily had flown down that night from Boston, as planned, but they wouldn't even let her on the hospital floor. The obstetrician who was on call that night got a flat tire on the way to the hospital, and they had kept Helen strapped up on the operating table, not knowing what was happening. Over her objections, they injected a drug that made her contractions stop. When the doctor finally arrived, he sent Jonathan out and said he had to do a Caesarean because the monitor showed the baby to be "stressed." But Helen felt sure that if only they had let her down, let her squat in the way she had been taught, she could have had the baby naturally. They had had a night of fear and terror, all of them, and I had not been there to help. But *the baby was fine*, Helen was fine (she looked terrible, still in shock, to me). Could I see the baby?

And Jonathan takes me to the nursery corridor. I study the baby through the glass. He looks *familiar*, that baby. He looks like Jonathan, as a baby—no, like Danny, my first-born—no, not quite like either of them. But familiar. Later, from a distance, I see Jonathan, scrubbed up in a hospital gown, shaken still but beaming now, his dimples showing, stiffly, proudly, self-consciously, tenderly carrying that baby, his son. (Even in such an Establishment hospital the new father is now allowed to fetch the baby in to the mother to nurse.)

Banished to the waiting room while the feeding takes place, I meet the baby's grandfather, from whom I have been divorced thirteen years now. He had shared their night of fear, while I had been on that plane. He had tried to get another doctor in. He had relived, obviously, another such night, over thirty years ago, when in similar shock and disbelief and outrage he and I had had to sign an agreement permitting our first-born, Jonathan's older brother, Daniel, to be taken by Caesarean. (To this day, just like Helen, I wonder if it was really necessary. If they had just let me try harder, longer, could I have done it naturally?)

There has been a great distance between us in the last dozen years, but there is healing in that shared memory, in this moment of shared support of our son, in the seriousness of new life going on from that shared beginning. "He seems so emotional," says my former husband of his son. "He was crying so. Do you think he's too emotional?" I don't, of course. Things might have been different if that older father, whom I no longer really know, had not been so afraid of feelings. There is pain for me in the distance, now, from all that happened between us, in knowing that we cannot really share this moment, and yet, there is the healing joy: "Hello, Grandma." "Hello, Grandpa."

In bedside conference, the whole family discusses boys' names. They had a girl's name ready but could not agree on a boy's. They do not decide for a week, until just before the naming, the *bris*. The baby's name is Rafael: "healer," it means. And then his mother's name, Nakdimen, which she has kept, hyphenated in accepted feminist style.

A postfeminist baby, with a traditional Jewish *bris* ceremony of circumcision and naming. My other son, Daniel, flies in from Chicago, where he is a theoretical physicist now, wearing, in lieu of a yarmulke, the beret he bought during his postdoctorate fellowship in Paris. And Jonathan's best friend, Michael, flies in from Lummi Island, off the coast of Washington, where he's still living in that log cabin he and Jonathan shared during their salmon-fisherman years, before Jon came back and finished college. And Steve, the third of those three musketeers, whose wife, Estelle, is now pregnant too—the boys intend to continue their friendship into the next generation! And those two boys' mothers, and my friend Natalie, and her kids, who grew up with mine, and Jon and Helen's new friends. It is moving, the gathering of this tribe linked by years of shared life and love, for this formal celebration of birth, of the glory of generation. We all feel it. "You will recognize it by its seriousness." I am a grandmother!

Since none of my close friends has had the experience of being a grandmother yet—we sometimes wondered if we ever would, given our daughters' preoccupation with their legal, publishing, banking, medical, and other careers, and our sons' seeming disinclination to marital commitment—I have no role model as a modern feminist grandmother. (My own achievement, finally, of this state, is not only envied by my friends but gives them hope!) "How does it feel, being a grandmother?" they keep asking me, curious, and so envious. Envious? An earlier convention assumed that if a woman allowed herself to be honest, she would feel some pain at such a public, undeniable announcement of the loss of her own youth. "Aren't you excited about being a grandfather?" Natalie asked my former husband. "I don't like to talk about it much," he said. "It would make the young women I take out think I was old." A new friend, male, who also recently achieved this state, said, "I don't *have* any feelings about it. I don't feel old enough to be a grandfather." But that's not, for some reason, the way the women I know feel. Not me. Turning another corner is the way I feel. Excited, curious. In my own moving from the battles of the women's movement to a new stage in my pursuit of personal and political truth, I welcome this new grounding in the land that is life. Generation is what I feel, the *goodness* of it.

There is a delight, a comfort, an easing of the burden, somehow, a renewal of joy in my own life, to feel the stream of life of which I am part going on like this. (I get a vaguely similar feeling when the daughters of the women's movement come up to me with their "it changed my whole life" and their new choices and problems, but that joy is less personal, less vivid.) "Face it," said Emily, "now that your children are getting married and having children of our own, we aren't your *children* anymore. You can't go on thinking of us that way." True? Yes, and no. . . . As research recently has shown, for women generally now, as for me, the empty nest is not traumatic, as it once was, or was assumed to be, back in the days of the feminine mystique, when woman was defined only as a wife and mother. Yet even now, surely part of our personhood is defined by that powerful experience as mother, which is far more than mystique. It is a sort of heavy joyous-painful shadow, under and over everything else we do during those mother years. For me, as for others, now that that part is nearly finished, there is relief, release, a lightening of shadow, as I see them make their own way into life at last, their own persons—my kids, so intensely, satisfyingly themselves, in work, in love, and now, beginning with kids of their own. As they enter this new cycle of generation, they even seem to come back home again, in a different way.

Jonathan is a lovely father. I like to watch him, tender, competent, responsible, enjoying, so sure, as he slings Rafi over his shoulder, feeds him bits of banana, and straps him into that backpack. I like to watch the flow between him and Helen as they share the concrete, omnipresent, never-finished mundane daily details of the feeding, undressing, wiping, patting, comforting, rocking, cleaning up, soothing, playing, laughing, endless watching, that is parenting. There is an evolution going on here. They share those details of parenting more consciously, and more organically, than we did. But his father and I shared them more than my father and mother did. Still, it is quite clear that Jonathan is not the baby's mother. She is breast-feeding, of course. I defiantly breast-fed all three of mine, for nearly a year each time, though it was not so fashionable then. But I was not nearly so confident a mother as she is.

She amazes and delights me, that young daughter-in-law of mine, in the clarity of her choices. She had just finished college, having dropped out for a while to go to Israel, and to work, as had my son. He was making up for lost time, doing two years' graduate work in one for his engineering degree. They agonized together over the decision, finally, to take what life was offering them, and have the baby. "I would have hated to feel I had to have the baby," she said. "Knowing that we really chose to have a baby, since I could have had an abortion, makes a big difference."

Watching her, I sense that this consciousness of chosen motherhood today gives, and requires, a sense of autonomy, identity, *self* in a woman that is different from the passive "anatomy is destiny" of past generations and the glorified feminine mystique of mine; beyond the pill and abortion, the consciousness of other choices, other women's career patterns, clarifies the values. This kind of chosen motherhood is a step beyond the ambivalent reactions and superwoman demands of first-stage feminism. There is, for sure, an evolution here.

My mother, who had to quit the newspaper job she loved when she married my father and started to have babies, covered some very conflictful feelings about herself as a woman by being the perfect housewife and perfect mother and shifting her own frustrated ambitions to excessive demands on her husband and children, which we never seemed to satisfy. She "raised" us compulsively by the book. The book, then, was Watson's behaviorism. No matter how much the baby cried, you "conditioned" by picking it (me) up to feed it only when the schedule said—every four hours, by the clock. Since I didn't want to be like my mother—and had no other image of what a woman could be or feel—I had very little confidence in myself as a mother. I had to blindly follow the book. Oh, how Dr. Spock could make me feel guilty! (Even today, the slightest hint from these grown-up children of mine about my lacks as a mother can arouse painful tremors of guilt in tough skin that hardly flinches at political abuse from the vicious likes of Phyllis Schlafly.) And I was fired from my newspaper job, when I was pregnant with Jonathan—I didn't have all that much choice. That firing would be a violation of the law against sex discrimination, today. Then, it wasn't even a grievance the union would take up.

Helen gets some of her strength from her own mother, who was a survivor of the Holocaust. But she has consciously repudiated the traditional passivity, the martyrdom to men, and the fears that she associates with her mother. She is, in her own mind, an independent, self-created woman.

I like to think that the new sense and possibilities of choice, and the new images of woman as person, that the movement opened have helped to give Helen and others of her postfeminist generation a good enough feeling about being a woman so that they can *trust themselves*. I've seen some books about parenting around Jonathan and Helen's apartment, but Helen doesn't consult any baby bible the slavish way I did Dr. Spock. She already feels she knows better than the experts about her own baby, and she probably does. My friends Jackie and Binky, who also had their first babies this year—from very conscious choice indeed, in their mid-thirties, in the midst of demanding careers—were confident enough to simply take the babies home from the hospital, ahead of schedule, when they seemed not to be doing well under hospital routine.

Given the strong feminist images of the family she married into, the fact that Helen felt no need to apologize for having taken a "hiatus" from any career to concentrate that first year on mothering bespeaks a real sureness of herself as a woman, which I applaud. "Sometimes I feel bored out of my skin," she admitted cheerfully, taking off for her class in karate (not a bad skill for a mother wheeling a baby in a tough city neighborhood, but also a way to vent those irritations of endless mothering which the feminine mystique used to deny). She also started studying graphology, which always fascinated her, and can now analyze handwriting with an accuracy that would probably stand up in court better than a lie detector. "You'd make a good psychotherapist," I tell her. "I'm not sure I want to waste the time getting all those degrees," she says. There's no sense whatsoever that she is martyring herself, or that she ever thought of herself as "just a housewife." But there is also no sense that she feels the need to be a superwoman. Her present, very part-time job is no "career." But her search is serious.

And she certainly takes no nonsense from Jonathan, who has his *macho* tendencies.

This same year, some of my friends having their first babies in their mid-thirties are having other problems. Barnard College, which still has no maternity-leave policy, made one of these women come back to work less than a month after her baby was born. Only 18 percent of women now working have the right to take a maternity leave, and come back to their jobs, to say nothing about men and paternity leave. Yet by the end of the decade, a Ford Foundation projection says, only one mother out of four will be able to stay home full time with a child. Luckily, Jonathan's engineering job pays enough so that they could choose to have Helen stay home for a while—at the price of crowding three people into a studio apartment meant for one.

Watching Jonathan with the baby, seeing his new confidence and sureness, I sense that he gets his own identity as a man at least as much from his new role as husband and father, and from the community he and Helen are building with other couples like themselves in New York's Upper West Side, as from his job as engineer. To his own surprise as a child of the 1960s, he puts on a suit now, and goes every morning to that job, which he even enjoys except for the rigid 9-to-5 schedule. "I'm really into something, and they all go out to lunch. Or I've just about got it licked, and it's five o'clock, time to go." Or the baby has kept them up all night, and the alarm clock still goes off. Would he do his job as well or better, even from his employer's point of view, if he had a more flexible schedule, geared to the needs of parenting?

I have never been forgiven for a certain excessively ambitious fantasy about that second son of mine, playing cowboy with such *command* in the Kennedy years, who could, for sure, grow up to be "the first Jewish president." That's not been my ambition for him for a long time, though he's probably still suspicious. Watching him come into his own now as a father, seeing his sensitivity to Rafi's needs, I think he really is a second-stage man, though it embarrasses him to have me say this.

You get the picture, maybe, that I take a special delight in my son— in all my kids. They were such special bonuses, such surprising undeserved pluses in my life—gifts. What did I *do* to deserve them? And they were so much *themselves*, from the very beginning. I can still remember how each one looked in the delivery room—how Jonathan as a flannel-wrapped newborn kicked with that lusty energy he still has. I remember Jonathan at three, in the cowboy hat he never took off, getting down from his little horse-on-wheels to climb into my lap; and all those businesses he and his friends started at eight and nine that were such a nuisance to cancel, with the mail-order houses.

I can still remember Danny, my first-born, smiling at me with *recognition* for the first time, under a streetlight as we were wheeling him home one dark night in his baby carriage after visiting friends. I can still remember making a game, swinging hands, he and I down the sidewalk, when he was four, going along with me to collect unemployment insurance, after I was fired for getting pregnant with Jonathan. I can still remember my walks with Emily, each afternoon after she got home from nursery school, swinging hands and singing our own song with many verses that we called "Swing High, Swing Low." I can still remember rocking them on my lap in the middle of the night, to soothe them back to sleep after a stomach-ache or a bad dream, the songs I would make up, each a personal running commentary on each child's life—"I have a little boy and his name is Jonathan" . . . his dog, his cat, his baby sister, his baseball bat. (The week after they brought Rafi home from the hospital, Emily took that red rocker, the only piece of furniture I still have from those days, from its corner in her old room to Jonathan's place, for them to nurse Rafi in.)

There is so much I remember still of the vivid intensity of those days of my own motherhood, which comes back to me as I watch them with Rafi now—and so much I realize is gone forever, lost even in memory. The omnipresent daily details of those mother years, which seemed so pressing then, so harassing, and sometimes so clouded with guilts and conflict and that "problem that had no name," in those cramped apartments, those houses so vivid in my memory and theirs, so crowded with life—I only wish now that I'd savored them all more, at the time.

This being a grandmother is not the same kind of experience, not at all. I marvel at this mysterious treasure, this grandbaby, suddenly with us, here, now, himself, a new person carrying on our lifestream; I stare at him, I take him in with my eyes and heart, but I don't have to change his diapers, or get up in the middle of the night with him, or feel responsible for him all the time. I have not exactly been overzealous in offering to baby-sit, though there have been many hints. Of course, I was up in Cambridge. And then I had to go to Rome and Paris and San Francisco to lecture. I

called them from the airport, on my way back to Sag Harbor from California in early winter, to see how things were going. "Great," they said.
"Where are you? Why don't you come over and baby-sit with your grand-
son? We could go out." But I had a dinner date that night—I was going out
myself.

I wonder at the men of my age and acquaintance who are starting over
again with new babies, second and third families of their own—new fathers, with the diapers and all, at fifty, sixty, almost seventy! Does replay
parenthood really make them feel younger, as they say? I wonder. I have
no wish to go through all that again, myself. Sour grapes maybe, since I
don't have that choice. But I've done that already! The one thing I envy
them—which I get a whiff of myself as grandmother—is the second
chance to enjoy it, without the hangups and the career pressures, or the
pressures from career avoidance or abeyance, that got in the way the first
time around.

They brought him to Sag Harbor for Thanksgiv-
ing. He was just beginning to crawl. It was not exactly over the hill and
through the trees to Grandma stuffing the turkey. Not this grandma. The
last few years, never knowing where my own kids are going to be and when
they are going to decide whether or not they want to come home for
Thanksgiving, I've developed a sort of tradition of communal Thanksgiving with my "family of friends." The ones I shared a weekend house with
in the first years after my divorce (we called it a commune, to the kids' annoyance—"aging would-be hippies!") have each now, remarried or alone,
acquired her or his own house within a ten-mile radius of my own beloved
little house on the cove in Sag Harbor. I seem to play the role of den mother
or matriarch in that loosely woven communal family, to which we readily
welcome each other's friends, new and old, whether recently separated, or
feeling stranded with children off at school, or newly on their own, or having such hassles with kids or spouse that they welcome the support of a
communal Thanksgiving.

So Cynthia was stuffing the turkey, and Natalie (Gittelson) and the
"Gitteldaughters" were baking the pies, and Arthur was bringing the wine,
and since Jonathan and Helen are vegetarians, I made a big production
with the vegetables. Baby onions and mushrooms from a recipe I got over
the phone from Joan Whitman, and garlicked brussels sprouts from Craig

Claiborne's recipe in the newspaper, and candied sweet potatoes the way I've always done them without any recipe at all, and two kinds of cranberry sauce from the can (vegetables are better cooked fresh, but cranberry sauce tastes fine from the can; I'd feel pretentious making it from scratch).

In the end, we seemed to have acquired an excess of stranded single men. Men are still more helpless, somehow, at times like Thanksgiving. It was our first Thanksgiving in my new dining room–studio that got built, finally, out of what had been a useless side stoop, back shed, and attic over the kitchen. I hadn't had space before for a dining table big enough for a holiday family dinner; we'd had to set up picnic tables in the living room, and when you wanted seconds you had to go out the front door and around the house to the back door to get into the kitchen.

Between courses, this Thanksgiving, at one point six adoring women were kneeling at Rafi's feet. Natalie, of course, is dying to be a grandmother. "It will all work out," I assure her, in my new smugness. The Gitteldaughters are positively possessive about Rafi. "We've checked out other babies," they report to me; "there's no comparison." It all reminds me of a prediction Isaac Asimov, my prophetic science-fiction-writer friend, once made—that having a baby was becoming so expensive, problem-laden, oft postponed, and in some parts of our society, rare, that the day would come when a baby would be regarded as a "national treasure."

In the last few months, in Cambridge and other cities, at least six women in their mid-thirties and early forties have asked my advice about having a baby "by myself." They are women who spent their twenties and thirties concentrating on careers, some of them after the disillusionment of too-early marriages, followed by divorce. Now, either they are involved with men who've had enough troubles with their own kids and want no more, or they are not in an intimate relationship with any man, and do not expect or even want to marry again. A few have become lesbian. But, up against the biological clock now, they seem to feel an overpowering urge to have a baby. "I give myself till I'm thirty-eight," one says. "Then, if I haven't found anyone, I'll go ahead anyhow, and have a kid by myself. The question is, shall I use a sperm bank and artificial insemination, or shall I ask a friend? But then, he might have a claim to the baby, and I wouldn't want that."

I'm not sure how I feel about all this. Remembering the pressures of my own mother years, watching the pressures on Jonathan and Helen, I think the care of a baby is tough enough with two parents. To start with, at least.

Don't get me wrong, I haven't gone back to the feminine mystique. I don't think having a baby is absolutely necessary, or even sufficient, for any and every woman's fulfillment. *Chosen motherhood* is the real liberation. The *choice* to have a child makes the whole experience of motherhood different, and the choice to be generative in other ways can at last be made, and is being made by many women now, without guilt. In those years of the feminine mystique, I saw too many women, who had no choice or had babies for the wrong reasons, cover up their own negative feelings about motherhood with compulsive smothering—or lash out in psychic or physical child abuse—to their own misery and their family's. But don't underestimate the power of that choice to be generative. I don't believe motherhood is a biological instinct in women, not as it is in animals. But it is a very basic human potential, in our genes and our psyches, that does somehow demand to be used.

The mystery and wonder of life renewing itself has been celebrated by all societies through all the ages of human history. An awe behind and beyond mystique forced men to invent elaborate rites to imitate, or compensate for not being able to have, the unique experience of birth. That experience seems intensified by choice, lifted from the realm of simple animal necessity to that of human freedom, as women and men now so clearly choose to take part in the stream of ongoing life when they do not really have to have children—not just because the pill and abortion are available, but because sons and daughters are no longer social security for old age, or needed extra hands to till the fields. And it costs so much, in time, energy, and money itself, to bring kids up now; trade-offs have to be made, in terms of career success, standard of living.

On a personal level, the postfeminist generation seems to me to be learning that one can't have it all perfectly, all at once. There are risks in the way Helen and Jon are doing it, and other risks in waiting till thirty-five to have a baby, or in combining motherhood with a full-time job. Tinka is getting so thin she looks almost anoretic from the pressures of her demanding agency partnership and the new insistence of two-year-old Max that only she can meet his demands. When they entertain clients at home, as they often must, she can no longer keep Max out of their hair with a babysitter. J. B. is a sharing father, sure, but Max just doesn't make those same demands on him. What Tinka desperately needs, she tells me, is some women friends who also have two-year-olds and will *understand*; but where, how, is she to make such friends, when she must rush home from the office at six to feed Max his supper, and trek with him to the country each weekend? I've heard the same complaint from my economist friend, Sylvia, the one who was denied maternity leave, so I do some mother-matching. Tinka and Sylvia now have an evening play group for their hyperactive two-year-olds, and that supportive woman friend in each other.

At the surprise party for Jon's thirtieth birthday, for which Helen borrowed my apartment, eight children, from a baby born after Rafi to a seven-year-old, were milling sweetly—at least, were not bawling nuisances—under the feet of some forty celebrating grown-ups at nearly midnight. Have baby-sitters gone out of style? I wondered. "It's not only that they're so expensive," said Ruthie, my niece-the-dentist, finally taking sleepy Mia home. "Because we can't be with Mia when we work, we want her with us the rest of the time. We'd miss too much otherwise."

The ways they are working things out over time, in this postfeminist generation—the how, when, why, and where of having children, or not, of family and work—are not the same for everyone and probably never will be again, as earlier family patterns seemed to be. That diversity seems a plus to me, compared to the single pattern of the perfect family, enshrined in the feminine mystique, that we tried to emulate, only to feel so guilty when we couldn't. But society doesn't provide enough support for the new patterns, or the old ones, when not even grandmothers have time to baby-sit, and not even women's colleges give enough maternity leave, and judges don't count the care of home and kids as equal to a wage contribution in divorce settlements or pension entitlement, and Reagan is cutting even the inadequate child-care programs that now exist. Still, given the great numbers of those sons and daughters of the postwar baby boom now having their own babies—late or soon—and the great numbers of their eager grandmothers, by 1984 some candidate for national or state office, some adviser to a would-be president, is going to realize how politically sexy such issues as maternity-paternity leave, flextime, job sharing, and child care might be.

F inally, I offer to baby-sit, myself. They have come up to Cambridge on my last weekend there, in January, to drive me and all my books and papers back home after my Harvard year. I haven't seen the baby for over a month. He's got hair now; he's lost the Buckminster

Fuller look. Have I told you how unusual, how exceptional, how objectively beautiful my grandbaby is? He has these intense blue eyes. He has these distinctive big ears, clones of Jonathan's. He can pull himself up by the coffee table and stands up now, his little behind fitting onto his cocky legs in a way that looks familiar indeed. His daddy's behind (if I remember correctly, his granddaddy's, too). "Hey, gene pool," I say, taking in the amazing energy of that baby, the intent way he grabs a crumb off the floor, studies it, makes a beeline—crawling fast across the room—to his daddy talking on the telephone, stares up at him, his whole face abeam. I get down on all fours myself, to make friends again. He studies me solemnly: *Who's this foolish lady? What is she to me?* He takes his own sweet time about it: *Where have I seen her before?* And finally, that smile, that enchanting smile that makes me melt.

I am a bit nervous about baby-sitting this priceless new being. It's a long time since I've taken care of a baby, after all. "You won't have any trouble," they assure me, studying the movie page. I catch their dubious glances. Am I really competent to leave him with? My brilliant young psychologist friend Ellen Langer calls to invite me for a farewell dinner. A tenured Harvard professor at thirty-five, she was married and divorced very young, and has lived a single life for many years, concentrating on her brilliant career. Two psychotherapist friends, also thirtyish, unmarried, are visiting for the weekend in her stunning modern triplex town house.

"I have to baby-sit for my grandbaby," I tell her.

"Wonderful," she says, with her usual zeal for novel psychological experiment. "We will help you baby-sit. It will be an interesting experience."

So Rafi, his stroller, a supply of those disposable snap-on diapers, a jar of baby carrots, and grandmother are deposited at Ellen's triplex, and the liberated parents assure me that they will telephone from the restaurant before they go into the movie, just to check. Rafi has fallen asleep in the car. He does not even seem to notice his parents leave. Those three psychological amazons devour him with unscientific attention. Soon, passed from arm to arm, lap to lap, he's wide awake, rising to the challenge of his audience, my gene pool all right. Ellen's gourmet meal is being nibbled in absent-minded bites; nobody even asks what's in the elaborate antipasto; three Ph.D.'s and one L.H.D. (Hon.) are cooing gibberish baby talk. "Why is it," says my experimental-psychologist hostess acidly, "that four otherwise brilliant adults are reduced to submoronic levels of communication by one small baby? If we could free ourselves from our stereotyped ideas of a baby, we would talk to him like a human being, and he would respond accordingly." I do find myself murmuring the most asinine endearments—"Rif Raf," "gush gosh," "sweet-potato pie"—but Rafi does not seem really to invite intellectual dialogue.

He is getting fretful. Whichever lap he's in, he keeps turning his head around, as if he's looking for something. "He's discovered his mother is gone," I say apprehensively. "He's looking for her."

"Don't be silly," says Ellen. "There you go with the stereotypes again. Why should he miss his mother? He's getting plenty of attention from us. He doesn't know the difference. He's probably wet." And before I can stop them, two of the amazons have carried Rafi off to the top floor of the triplex to experiment with diapering.

"Hey, wait a minute," I start to object. "He's my grandbaby."

"Ah, let them," says the other guest. "You've done it already. Let them have the experience." Hearing his little cries, I am about to go to the rescue when they bring him down triumphantly—diapered, dry, stunned into momentary silence. Now he starts looking around again, and begins to cry a little more vociferously. I suddenly realize he may be thirsty. Panic, no milk in the breasts here! Then, I remember they said to give him juice. Apple? Orange? She only has cranberry. I don't remember giving that to my babies, but cranberry juice is very healthy, good for the kidneys. I start to tear open the container. "Could I have a cup or glass?" I ask.

"You drink it from the container with a straw," Ellen says.

"A baby can't drink from a straw," I tell her.

"Oh, there you go again with those stereotypes," says my brilliant psychologist friend. "How do you know he couldn't drink from a straw if you didn't expect him not to? Let's try it." I am in no mood for such experiments with my grandbaby. I'm not sure I could stop serious crying. I've just seen *Tootsie*; I'd rather leave that scene to Dustin Hoffman. I pour the juice into a highball glass, and he clutches it eagerly with both hands and slurps away. Holding him on my lap, I keep tilting the glass, so he won't drown. Success!

With Rafi restored to cheer and charm, I notice all that beautiful veal and salad still hardly touched and suggest that he can now be put down for crawling exercise while we finish eating. I make a fence of three of Ellen's chrome-and-leather chairs in front of the fireplace, and upend a fourth to block the stairwell. "Aren't you being a bit obsessively overprotective?" one of the visiting psychotherapists protests. Ellen is smiling caustically. Perhaps she feels disillusioned, seeing her fearless feminist mentor turn into a baby-talking fuss-budget. Rafi does a quick exploratory tour of the premises. I *swear* he's looking for someone. He starts to whimper again. One of the guests has long curly brown hair like Helen's, and a similar build. From the far end of the kitchen, he suddenly catches sight of her, smiles that enchanting beam of recognition, and makes a beeline for her lap. She is dazzled at being thus singled out. But on her lap—which is not his mother's, after all—he starts whimpering again, more seriously. All three are now trying to distract him with stimulating, noisy tricks. I can just see that frantic scene from *Tootsie*, with the four of us playing Dustin Hoffman.

Inchoate stirrings of knowledge long unused awake in whatever brain cells still carry the imprints left by my own mothering. I stand on grandmotherly personal privilege, and rescue my grandbaby from that high-powered adoring clique. I carry him off to be quiet in the space under the spiral staircase where tall green plants make shadows on the white walls. I walk around with him among the plants; he stops crying and reaches to touch the green leaves. I murmur little singsongs, the way I used to do with them, and he puts his head down on my shoulder, quiet and mellow. He falls asleep. The stroller I gave them for a baby present opens out into a slanting little bed. I put him gently down in it, turn its back to the light, and push it back and forth, gently rocking with one hand as we finish dinner.

It seems that Jonathan has called in the middle of all that, but Ellen has said everything is under control and I don't need to talk to him. Later, she drives us home. And that night, in my bedroom in Cambridge, Rafi, to his parents' amazement, for the first time sleeps the night through. I take no credit. It is simply a developmental coincidence. But the next morning, as I frantically pack the dozen boxes of papers and books accumulated during that year in Cambridge—the research for my next book, *The Fountain of Age*—I look up now and then and catch my grandbaby staring at *me* with that smile of recognition. He knows me now! "We're going to be friends, you and I," I venture, now that we've been tested. I wonder how long before I can take him with me on a trip. Maybe, when he's eight? "Venice," I tell him. "What do you say to Venice?" He smiles, mysteriously . . .

There was no room in the station wagon, on top of my books, papers, and other junk, beside the baby and all his paraphernalia, for my plants. I've never had a green thumb, but there in my otherwise bleak Cambridge apartment on top of that new concrete-block Harvard dormitory, I'd somehow made flourish two tree-bushes in baskets, three jade plants, and a hanging fern. I decided to hand them on to Ellen. When she came to pick them up, she said they'd stayed up half the night, she and her friends, discussing the pros and cons of having babies, with or without husbands. "It would be hard to do it alone," I said. "If you didn't have a husband, you'd need some other kind of support system." Maybe she's brilliant enough to dream up a support system better than a husband, but maybe not. I wonder how she and my son Danny would get along . . .

Someone has suggested that women are so anxious to become grandmothers because they want revenge on their children—they just can't wait to relish, with vicious glee, the spectacle of those loved-hated children as victims of the martyrdom they suffered as mothers. (Men, by contrast, don't pay that suffering price as fathers, and aren't anxious to be grandfathers, because they don't want to feel old. Of course, I have a hunch from my research for *The Fountain of Age* that the very embrace of changing, evolving life that makes women relish even becoming grandmothers is what helps keep women alive longer than men. But that's another story.)

About that vicious glee. Back now in New York, I have dinner one night in Jonathan and Helen's crowded apartment. They've appropriated the screen I brought back from Haiti—jungle animals on one side, flowers on the other, I was going to use it to hide my messy desk when I entertain in my Sag Harbor studio—to make a semiprivate space around Rafi's crib. But he still won't go to sleep as long as he senses them, us, in the room, talking. He loves life too much, that kid. Finally, as he gets very peevish, his sweet mother and daddy give up on the rocking, the patting, the songs, and simply turn out all the lights, and we sit there grimly around the dining table, not even talking, while our lentil soup gets cold, just letting him cry till he falls asleep. Which he finally does. They light some candles, we eat the zucchini soufflé, which by now has fallen a bit, and Jon grins at me sheepishly. "Well, now you know he isn't always such an angel," he says. *He's also a pain in the ass. What else is new?* I forbear to say. They wanted to show him off, in all his perfection, and he didn't oblige! Oh well, I enjoy watching them *enjoy*, and *suffer*, as parents themselves.

I'm just waiting for the day when that strong-minded Rafi, and his future siblings and cousins, reach the critical age and start giving those irritatingly superior children of mine some of the same flak they gave me, getting under their skin about not being such perfect parents. I never really *suffered* from the diapering, the dirt, the sleepless nights, their inexhaustible energy as children; it was only that superior condescension and those guilt-producing accusations they occasionally turned on me in their adolescence—and their own times of misery, in love or work, which still cause pangs of pain and guilt in me—that made my kids cease to be unalloyed joys. I told myself, of course, that they had to turn on me that way, to deny their dependence and cut their mother-strings, to grow up! But it didn't really help, when Emily, for instance, reminded me of the time she brought me home a May basket she'd made at school, and rang the doorbell and hid, but I was in the middle of a paragraph of *The Feminine Mystique,* and kept yelling at *her* to answer the door, so she never gave me the May basket, and now she never would! Jonathan and his sister and brother may not make the same mistakes as I did, but there's no way they can be such perfect angelic parents—with Rafi, and the others to come—that they will not get some of that guilt flak back from their children someday. I expect it's realizing this already that's made them so much sweeter to their old mother since the baby came.

"What's he going to call you?" the baby's parents keep asking. My kids called their Massachusetts grandmother "Grandma" and the one in California "Granny," but they didn't really know either one. Both my grandmothers were dead when I was five. I want this little Rafi to know me, I want to know this little person, who is carrying my blood and energy and spirit into new life. His being gladdens my heart. I can't wait for him to start talking to me. He can call me any name he wants.

1983

PART TWO

Inside Passages

Essays on Self-Identity

The great epiphany was our realization that we were

beautiful—every one of us in her own way.

CHINA ALTMAN

Names

Anna Lyons, Mary Louise Lyons, Mary von Phul, Emilie von Phul, Eugenia McLellan, Marjorie McPhail, Marie-Louise L'Abbé, Mary Danz, Julia Dodge, Mary Fordyce Blake, Janet Preston—these were the names (I can still tell them over like a rosary) of some of the older girls in the convent: the Virtues and Graces. The virtuous ones wore wide blue or green moiré good-conduct ribbons, bandoleer-style, across their blue serge uniforms; the beautiful ones wore rouge and powder or at least were reputed to do so. Our class, the eighth grade, wore pink ribbons (I never got one myself) and had names like Patricia ("Pat") Sullivan, Eileen Donohoe, and Joan Kane. We were inelegant even in this respect; the best name we could show, among us, was Phyllis ("Phil") Chatham, who boasted that her father's name, Ralph, was pronounced "Rafe" as in England.

Names had a great importance for us in the convent, and foreign names, French, German, or plain English (which, to us, were foreign, because of their Protestant sound), bloomed like prize roses among a collection of spuds. Irish names were too common in the school to have any prestige either as surnames (Gallagher, Sheehan, Finn, Sullivan, McCarthy) or as Christian names (Kathleen, Eileen). Anything exotic had value: an "olive" complexion, for example. The pet girl of the convent was a fragile Jewish girl named Susie Lowenstein, who had pale red-gold hair and an exquisite retroussé nose, which, if we had had it, might have been called "pug." We liked her name too and the name of a child in the primary grades: Abbie Stuart Baillargeon. My favorite name, on the whole, though, was Emilie von Phul (pronounced "Pool"); her oldest sister, recently graduated, was called Celeste. Another name that appealed to me was Genevieve Albers, Saint Genevieve being the patron saint of Paris who turned back Attila from the gates of the city.

All these names reflected the still-pioneer character of the Pacific Northwest. I had never heard their like in the parochial school in Minneapolis, where "foreign" extraction, in any case, was something to be ashamed of, the whole drive being toward Americanization of first name and surname alike. The exceptions to this were the Irish, who could vaunt such names as Catherine O'Dea and the name of my second cousin, Mary Catherine Anne Rose Violet McCarthy, while an unfortunate German boy named Manfred was made to suffer for his. But that was Minneapolis. In Seattle, and especially in the convent of the Ladies of the Sacred Heart, foreign names suggested not immigration but emigration—distinguished exile. Minneapolis was a granary; Seattle was a port, which had attracted a veritable Foreign Legion of adventurers—soldiers of fortune, younger sons, gamblers, traders, drawn by the fortunes to be made in virgin timber and shipping and by the Alaska Gold Rush. Wars and revolutions had sent the defeated out to Puget Sound, to start a new life; the latest had been the Russian Revolution, which had shipped us, via Harbin, a Russian colony, complete with restaurant, on Queen Anne Hill. The English names in the convent, when they did not testify to direct English origin, as in the case of "Rafe" Chatham, had come to us from the South and represented a kind of internal exile; such girls as Mary Fordyce Blake and Mary McQueen Street (a class ahead of me; her sister was named Francesca) bore their double-barreled first names like titles of aristocracy from the antebellum South. Not all our girls, by any means, were Catholic; some of the very prettiest ones—Julia Dodge and Janet Preston, if I remember rightly— were Protestants. The nuns had taught us to behave with special courtesy to these strangers in our midst, and the whole effect was of some superior hostel for refugees of all the lost causes of the past hundred years. Money could not count for much in such an atmosphere; the fathers and grandfathers of many of our "best" girls were ruined men.

Names, often, were freakish in the Pacific Northwest, particularly girls' names. In the Episcopal boarding school I went to later, in Tacoma, there was a girl called De Vere Utter, and there was a girl called Rocena and another called Hermoine. Was Rocena a mistake for Rowena and Hermoine for Hermione? And was Vere, as we called her, Lady Clara Vere de Vere? Probably. You do not hear names like those often, in any case, east of the Cascade Mountains; they belong to the frontier, where books and libraries were few and memory seems to have been oral, as in the time of Homer.

Names have more significance for Catholics than they do for other people; Christian names are chosen for the spiritual qualities of the saints they are taken from; Protestants used to name their children out of the Old Testament and now they name them out of novels and plays, whose heroes and heroines are perhaps the new patron saints of a secular age. But with Catholics it is different. The saint a child is named for is supposed to serve, literally, as a model or pattern to imitate; your name is your fortune and it tells you what you are or must be. Catholic children ponder their names for a mystic meaning, like birthstones; my own, I learned, besides belonging to the Virgin and Saint Mary of Egypt, originally meant "bitter" or "star of the sea." My second name, Therese, could dedicate me either to Saint Theresa or to the saint called the Little Flower, Soeur Thérèse of Lisieux, on whom God was supposed to have descended in the form of a shower of roses. At Confirmation, I had added a third name (for Catholics then rename themselves, as most nuns do, yet another time, when they take orders); on the advice of a nun, I had taken "Clementina," after Saint Clement, an early pope—a step I soon regretted on account of "My Darling Clementine" and her number nine shoes. By the time I was in the convent, I would no longer tell anyone what my Confirmation name was. The name I had nearly picked was "Agnes," after a little Roman virgin martyr, always shown with a lamb, because of her purity. But Agnes would have been just as bad, I recognized in Forest Ridge Convent—not only because of the possibility of "Aggie," but because it was subtly, indefinably *wrong*, in itself. Agnes would have made me look like an ass.

The fear of appearing ridiculous first entered my life, as a governing motive, during my second year in the convent. Up to then, a desire for prominence had decided many of my actions and, in fact, still persisted. But in the eighth grade, I became aware of mockery and perceived that I could not seek prominence without attracting laughter. Other people could, but I couldn't. This laughter was proceeding, not from my classmates, but from the girls of the class just above me, in particular from two boon companions, Elinor Heffernan and Mary Harty, a clownish pair—oddly assorted in size and shape, as teams of clowns generally are, one short, plump, and baby-faced, the other tall, lean, and owlish—who entertained the high-school department by calling attention to the oddities of the younger girls. Nearly every school has such a pair of satirists, whose marks are generally low and who are tolerated just because of their laziness and nonconformity; one of them (in this case, Mary Harty, the plump one) usually appears to be half asleep. Because of their low standing, their indifference to appearances, the sad state of their uniforms, their clowning is taken to be harmless, which, on the whole, it is, their object being not to wound but to divert; such girls are bored in school. We in the eighth grade sat directly in front of the two wits in study hall, so that they had us under close observation; yet at first I was not afraid of them, wanting, if anything, to identify myself with their laughter, to be initiated into the joke. One of their specialties was giving people nicknames, and it was considered an honor to be the first in the eighth grade to be let in by Elinor and Mary on their latest invention. This often happened to me; they would tell me, on the playground, and I would tell the others. As their intermediary, I felt myself almost their friend and it did not occur to me that I might be next on their list.

I had achieved prominence not long before by publicly losing my faith and regaining it at the end of a retreat. I believe Elinor and Mary questioned me about this on the playground, during recess, and listened with serious, respectful faces while I told them about my conversations with the Jesuits. Those serious faces ought to have been an omen, but if the two girls used what I had revealed to make fun of me, it must have been behind my back. I never heard any more of it, and yet just at this time I began to feel something, like a cold breath on the nape of my neck, that made me wonder whether the new position I had won for myself in the convent was as secure as I imagined. I would turn around in study hall and find the two girls looking at me with speculation in their eyes.

It was just at this time, too, that I found myself in a perfectly absurd situation, a very private one, which made me live, from month to month, in horror of discovery. I had waked up one morning, in my convent room, to find a few small spots of blood on my sheet; I had somehow scratched a trifling cut on one of my legs and opened it during the night. I wondered what to do about this, for the nuns were fussy about bedmaking, as they were about our white collars and cuffs, and if we had an inspection those spots might count against me. It was best, I decided, to ask the nun on dormitory duty, tall, stout Mother Slattery, for a clean bottom sheet, even though she might scold me for having scratched my leg in my sleep and order me to cut my toenails. You never know what you might be blamed for. But Mother Slattery, when she bustled in to look at the sheet, did not scold me at all; indeed, she hardly seemed to be listening as I explained to her about the cut. She told me to sit down: she would be back in a minute. "You can be excused from athletics today," she added, closing the door. As I waited, I considered this remark, which seemed to me strangely munificent, in view of the unimportance of the cut. In a moment, she returned, but without the sheet. Instead, she produced out of her big pocket a sort of cloth girdle and a peculiar flannel object which I first took to be a bandage, and I began to protest that I did not need or want a bandage; all I needed was a bottom sheet. "The sheet can wait," said Mother Slattery, succinctly, handing me two large safety pins. It was the pins that abruptly enlightened me; I saw Mother Slattery's mistake, even as she was instructing me as to how this flannel article, which I now understood to be a sanitary napkin, was to be put on.

"Oh, no, Mother," I said, feeling somewhat embarrassed. "You don't understand. It's just a little cut, on my leg." But Mother, again, was not listening; she appeared to have grown deaf, as the nuns had a habit of doing when what you were saying did not fit in with their ideas. And now that I knew what was in her mind, I was conscious of a funny constraint; I did not feel it proper to name a natural process, in so many words, to a nun. It was like trying not to think of their going to the bathroom or trying not to see the straggling iron-grey hair coming out of their coifs (the common notion that they shaved their heads was false). On the whole, it seemed better just to show her my cut. But when I offered to do so, and unfastened my black stocking, she only glanced at my leg, cursorily. "That's only a scratch, dear," she said. "Now hurry up and put this on or you'll be late for chapel. Have you any pain?" "No, no, Mother!" I cried. "You don't understand!" "Yes, yes, I understand," she replied soothingly, "and you will too, a little later. Mother Superior will tell you about it some time during the morning. There's nothing to be afraid of. You have become a woman."

"I know all about that," I persisted. "Mother, please listen. I just cut my leg. On the athletic field. Yesterday afternoon." But the more excited I grew, the more soothing, and yet firm, Mother Slattery became. There seemed to be nothing for it but to give up and do as I was bid. I was in the grip of a higher authority, which almost had the power to persuade me that it was right and I was wrong. But of course I was not wrong; that would have been too good to be true. While Mother Slattery waited, just outside my door, I miserably donned the equipment she had given me, for there was no place to hide it, on account of drawer inspection. She led me down the hall to where there was a chute and explained how I was to dispose of the flannel thing, by dropping it down the chute into the laundry. (The convent arrangements were very old-fashioned, dating back, no doubt, to the days of Louis Philippe.)

The Mother Superior, Madame MacIllvra, was a sensible woman, and all through my early morning classes, I was on pins and needles, chafing for the promised interview with her which I trusted would clear things up. "*Ma Mère*," I would begin, "Mother Slattery thinks . . ." Then I would tell her about the cut and the athletic field. But precisely the same impasse confronted me when I was summoned to her office at recess time. *I* talked about my cut, and *she* talked about becoming a woman. It was rather like a round, in which she was singing "Scotland's burning, Scotland's burning," and I was singing "Pour on water, pour on water." Neither of us could hear the other, or, rather, I could hear her, but she could not hear me. Owing to our different positions in the convent, she was free to interrupt me, whereas I was expected to remain silent until she had finished speaking. When I kept breaking in, she hushed me, gently, and took me on her lap. Exactly like Mother Slattery, she attributed all my references to the cut to a blind fear of this new, unexpected reality that had supposedly entered my life. Many young girls, she reassured me, were frightened if they had not been prepared. "And you, Mary, have lost your dear mother, who could have made this easier for you." Rocked on Madame MacIllvra's lap, I felt paralysis overtake me and I lay, mutely listening, against her bosom, my face being tickled by her white, starched, fluted wimple, while she explained to me how babies were born, all of which I had heard before.

There was no use fighting the convent. I had to pretend to have become a woman, just as, not long before, I had had to pretend to get my faith back—for the sake of peace. This pretense was decidedly awkward. For fear of being found out by the lay sisters downstairs in the laundry (no doubt an imaginary contingency, but the convent was so very thorough), I reopened the cut on my leg, so as to draw a little blood to stain the napkins, which were issued me regularly, not only on this occasion, but every twenty-eight days thereafter. Eventually, I abandoned this bloodletting, for fear of lockjaw, and trusted to fate. Yet I was in awful dread of detection; my only hope, as I saw it, was either to be released from the convent or to become a woman in reality, which might take a year, at least, since I was only twelve. Getting out of athletics once a month was not sufficient compensation for the farce I was going through. It was not my fault; they had forced me into it; nevertheless, it was I who would look silly—worse than silly; half mad—if the truth ever came to light.

I was burdened with this guilt and shame when the nickname finally found me out. "Found me out," in a general sense, for no one ever did learn the particular secret I bore about with me, pinned to the linen band. "We've got a name for you," Elinor and Mary called out to me, one day on the playground. "What is it?" I asked, half hoping, half fearing, since not all their sobriquets were unfavorable. "Cye," they answered, looking at each other and laughing. "Si?" I repeated, supposing that it was based on Simple Simon. Did they regard me as a hick? "C.Y.E.," they elucidated, spelling it out in chorus. "The letters stand for something. Can you guess?" I could not and I cannot now. The closest I could come to it in the convent was "Clean Your Ears." Perhaps that was it, though in later life I have wondered whether it did not stand, simply, for "Clever Young Egg" or "Champion Young Eccentric." But in the convent I was certain that it stood for something horrible, something even worse than dirty ears (as far as I knew, my ears were clean), something I could never guess because it represented some aspect of myself that the world could see and I couldn't, like a sign pinned on my back. Everyone in the convent must have known what the letters stood for, but no one would tell me. Elinor and Mary had made them promise. It was like halitosis; not even my best friend, my deskmate, Louise, would tell me, no matter how much I pleaded. Yet everyone assured me that it was "very good," that is, very apt. And it made everyone laugh.

This name reduced all my pretensions and solidified my sense of *wrongness*. Just as I felt I was beginning to belong to the convent, it turned me into an outsider, since I was the only pupil who was not in the know. I liked the convent, but it did not like me, as people say of certain foods that disagree with them. By this, I do not mean that I was actively unpopular, either with the pupils or with the nuns. The Mother Superior cried when

I left and predicted that I would be a novelist, which surprised me. And I had finally made friends; even Emilie von Phul smiled upon me softly out of her bright blue eyes from the far end of the study hall. It was just that I did not fit into the convent pattern; the simplest thing I did, like asking for a clean sheet, entrapped me in consequences that I never could have predicted. I was not bad; I did not consciously break the rules; and yet I could never, not even for a week, get a pink ribbon, and this was something I could not understand, because I was trying as hard as I could. It was the same case as with the hated name; the nuns, evidently, saw something about me that was invisible to me.

The oddest part was all that pretending. There I was, a walking mass of lies, pretending to be a Catholic and going to confession while really I had lost my faith, and pretending to have monthly periods by cutting myself with nail scissors; yet all this had come about without my volition and even contrary to it. But the basest pretense I was driven to was the acceptance of the nickname. Yet what else could I do? In the convent, I could not live it down. To all those girls, I had become "Cye McCarthy." That was who I was. That was how I had to identify myself when telephoning my friends during vacations to ask them to the movies: "Hello, this is Cye." I loathed myself when I said it, and yet I succumbed to the name totally, making myself over into a sort of hearty to go with it—the kind of girl I hated. "Cye" was my new patron saint. This false personality stuck to me, like the name, when I entered public high school, the next fall, as a freshman, having finally persuaded my grandparents to take me out of the convent, although they could never get to the bottom of my reasons, since, as I admitted, the nuns were kind, and I had made many nice new friends. What I wanted was a fresh start, a chance to begin life over again, but the first thing I heard in the corridors of the public high school was that name called out to me, like the warmest of welcomes: "Hi, there, Si!" That was the way they thought it was spelled. But this time I was resolute. After the first weeks, I dropped the hearties who called me "Si" and I never heard it again. I got my own name back and sloughed off Clementina and even Therese—the names that did not seem to me any more to be mine but to have been imposed on me by others. And I preferred to think that Mary meant "bitter" rather than "star of the sea."

1951

Hair

I've been around and seen the Taj Mahal and the Grand Canyon and Marilyn Monroe's footprints outside Grauman's Chinese Theater, but I've never seen my mother wash her own hair. After my mother married, she never washed her own hair again. As a girl and an unmarried woman—yes—but, in my lifetime, she never washed her hair with her own two hands. Upon matrimony, she began weekly treks to the beauty salon where Julie washed and styled her hair. Her appointment on Fridays at two o'clock was never canceled or rescheduled; it was the bedrock of her week, around which she pivoted and planned. These two hours were indispensable to my mother's routine, to her sense of herself and what, as a woman, she should concern herself with—not to mention their being her primary source of information about all sorts of things she wouldn't otherwise come to know. With Julie my mother discussed momentous decisions concerning hair color and the advancement of age and what could be done about it, hair length and its effect upon maturity, when to perm and when not to perm, the need to proceed with caution when a woman desperately wanted a major change in her life like dumping her husband or sending back her newborn baby and the only change she could effect was a change in her hair. That was what Julie called a "dangerous time" in a woman's life. When my mother spoke to Julie, she spoke in conspiratorial, almost confessional, tones I had never heard before. Her voice was usually tense, on guard, the laughter forced, but with Julie it dropped much lower, the timbre darker than the upper-register shrills sounded at home. And most remarkably, she listened to everything Julie said.

As a child I was puzzled by the way my mother's sense of self-worth and mood seemed dependent upon how she thought her hair looked, how the search for the perfect hair style never ended. Just as Mother seemed to like her latest color and cut, she began to agitate for a new look. The cut seemed to have become a melancholy testimony, in my mother's eyes, to time's inexorable passage. Her hair never stood in and of itself; it was always moored to a complex set of needs and desires her hair couldn't in itself satisfy. She wanted her hair to illuminate the relationship between herself and the idea of motion while appearing still, for example. My mother wanted her hair to be fashioned into an event with a complicated narrative past. However, the more my mother attempted to impose a hair style pulled from an idealized image of herself, the more the hair style seemed to be at odds with my mother. The more the hair style became substantial, the more the woman underneath was obscured. She'd riffle through women's magazines and stare for long dreamy hours at a particular woman's coiffure. Then she'd ask my father in an artificially casual voice: "How do you think I'd look with really short hair?" or "Would blonde become me?" My father never committed himself to an opinion. He had learned from long experience that no response he made could turn out well; anything he said would be used against him, if not in the immediate circumstances, down the line, for my mother never forgot anything anyone ever said about her hair. My father's refusal to engage the "hair question" irritated her.

So too, I was puzzled to see that unmarried women washed their own hair, and married women, in my mother's circle at least, by some unwritten dictum never touched their own hair. I began studying before and after photographs of my mother's friends. These photographs were all the same. In the pre-married mode, their hair was soft and unformed. After the wedding, the women's hair styles bore the stamp of property, looked constructed from grooming talents not their own, hair styles I'd call produced, requiring constant upkeep and technique to sustain the considerable loft and rigidity—in short, the antithesis of anything I might naively call natural. This was hair no one touched, crushed, or ran fingers through. One poked and prodded various hair masses back into formation. This hair presented obstacles to embrace, the scent of the hair spray alone warded off man, child, and pests. I never saw my father stroke my mother's head. Children whimpered when my mother came home fresh from the salon with a potent do. Just when a woman's life was supposed to be opening out into daily affection, *the* sanctioned affection of husband and children, the women of my mother's circle encased themselves in a helmet of hair not unlike Medusa's.

In so-called middle age, my mother's hair never moved, never blew, never fell in her face: her hair became a museum piece. When she went to bed, she wore a blue net, and when she took short showers, short because, after all, she wasn't washing her hair and she was seldom dirty, she wore a blue plastic cap for the sake of preservation. From one appointment to the next, the only change her hair could be said to undergo was to become crestfallen. Taking extended vacations presented problems sufficiently troublesome to rule out countries where she feared no beauty parlors existed. In the beginning, my parents took overnighters, then week jaunts, and thereby avoided the whole hair dilemma. Extending their vacations to two weeks was eventually managed by my mother applying more hair spray and sleeping sitting up. But after the two-week mark had been reached, she was forced to either return home or venture into an unfamiliar salon and subject herself to scrutiny, the kind of scrutiny that leaves no woman unscathed. Then she faced Julie's disapproval, for no matter how expensive and expert the salon, my mother's hair was to be lamented. Speaking just for myself, I had difficulty distinguishing Julie's cunning from the stranger's. In these years my mother's hair looked curled, teased, and sprayed into a waved tossed monument with holes poked through for glasses. She believed the damage done to her hair was tangible proof she had been somewhere, like stickers on her suitcases.

My older sisters have worked out their hair positions differently. My oldest sister's solution has been to fix upon one hair style and never change it. She wants to be thought of in a singular fashion. She may vary the length from long to longer, but that is the extent of her alteration. Once, after having her first baby, the "dangerous time" for women, she recklessly cut her hair to just below the ear. She immediately regretted the decision and began growing it back as she walked home from the salon, vowing not to repeat the mistake. Her signature is dark, straight hair pulled heavily off her face in a large silver clip, found at any Woolworth's. When one clip breaks, she buys another just like it. My mother hates the timelessness of my sister's hair. She equates it with a refusal to face growing old. My mother says, "It's immature to wear your hair the same way all your life." My sister replies,

"It's immature to never stop thinking about your hair. If this hair style was good enough when I was twenty, it's good enough when I'm forty, if not better."

"But what about change?" my mother asks.

"Change is overrated," my sister says, flipping her long hair over her shoulder definitively. "I feel my hair."

My other sister was born with thin, lifeless, nondescript hair: a cross she has had to bear. Even in the baby pictures, the limp strands plastered on her forehead in question marks wear her down. Shame and self-effacement are especially plain in the pictures where she posed with our eldest sister, whose dark hair dominates the frame. She's spent her life attempting to disguise the real state of her hair. Some years she'd focus on style, pulling it back in ponytails so that from the front no one could see there wasn't much hair in the back. She tried artless, even messy styles— as if she had just tied it up any old way before taking a bath or bunched it to look deliberately snarled. There were the weird years punctuated by styles that looked as if she had taken sugar water and lemon juice and squeezed them onto her wet hair and then let them crystallize. The worst style was when she took her hair and piled it on the top of her head in a cone shape and then crimped the ponytail into a zigzag. Personally, I thought she had gone too far. No single approach solved the hair problem, and so now, in maturity, she combines the various phases of attack in hope something will work. She frosts both the gray strands and the pale brown, and then perms for added body and thickness. She's forced to keep her hair short because chemicals do tend to destroy. My mother admires my sister's determination to transform herself, and never more than in my sister's latest assault upon middle age. No one has known for many years nor does anyone remember what the untreated color or texture of either my mother's or my sister's hair might be.

As the youngest by twelve years, there was little to distract Mother's considerable attention from the problem of my hair. I had cowlicks, a remarkable number of them, which like little arrows shot across my scalp. They refused to be trained, to lie down quietly in the same direction as the rest of my hair. One at the front insisted on sticking straight up while two on either side of my ears jutted out seeking sun. The lack of uniformity, the fact that my hair had a mind of its own, infuriated my mother and she saw to it that Julie cut my hair as short as possible in order to curtail its wanton expression. Sitting in the swivel chair before the mirror while Julie snipped, I felt invisible, as if I was unattached to my hair.

Just when I started to menstruate, my mother decided the battle plan needed a change, and presto, the page boy replaced the pixie. Having not outgrown the thicket of cowlicks, Mother bought a spectrum of brightly colored stretch bands to hold my hair back off my face. Then she attached thin pink plastic curlers with snap-on lids to the ends of my hair to make them flip up or under, depending on her mood. The stretch bands pressed my hair flat until the very bottom, at which point the ends formed a tunnel with ridges from the roller caps—a point of emphasis, she called it. Coupled with the aquamarine eyeglasses, newly acquired, I looked like an overgrown insect that had none of its kind to bond with.

However, I was not alone. Unless you were the last in a long line of sisters, chances were good that your hair would not go unnoticed by your mother. Each of my best friends was subjected to her mother's hair dictatorship, although with entirely different results. Perry Jensen's mother insisted that all five of her daughters peroxide their hair blonde and pull it back into high ponytails. All the girls' hair turned green in the summer from chlorine. Melissa Matson underwent a look-alike "home perm" with her mother, an experience she never did recover from. She developed a phobic reaction to anything synthetic, which made life very expensive. Not only did mother and daughter have identical tight curls and wear mother-daughter outfits, later they had look-alike nose jobs.

In my generation, many women who survived hair bondage to their mothers now experiment with hair styles as one would test a new design: to see how it works, what it will withstand, and how it can be improved. Testing requires boldness, for often the style fails dramatically, as when I had my hair cut about a half inch long at the top, and it stood straight up like a tacky shag carpet. I had to live with the results, bear daily witness to the kinks in its design for nine months until strategies of damage control could be deployed. But sometimes women I know create a look that startles in its originality and suggests a future not yet realized.

The women in my family divide into two general groups: those who fasten upon one style, become identified with a look, and are impervious to change, weathering the years steadfastly, and those who, for a variety of reasons, are in the business of transforming themselves. In my sister's case, the quest for perfect hair originates in a need to mask her own appearance; in my mother's case, she wants to achieve a beauty of person unavailable in her own life story. Some women seek transformation, not out of dissatisfaction with themselves, but because hair change is a means of moving along in their lives. These women create portraits of themselves that won't last forever, a new hair style will write over the last.

Since my mother dictated my hair, I never took a stand on the hair issue. In maturity, I'm incapable of assuming a coherent or consistent philosophy. I have wayward hair: it's always becoming something else. The moment it arrives at a recognizable style, it begins to undo itself, it grows, the sun colors it, it waves. When one hair pin goes in, another seems to come out. Sometimes I think I should follow my oldest sister—she claims to never give more than a passing thought to her hair and can't see what all the angst is about. She asks, "Don't women have better things to think about than their hair?"

I bite back: "But don't you think hair should reflect who you are?"

"To be honest, I've never thought about it. I don't think so. Cut your hair the same way, and lose yourself in something else. You're distracted from the real action."

I want to do what my sister says, but when I walk out into shop-lined streets, I automatically study women's hair and always with the same question: How did they arrive at their hair? Lately, I've been feeling more and more like my mother. I hadn't known how to resolve the dilemma until I found Rhonda. I don't know if I found Rhonda or made her up. She is not a normally trained hairdresser: she has a different set of eyes, unaffected. One day while out driving around to no place in particular, at the bottom of a hill, I found: "Rhonda's Hair Salon—Don't Look Back" written on a life-size cardboard image of Rhonda. Her shop was on the top of this steep orchard-planted hill, on a plateau with a great view that opened out and went on forever. I parked my car at the bottom and walked up. Zigzagging all the way up the hill, leaning against or sticking out from behind the apple trees, were more life-size cardboard likenesses of Rhonda. Except for the explosive sunbursts in her hair, no two signs were the same. At the bottom, she wore long red hair falling below her knees and covering her entire body like a shawl. As I climbed the hill, Rhonda's hair gradually became shorter and shorter, and each length was cut differently, until when I reached the top, her head was shaved and glistening in the sun. I found Rhonda herself out under one of the apple trees wearing running shoes. Her hair was long and red and looked as if it had never been cut. She told me she had no aspirations to be a hairdresser, "she just fell into it." "I see hair," she continued, "as an extension of the head and therefore I try to do hair with a lot of thought." Inside there were no mirrors, no swivel chairs, no machines of torture with their accompanying stink. She said, "Nothing is permanent, nothing is forever. Don't feel hampered or hemmed in by the shape of your face or the shape of your past. Hair is vital, sustains mistakes, can be born again. You don't have to marry it. Now tip back and put your head into my hands."

1992

A Friendship
Forged on Concrete

NEW YORK CITY

A man comes loping toward me, looks at me with pure hate and, without missing a step, spits in my face; jogs past. Suddenly, I am *female*. I'm his mama who almost swallowed him up; his girlfriend who just left him; I'm the woman in a magazine showing my thighs, smiling with a hint of tongue.

Another time on another avenue in New York, a man urinates on the wall and his friends, seeing me approach, start laughing—"I want to see her face," one says, and they all turn expectantly as a raggedy stream darkens the sidewalk in front of me.

My eleven-year-old neighbor is also a traveler of Brooklyn's streets. Half black, half Jewish, he has lived with his mother, then with relatives in foster care, then in a couple of group homes, and now with his father.

We trade wishes: "If you could choose three powers, what would they be?"

He goes first, and chooses arms that stretch across the world and can grab whatever he wants (like Spiderman's web-shooting hands); incredible strength (like the superhero Rage); a body that heals its own wounds. I chose invisibility and flight and the power to move objects with words.

I met Ali two years ago when he and his friends came to my door looking for work. Did I want my walk swept? Ali just kept coming back—sometimes twice a day. On the second visit, he'd knock out some song on the doorbell, hoping to soften me with a serenade. I remember opening the door once, angry and ready to send him away, and he was laying flat on the ground, chin in his hand, elbow on the doorstep—"What's up?" he said. Ali was definitely willing to be a clown for love. We became fast friends. He lived in an apartment one block away with an aunt and stepuncle— "like Cinderella," he said, sitting on his skateboard in my kitchen.

Ali brought me stories of his streets: He spotted a pigeon squashed dead in front of the Key Food supermarket; saw a cat get hit by a car and then hobble furiously away on three legs. He watched two men in Prospect Park catch a squirrel and, laughing, throw it in their barbecue; saw a neighborhood guy tie a stray dog to a bus and watched the dog run as long and as hard as it could. In his ninth year, Ali's street reporting was often brutal and short.

He traveled with a turtle—a box turtle he named Snapper. One day he called me on the phone to ask if he could come over, and when I said no, he yelled: "But I'm on the street and I've got a turtle in my pocket!" Another time he called up to see if I wanted another cat, and when I didn't, he protested: "But he's homeless!"

He wanted to be loved; he wanted to be essential. At night when I sent him home, he'd make a show of running down the street—slow motion, then scampering, then swishing his butt and poking his fingers in the air, then clutching his heart and falling to the ground, arms splayed. The street was his theater—he played a child running happily, dancing unaware; fire crackers became gunshots; he was leaving me, he was motherless, he was struck down and lying there dead. I applauded; cheered him on home.

I loved Ali's streets. He flew down them on sneakered feet, on a skateboard, on a bike he put together from the discarded bones of other bikes and then painted in glow-in-the-dark zebra stripes. He was fast—fast enough to duck bullies. One evening when he and I were coming out of the grocery store, a black man stopped Ali, clapping his hand on top of Ali's head. "Who's she?" he asked, jerking his chin in my direction, obviously angry. Ali slipped out from under his heavy hand, ran a few steps away and then yelled: "My adopted mother," a mischievous grin on his face. He's braver than I am.

When I came to New York, I thought I would find the freedom of anonymity. I was seventeen, and like a lot of other immigrants from suburbs and small towns, I wanted to escape the role assigned me by my home town. I was labeled the "bad girl." Actually, I was a very shy girl, assigned the wrong role.

In my early years in New York, I walked everywhere. I also moved in and out of jobs, boyfriends, apartments. It's been fourteen years. Now I have a home; I have friends. And now the city's dangerous. There's a lot of sickness on the streets. On a bad day, a vulnerable day, I don't like to walk around alone. It seems fitting somehow that intimacy and danger have grown at an equal pace in my life.

Ali was put in a group home last year, surprising us both. When he called me, he could barely speak. I had to pull him slowly from his shock—I recalled our history, anecdote by anecdote, and promised him I'd get him out. When he finally found his tongue, he asked: "What's the cat doing?" I told him, and then he wanted to know what each of my roommates was doing; then where was I sitting while I talked to him—summoning the scene of home as he talked on a public pay phone.

I met his father, who wanted him back, and we got him out. He took Ali to a new neighborhood, fifteen minutes away, up on the hills where they built Prospect Park. It's a middle-class brownstone neighborhood, where the kids have Nintendo dates arranged by their parents. "It's boring," Ali complains. "Nobody's outside."

He returns to the old neighborhood whenever he can. On his bicycle, downhill, the streets become rivers. He arrives at my door ten minutes after calling. "How'd you get here so fast?" I ask. "No traffic," he says.

Every time I think that public life has become too intrusive and hateful—not at all what I expected when I moved here—I remember Ali dancing out his vulnerability on the pavement outside my door. When I was twenty-nine my child sprang from the city streets full grown and hungry. Our relationship is completely urban. Out of the public space—howling and mad—he and I made a better family than the ones we were born into; fluid and light on our feet, we made the concrete flow and escaped loneliness.

1991

An American
in New York

The first thing I realized when I went to New York City was that everyone is something different from what they seem: JAPs are Jewish American Princesses; Arabs are Towel Heads; and Haitians are cab drivers.

I was sent to New York on financial business. The high-stakes bond business. There's something hypocritical about an Indian selling and trading U.S. Treasury Bonds. Even the word *bond* connotes servitude. To bond, to bind, to restrain, to obligate, to indebt, to enslave.

Bonds also help prop up, and perpetuate, the country's economy. They're printed on 100 percent white bonded paper by the government, so the government will be able to pay interest on the other bonded pieces of paper they printed last year. The government's bonds are its words to its people. This is what we're worth. Our word is our bond.

"We're all bonded," said the head of government operations at Saloman Brothers. "When you're responsible for receiving and delivering four billion dollars a day worth of government bonds you have to be bonded."

I was sent to New York with a wad of expense money to entertain, beguile, and prepare the hogs (our operations people) for the slaughter. My boss gave me a pep talk before I left for the Big Apple.

"Show 'em a good time, take 'em out to eat, get 'em drunk, take 'em to a show. Do whatever you have to do to get 'em to handle our bond trades more efficiently."

Yes, Kimosabe. Me go to New York. Me make 'em like Indian.

I saw this assignment as a kind of reversal of historic roles. This time an Indian was going to buy immigrants. And I thought it a perfect opportunity to trot out my Tonto-with-tits garb. I'd learned a long time ago that even in Texas people don't recognize you as an Indian unless you're wearing a costume. They've seen too many Hollywood movies. So I packed my leather and feathers and flew back East.

For most of the three days I was in Manhattan, I wore my hawk feathers for protection from the enemy and as a way of advertisement. An American in New York. No one caught the irony.

Now that I put the whole episode in perspective, I think I saw myself as some kind of native sojourner on a vision quest, in search of that magical ambience Frank Sinatra sings about in "New York, New York."

I wanted to see the Empire State Building, Fifth Avenue, the Garment District, Central Park, Broadway, Rockefeller Center, the World Trade Center, Radio City, the Statue of Liberty, and Hell's Kitchen.

No wonder we sold the whole place for twenty-six bucks and some beads. I wouldn't give you twenty-six cents for the entire island right now. It stinks. There's trash piled higher than your head on every corner. Old men and women are puking and peeing all over the place. You can't see the sky. Everywhere you look there's black grunge growing up the walls on the buildings, and there are rats the size of small coyotes climbing trees in Central Park. It's horrible.

Outside my hotel at the World Trade Center there was a young man who thought he was a bird. He ran day and night, up and down the concrete median between the streets, flapping his arms trying to fly away.

I asked the hotel doorman what was going to happen to the Bird Man. He told me when the Bird Man dies the city health department will pick up his body and bury it.

Sonofabitch. Those scenes from Woody Allen's film *Manhattan*, where he and Mariel Hemingway are taking a romantic carriage ride around Central Park, are as fabricated as those where Ward Bond is looking for smoke signals in *Wagon Train*.

I was as surprised by what I saw as the New Yorker who landed at Oklahoma City's airport and asked me where all the Indians and tepees were. I was working as a waitress at the airport coffee shop.

I stood there proudly pouring him a cup of coffee and said, "Right here, sir. I'm an Indian."

As I stood there in my stiffly starched yellow and white SkyChef's uniform, the New Yorker looked me up and down and asked, "You're it? I've come all this way to see Indians and you're telling me you're it? My God, darling, you mean you live in houses just like the rest of us?"

I said, "Well . . . I live in an apartment."

While I was working with the people in government operations during the day, my friend Sheree Turner, who'd flown to New York with me, was learning a lot about the city and its residents.

She told me that more than two million of the city's seven million residents are from overseas. There are more Dominicans in New York City, some 350,000, than in any city but Santo Domingo, more Greeks than anywhere but Athens, more Haitians than anywhere but Port au Prince. She told me most immigrants come to New York City because they know they can find fellow countrymen in this city, where everyone is an alien and no one is an alien.

On our last night in Manhattan, Sheree and I decided to see a show and do some exploring on our own.

We dressed up like some kind of tourists in semi-evening clothes. Again, the victims of commercialism. We thought you dressed for the theater. Sheree wore a backless dress with feathers and I wore a shirt that was slit down to my navel (sans feathers).

Most everyone else attending that evening's performance of A Chorus Line looked like they were going to a Texas Ranger baseball game, except two little old ladies from Kansas City who were wearing synthetic velvet.

After the show, I flagged down a horse-drawn taxi. A man steered his carriage toward us and stopped. Sheree jumped in back and the driver asked me if I'd like to ride up front with him. I was ecstatic.

As I was climbing into the coach, I realized why he asked me to ride up front. Both my tits were hanging out of my shirt as I'd flagged him down.

"Where you be wantin' to go, Miss?"

God! A real Irishman with a thick Irish brogue, complete with auburn hair and freckles. I imagined him a cross between Barry Fitzgerald and John Kennedy. (My faith in Woody Allen was restored.)

"We want to see everything, go everywhere, and spend some of my company's money."

He gave me a delicious grin and said to my tits, "Okay, Miss, we're off."

Seamus MacDonald was a wonderful guide. I loved the way he talked. He dutifully drove us around the Rockefeller Center and seemed to genuinely enjoy pointing out the sights. He told us where we could catch the Staten Island Ferry to see the Statue of Liberty after he dropped us off. He pointed out some hot night spots, and asked me where I was from.

We got on very well. I played the part of an investigative reporter, asking him everything from how long he had been in this country to what kind of girls he dated.

He was Catholic. His three older brothers were in this country going to law school. There were ten children in his family and his mother was still in Ireland raising the other six. His father worked in America and sent money to Ireland. Seamus said he was a boxer and eventually wanted to go professional. He planned to win the New York City Golden Glove Heavyweight Championship coming up in the fall. He said he loved to fight. (I knew we'd get along.) He dated girls who weren't Catholic. He was openminded, but knew he would never marry outside the church.

I said I didn't believe he was big enough to be a heavyweight boxer.

"How tall are you? You don't look like you weigh enough to be a heavyweight."

I was baiting him. I like to symbolically challenge men. Whether it's a question of their manhood, their physical stature, strength, or just a game of trivia questions, they can never resist a challenge. Then, once they've proven they're stronger, taller, bigger, faster, or smarter, you have them hooked.

Women are no fun at this little ritual. They'll never meet a challenge head-on with another woman; they'll just go in another room and talk bad about you behind your back.

Anyway, Seamus fell for it. Putty in my hands. He laughed at me, gave me the reins, and stood up as we were going around 42nd Street.

He was big. (I'm attracted to big men.) Standing up in the carriage seat, his crotch was at eye level. He was also thick and very tall. He had a good size butt on him, too.

I bit my lip. My eyes glazed over and I swallowed hard. I began to struggle with my conscience. I was married. I was also averse to fucking someone only five years older than my son. (I wondered if my deodorant was still working? Was I wearing clean panty hose?) He probably had AIDS, or herpes. Besides, I hadn't lost that twenty pounds or so I was going to lose before coming to New York.

I looked around at Sheree sitting in the back seat of the carriage. I'd been ignoring her ever since I'd climbed in the driver's seat. She'd passed out with a grin on her face.

Just as I looked up at Seamus, our eyes met. He was still standing up in the carriage. His eyes were green and heavy-lidded. He smiled wide, revealing deep dimples and brilliant white teeth. I let my gaze match his and he said softly, "Your time's up. This is where you get off."

Oh shit. How humiliating. He'd just been play-ing the game, too. I wanted to kick myself. What am I going to be like in twenty years, a heavy-breathing old broad lusting after young boys with supple bodies?

"Wait a minute. I have more money and you didn't take us anywhere except around Central Park. I want to see things other tourists don't get to see. This is my last night in New York, and goddammit, I wanna see everything."

"Okay. For another twenty dollars I'll drive you places I don't take out-of-towners, then I'll drop you near a cab stand so you can get back to your hotel."

He headed toward streets partially lit by dim street lamps. We passed small, all-night coffee shops with outdated 10, 2 & 4 Dr. Pepper signs in the windows. Our carriage stopped behind a delivery truck and I watched a man with no shirt, and what looked like a dirty, wet towel on his head, rummage through piles of garbage. He picked up a crate covered with wilted lettuce leaves, shook them off, and carried it somewhere toward the dark end of the street.

"They are everywhere," said Seamus. "New York nobility used to bewail each succeeding wave of Irish immigrants. Now there's a lot of concern around here that the new immigrants, these Middle Easterners, these Haitian boat people, these wandering Hispanics, can't be assimilated into our society."

"Our society?"

"Yes, our society. I'm going to get my American citizenship one day soon. Most everyone wants the same things. We wanna eat hamburgers, and pizza, buy designer clothes, and Swiss-made watches. Maybe that's materialistic but that is why everyone comes here."

"But there's more to life, and more to America than just things."

"More to life than expensive carriage rides and Broadway theatre, you mean."

I shut up.

We continued our trip around a curve and slowed behind several cars that were in some kind of a line.

Standing on both sides of the street were women with strangely exaggerated facial expressions. Painted women. Women with day-glo faces.

"Whores," he said softly. "You wanted to see unusual sights. Here they are."

"Where are we?"

"We're close to what used to be Hell's Kitchen."

The whole scene became surrealistic. The women, some wearing bras and panties, some completely naked, reminded me of South African baboons I'd seen in film clips on Channel 13. Like wild animals running down from the hills to beg tourists for sweets, the women ran from behind massive iron trash dumpsters and empty warehouses to beat on the sides of the cars and throw themselves on the car hoods.

It was another kind of feeding frenzy. There were thin-lipped, gaunt, white girls; pregnant older women; kinky-haired Asians; flat-chested black/white girls with gray, anemic skin and bleached hair. They were pandering, competing, cajoling, and hustling up their dinner money from the car men in line.

When the Ford Pinto in front of us finally came to a dead stop, I grabbed Seamus's arm.

"Don't worry. They won't come over here, we're not customers."

The white man rolled down his window and the tall, black/white girl in a red garter belt, red hose, and heels with waist-length, mica-white hair leaned through the driver's window. I was drawn to her and the moment in a way I'd never felt before. My breathing quickened and my palms felt sweaty. I reckoned this was what it felt like to be a voyeur peeking into someone's night room.

All we could see were the buttocks and legs of the girl leaning through the car window. The engine sputtered for lack of gas. The whole car body shook for a brief instant, then went dead.

My eyes watered from staring at the girl's legs and then she raised up out of the car and looked in our direction.

Her mouth was open and she spit on the sidewalk.

I stood up. I was amazed. "God, she's spitting cum on the sidewalk."

Seamus pulled me down in the seat.

"Shut up."

The woman-whore met my gaze.

"You want some of this?"

She rubbed her stomach and then rubbed the wadded bills between her fingers. Her gaze pulled me into her circle. The Pinto engine started up and from the distance we heard an ambulance turn the corner. I looked toward the sound and then looked back toward the black/white girl. She was gone. They were all gone. There were only the cars in front of us pulling out one by one.

"Where'd they go?"

"They're like rats. They run and hide when a city car comes. If they get picked up by the police, their pimps pay their bond."

We spent the rest of the ride in silence. Seamus gave me his address and promised to call me when he won the Golden Glove Championship, so I could write a story on him. I've never heard from him.

He dropped Sheree and me off at a taxi station and we waited for someone to pick us up. It was two in the morning.

I put on my hawk feathers for protection while we were waiting for a cab to come along. About twenty-five minutes later, one stopped and we asked the cabby to drive us around Greenwich Village. He was very black and slight. He must have thought we were lesbians because on the way to

Greenwich Village he pointed out every lesbian bar we passed. He stopped in front of a building with a giant plaster head of the Statue of Liberty and said, "Largest lesbian club in New York. Men not allowed there. You like?"

When we told him we didn't want to stop, he gave up. I asked him where he was from and he said Nigeria.

"I been in America seese months."

He looked at me with my feathers and asked where I was from. I told him I was born here, that I was an American Indian. He pulled the cab over to the corner and stopped.

"Oh, how much would I like to talk to you. You are the real Americans. This was all your home before we started coming here. I am learning about you in my classes. Right now, you are having a lot of problems with the government discriminating against you. To me, it's so sad. I want to do something."

I was stunned and a little ashamed. For a moment I couldn't decide whether to say something flippant or believe his sincerity. I believed he meant what he was saying, even if it was just a temporary state of naiveté. I answered lamely that there was always hope or something stupid like that. Here was this black Nigerian who barely spoke English, guiding us around New York City in the early morning hours, trying to comfort me about the problems of the American Indian.

He again said he wished he could talk to us but he must go home to his family. We were his last fare. We asked him to drop us off at the Staten Island Ferry. As he drove away, I thought about my ambivalence toward newcomers. Ambivalence at best; racism at worst.

After all, the flood of white people is responsible for my being alive. (I am part white.) And yet, according to the melting-pot theorists, turning "us" into "them" has not been easy. Even after 210 years of worldwide immigration into the United States, Indians still exist, numbering two million people in some 846 tribes. About the same number of new immigrants living in New York City.

We took the ferry to see the Statue of Liberty. The Nigerian had made my feelings toward immigrants soften. Maybe more newcomers was a good thing. In a way, newcomers have forced us, at least some of us, to be stronger.

I've always believed that mixing white and Indian blood makes first-generation half-breeds unpredictably mean, and often confused. Confused by their misdirected anger, confused by their choices, confused by their inherited instincts which the scientists say don't exist.

Man is a thinking animal therefore he suppresses any instincts and he learns from his environment. Take an Indian child from a reservation and put him with a white family in Boston and chances are that he'll become a Bostonian and a working member of society. Eventually the Indian child will forget about his home and ancestry.

That's the theory I learned from a behavioral psychologist at the University of Oklahoma. But that was ten years ago. Now a recent university study, completed in 1986, says that your genes determine whether or not you can do mathematics. I believe if your genes can help you find the answer to a trigonometry problem, then they can likewise make you crazy.

John Stuart says it more directly: "You never know what you're gonna get when you breed two different kinds of dogs. Most of the time, the dog is smarter than its parents, but then there are those times when the dog is born a complete idiot. You just never know when it comes to breeding."

Half-breeds live on the edge of both races. You feel like you're split down the middle. Your right arm wants to unbutton your shirt while your left arm is trying to keep your shirt on. You're torn between wanting to kill everyone in the room, or buying 'em all another round of drinks.

Our erratic behavior is often explained away by friends and family as "trying to be." If you're around Indians, you're trying to be white. If you're around white friends, you're trying to be Indian. Sometimes I feel like the blood in my veins is a deadly mixture of Rh positive and Rh negative and every cell in my body is on a slow nuclear melt-down.

As we approached America's statue of freedom, the only sound on the ferryboat was the muffled churning of its engines.

I thought about all the Indians huddled on reservations, the tired women-whores bound to their pimps, the Irish boxer, the poor Nigerian cabdriver. I thought about our relationship to each other. Now almost two years have passed and still the images of those people have stayed with me through all the July Fourth hoopla and one-hundredth birthday celebration of the Statue of Liberty. Even though not one word was mentioned about America's natives, only about the immigrants who've been coming here because they believed our country was better than theirs, I've decided Emma Lazarus, who wrote the Statue's welcoming inscription, was really an Indian: "Give me your tired, your poor, your huddled masses yearning to breathe free . . ."

You did. Now where do we go from here?

1986

GWENDOLYN BROOKS

Dreams of a Black Christmas

When I was a child, it did not occur to me, even once, that the black in which I was encased (I called it brown in those days) would be considered, one day, beautiful. Considered beautiful and called beautiful by great groups.

I had always considered it beautiful. I would stick out my arm, examine it, and smile. Charming! And convenient, for mud on my leg was not as annunciatory as was mud on the leg of light Rose Hurd.

Charm—and efficiency.

This delight in my pigmentation was hardly a feature of my world. One of the first "world"-truths revealed to me when I at last became a member of SCHOOL was that, to be socially successful, a little girl must be Bright (of skin). It was better if your hair was curly, too—or at least Good Grade (Good Grade implied, usually, no involvement with the Hot Comb)—but Bright you marvelously *needed* to be. Exceptions? A few. Wealth was an escape passport. If a dusky maiden's father was a doctor, lawyer, City Hall employee, or Post Office man, or if her mother was a School-teacher, there was some hope: because that girl would often have lovelier clothes, and more of them, than her Bright competitors; and her hair was often long, at *least*, and straight—oh so Hot Comb straight! Such a damsel, if she had virtually nothing to do with the *ordinary* black women of the class, might be favored, might be Accepted.

My father was a janitor. My mother had been a schoolteacher in To-peka before her marriage, but that did not count. Who knew it, anyhow? Of course, not many knew of my father's lowly calling. Still, there was something about me—even though in the early years I wore decent dresses because my Aunt Beulah, a sewing teacher at the Booker Washington High School in Tulsa, was making them for me, sending, on occasion, five at a time—SOMETHING—that stamped me "beyond the pale." And thereby doubly.

All I could hope for was achievement of reverence among the Lesser Blacks. Alas. Requisites for eminence among these I had not. I had not brass or sass. I did not fight brilliantly, or at all, on the playground. I was not ingenious in gym, carrying my team single-handedly to glory. I could not play jacks. I could not ride a bicycle. I did not whisper excitedly about my Boyfriends. For the best of reasons. I did not have any. Among the Lesser Blacks my decent dresses were hinderers to my advance. The girls who did not have them loathed me for having them. When they bothered to remember that I was alive, that is. When they bothered to remember that I was alive, they called me "ol' stuck-up heifer"; and they informed me that they wanted "nothin' t' do with no rich people's sp'iled chirren." Doubtless, this decision amazed the Bright and the *truly* rich, whom the critics openly adored.

As for the Men in the world of School—the little Bright ones looked through me as if I happened to inconvenience their vision, and those of my own hue rechristened me Ol' Black Gal.

These facts of my eight-year membership in school served to sully the truly nice delights of crayon and chalk and watercolor, of story time, and textbooks with cheery pictures of neat, gay-colored life-among-the-white-folks.

Home, however, always warmly awaited me. Welcoming, envelop-ing. Home meant a quick-walking, careful, Duty-Loving mother, who played the piano, made fudge, made cocoa and prune whip and apricot pie, drew tidy cows and trees and expert houses with chimneys and chim-ney smoke, who helped her children with arithmetic homework, and who sang in a high soprano:

> *Brighten the corner where you are!—*
> *Br-rrr-righten the corner where you are!—*

Someone far from harbor you may guide
across the bar—
Bright-TEN the cor-nerr—
where
you
are.

Home meant my father, with kind eyes, songs, and tense recitations for my brother and myself. A favorite of his, a wonderful poem about a pie-making lady. Along had come a man, weary, worn, to beg of the lady a pie. Those already baked, she informed him, were too large for the likes of him. She said she would bake another. It, too, was "large." And the next was large. And the next, and the next. Finally the traveler, completely out of patience, berated her and exclaimed that henceforth she should draw her own sustenance from the bark of trees. And she became, *mirabile dictu,* a woodpecker and flew off. We never tired of that. My father seemed to Gwendolyn and Raymond a figure of power. He had those rich Artistic Abilities, but he had more. He could fix anything that broke or stopped. He could build long-lasting fires in the ancient furnace below. He could paint the house, inside and out, and could whitewash the basement. He could spread the American Flag in wide loud magic across the front of our house on the Fourth of July and Decoration Day. He could chuckle. No one has ever had, no one will ever have, a chuckle exactly like my father's. It was gentle, it was warmly happy, it was heavyish but not hard. It was secure, and seemed to us an assistant to the Power that registered with his children. My father, too, was almost our family doctor. We had Dr. Carter, of course, precise and semitwinkly and effective—but it was not always necessary to call him. My father had wanted to be a doctor. Thwarted, he read every "doctor book" (and he remembered much from a black tradition) he could reach, learning fine secrets and curing us with steams, and fruit compotes, and dexterous rubs, and, above all, with bedside compassion. "Well, there, young lady! How's that throat now?" "Well, let's see now. This salve will take care of that bruise! Now, we're going to be all right." In illness there was an advantage: the invalid was royalty for the run of the seizure.

And of course my father furnished All the Money. The "all" was inadequate, felt Keziah Wims Brooks: could he not leave the McKinley Music Publishing Company, which was paying him about twenty-five dollars a week (from thirty to thirty-five when he worked overtime)? Uncle Paul, her sister Gertrude's husband, worked at City Hall—had a "snap" job— made *fifty* dollars a week. . . . True, during the bad times, during the Depression, when McKinley, itself stricken, could pay my father only in part—sometimes eighteen dollars, sometimes ten dollars—my family ate beans. But children dread, often above all else, dissension in the house, and we would have been quite content to entertain a beany diet every day, if necessary, and not live in Lilydale as did bungalow-owning Aunt Gertrude and Uncle Paul, if only there could be, continuously, the almost musical Peace that we had most of the time.

Home. Checker games. Dominoes. Radio (Jack Benny, Ben Bernie, and Kate Smith; "Amos and Andy"; Major Bowes's "Amateur Hour"; Wayne King, the Waltz King; and "Ladies and Gentlemen: Ea-sy Aces"). Christmases. I shall stop right here to tell about those. They were important.

The world of Christmas was firm. Certain things were done. Certain things were not done.

We did not put Christmas trees outdoors.

We did not open Christmas presents on Christmas Eve.

And we had *not* made fruitcakes two or three months ahead of time.

A Christmas tree, we felt—my mother, my father, my brother, and I—belonged in the living room. Green, never silver or gold or pink. Full-branched and aspiring to the ceiling.

Christmas presents were wrapped and hidden on Christmas Eve. Oh, the sly winks and grins. The furtive rustle of tissue, the whip of ribbon off the spool, semiheard. The trippings here and there in search of secure hiding places. Our house had nooks and crannies, a closet, a pantry, alcoves, "the little room," an extensive basement: There were hiding places aplenty.

Fruitcakes were made about a week before Christmas. We didn't care what the recipe books said. We liked having all the Christmas joy as close together as possible. Mama went downtown, as a rule, for the very freshest supplies, for then, as now, distributors sent their *worst* materials to "the colored neighborhood." Candied cherries and pineapple but no citron. Mama didn't like citron (*I* did and do), so that was out. Candied orange and lemon, however. Figs galore. Dates galore. Raisins, raisins, raisins.

We children had the bake-eve fun of cutting up the candied fruit, shelling and chopping the nuts, and mixing everything together. Our fingers got tired, our teeth and tongues never. We tasted and tasted and took gay tummy aches to bed. Next day, the house was rich with the aroma of brandied fruit and spice. How wonderful. How happy I was.

It was the baking of the fruitcakes that opened our Christmas season. After that, there was the merriest playing of Christmas carols on the piano by my mother and me, with everybody singing; mysterious shopping jaunts; the lingering, careful purchase of Christmas cards; the visit to Santa Claus; the desperately scrupulous housecleaning; for my mother and myself, the calls at the beauty shop for Christmas hairdos (you had to look your very best on Christmas Day); the Christmas-tree hunt, undertaken by all, with the marvelous pungent symbol *found* and borne back triumphantly through the dusk of the third or fourth day before Christmas.

All this. So much more that fades, and fades. I almost forgot the high, high angel-food cake, made a day or two before Christmas. We were, somehow, not great Christmas-cookie advocates, but there would be a few frosted cookies about. We had Christmas candy. And filled candies and Christmas mints. Some of those dates, too, were stuffed with nuts and sugared over, to make another sort of confection.

On Christmas Eve we decorated the Christmas tree. So much silver tinsel. And ropes of fringed gold, and red, silver, blue, and gold balls, and a star on top. We children hung our stockings on the mantel—in the morning they would ache with apples, oranges, nuts, and tiny toys—over our, yes, *real* fireplace! That night we were allowed to "sample the sample"— that is, "test" fruitcake that my mother always made in a shallow pan, along with the proper proud giants—and with it we had eggnog with nutmeg on top.

With what excited pleasure my brother and I went to bed, trying to stay awake to hear Santa Claus come down our chimney, but always failing, for Santa was a sly old soul. We went to sleep with radio carols in our ears, or to the sweet sound of Mama playing and singing "Silent Night," or "Hark! The Herald Angels Sing," or "O Little Town of Bethlehem."

Next day it was so hard to wait for the sky to turn on its light. As soon as it did, out of bed we children threw ourselves and rushed into the living room. There we found, always, that Papa had turned on the Christmas-tree lights, and under the tree shone *just about* everything we had asked of Santa Claus. (Of course, Mama *always* "helped" us with our letters to

Santa Claus.) My brother remembers trains and tracks, baseball equipment, wagons, skates, games. Various Christmases brought me dishes, a rocking chair, a doll house, paper dolls which I liked better than hard dolls because so much more could be done with the paper ones. My most delicate and exquisite Christmas-gift memory is of a little glass deer, dainty-antlered, slender-legged, and filled with perfume.

Of course, there were clothes—"secondary" gifts.

And BOOKS.

About books. My "book Christmas" had already begun, on Christmas Eve, soon after the Christmas tree was strung with lights. It was for long my own personal tradition to sit behind the tree and read a paper book I still own: *The Cherry Orchard*, by Marie Battelle Schilling, and published by the David C. Cook Publishing Company. It had been given me by Kayola Moore, my Sunday school teacher. I don't know why I enjoyed reading that book, Christmas Eve after Christmas Eve, to the tune of black-walnut candy crunching.

And back I went—to the back of the Christmas tree—with my new books. Late, late. After the relatives, after the Christmas turkey, after the cranberries—fresh!—none of your canned cranberries for us—and the mashed potatoes and gravy and baked macaroni and celery and candied sweet potatoes and peas-and-carrots, and the fruitcake and angel cake and eggnog. Back, while the rest of the family forgot it all in bed, to the else-dark room. The silence. The black-walnut candy. And the books that began the giving again.

It did not trouble me, then, that Santa was white and Christ and Christmas were offered as white, except for That One of the "wise men," with role ever slurred, ever understated.

Today, *my* house has not yet escaped the green-tree-fruit-cake-eggnog-gifts-on-Christmas-morning "esthetic," even in this our time of black decision and ascent. The human heart delights in "celebration." Human beings delight in the Day set apart for singing and feasting and dancing and fancy dress—or "best" apparel—and the special giving of gifts and twenty-four-hour formalized love. An urgent need is a holiday for blacks, to be enjoyed by blacks everywhere. Worldwide . . .

In those old days we honored Easter, too. Easter, heralded by hot cross buns on Good Friday, was a time for true newness. On Easter Sunday we did not put on our winter heaviness even if the snow fell and the temperature plunged. No more the long underwear. My brother had white sleeveless undershirts and white shorts, new "oxfords." He had a new suit, a new coat, a new cap. I had patent leather shoes, white socks, girls' b.v.d.'s, light petticoats, a new dress, a new coat, a hat made of straw and ribbons. My self-sacrificing mother rarely had more than a new hat; my father had nothing. We—my mother, my brother, and I, *never* my father —trotted off to Sunday School. Carter Temple Colored Methodist Episcopal Church was at the northwest corner of our block. After Sunday School we went home, returning in the afternoon to take part in the Easter Program. Before coming back we had found our hidden Easter eggs, and had received our Easter baskets full of chocolate rabbits and cotton rabbits and jelly beans and bright marshmallow eggs and lots of green straw.

Birthdays. Large frosted cakes, strawberry and vanilla ice cream (sometimes little ice cream fruit and flower or animal forms found at Frozen Arts, just off 43rd and Cottage Grove); presents, beautifully ribboned; the half-hysterical little guests squeakily singing "Happy Birthday to you!" in honor of the half-hysterical little host or hostess; the wee pink or white candles doomed to be quickly lit, blown out, and forgotten.

Another loved special was Halloween. Pumpkin lanterns. Sheets for ghost costumes. Polished red apples. Trick-or-treating. Angry neighbors.

The Thanksgiving Day menu was exactly the same as the Christmas menu, except that there were mince, pumpkin, and apple pies instead of cakes. Every Thanksgiving Day, as a prelude to the feast, I read Palmer Cox's "The Brownies' Thanksgiving."

Are you aware of a fact-that-should-be-startling about the High Days of my youth? All were Europe-rooted or America-rooted. Not one celebration in my black household or in any black household that I knew featured any black glory or greatness or grandeur.

A capricious bunch of entries and responses has brought me to my present understanding of fertile facts. Know-nows: I know now that I am essentially an essential African, in occupancy here because of an indeed "peculiar" institution. I know now that the Indian is the authentic American, unless *he* did some forcible country-taking, too. I know that I am in that company of thousands now believing that black tragedy is contrived. I know now that black fellow-feeling must be the black man's encyclopedic Primer. I know that the black-and-white integration concept, which in the mind of some beaming early saint was a dainty spinning dream, has wound down to farce, to unsavory and mumbling farce, and that Don L. Lee, a major and muscular black voice of this day, is correct in "The New Integrationist":

> *I*
> *seek*
> *integration*
> *of*
> *negroes*
> *with*
> *black*
> *people.*

I know that the black emphasis must be, not *against white*, but *FOR black*. I know that a substantial manner of communication and transaction with whites will be, eventually, arrived at, arranged—*if* blacks remain in this country; but the old order shall not prevail; the day of head pats for nice little niggers, bummy kicks for bad bad Biggers, and apparent black acceptance of both, is done. In the Conference-That-Counts, whose date may be 1980 or 2080 (woe betide the Fabric of Man if it is 2080), there will be no looking up nor looking down.

It frightens me to realize that, if I had died before the age of fifty, I would have died a "Negro" fraction . . .

Yes, needed is a holiday for blacks everywhere, a Black World Day, with black excitement and black trimmings in honor of the astounding strength and achievement of black people. A yearly Black People's Day—akin, perhaps, to the black concept Kwanza, which, based on a traditional African holiday, is considered by many black people an alternative to commercial Christmas; for the week beginning December twenty-sixth, homes are decorated in red and black and green, the black representing the black nation, the red representing our shed blood, the green featured as a symbol of land for nation-establishment and a symbol, too, for live faith in our young.

I see, feel, and hear a potential celebration as Africa colors—thorough, direct. A thing of shout but of African quietness, too, because in Africa these tonals can almost coincide. A clean-throated singing. Drums;

and perhaps guitars. Flags or a flag. Costumery, wholesomely gaudy; costumery which, for the African, is not affectation but merely a right richness
that the body deserves. Foods; not pate de foie gras or creamed lobster de
bon bon, but figs and oranges, and vegetables. . . . AND the profound and
frequent shaking of hands, which in Africa is so important. The shaking of
hands in warmth and strength and union.

1972

TONI MORRISON

A Knowing So Deep

I think about us, Black women, a lot. How many of us are battered and how many are champions. I note the strides that have replaced the tiptoe; I watch the new configurations we have given to personal relationships, wonder what shapes are forged and what merely bent. I think about the sisters no longer with us, who, in rage or contentment, left us to finish what should never have begun: a gender/racial war in which everybody would lose, if we lost, and in which everybody would win, if we won. I think about the Black women who never landed who are still swimming open-eyed in the sea. I think about those of us who did land and see how their strategies for survival became our maneuvers for power.

I know the achievements of the past are staggering in their everydayness as well as their singularity. I know the work undone is equally staggering, for it is nothing less than to alter the world in each of its parts: the distribution of money, the management of resources, the way families are nurtured, the way work is accomplished and valued, the penetration of the network that connects these parts. If each hour of every day brings fresh reasons to weep, the same hour is full of cause for congratulations: Our scholarship illuminates our past, our political astuteness brightens our future, and the ties that bind us to other women are in constant repair in order to build strength in this present, now.

I think about us, women and girls, and I want to say something worth saying to a daughter, a friend, a mother, a sister—my self. And if I were to try, it might go like this:

Dear Us: You were the rim of the world—its beginning. Primary. In the first shadow the new sun threw, you carried inside you all there was of startled and startling life. And you were there to do it when the things of the world needed words. Before you were named, you were already naming.

Hell's twins, slavery and silence, came later. Still you were like no other. Not because you suffered more or longer, but because of what you knew and did before, during, and following that suffering. No one knew your weight until you left them to carry their own. But you knew. You said, "Excuse me, am I in the way?" knowing all the while that you were the way. You had this canny ability to shape an untenable reality, mold it, sing it, reduce it to its manageable, transforming essence, which is a knowing so deep it's like a secret. In your silence, enforced or chosen, lay not only eloquence but discourse so devastating that "civilization" could not risk engaging in it lest it lose the ground it stomped. All claims to prescience disintegrate when and where that discourse takes place. When you say "No" or "Yes" or "This and not that," change itself changes.

So the literature you live and write asks and gives no quarter. When you sculpt or paint, organize or refute, manage, teach, nourish, investigate or love, you do not blink. Your gaze, so lovingly unforgiving, stills, agitates, and stills again. Wild or serene, vulnerable or steel trap, you are the touchstone by which all that is human can be measured. Porch or horizon, your sweep is grand.

You are what fashion tries to be—original and endlessly refreshing. Say what they like on Channel X, you are the news of the day. What doesn't love you has trivialized itself and must answer for that. And anybody who does not know your history doesn't know their own and must answer for that too.

You did all right, girl. Then, at the first naming, and now at the renaming. You did all right. You took the hands of the children and danced with them. You defended men who could not defend you. You turned grandparents over on their sides to freshen sheets and white pillows. You made meals from leavings, and leaving you was never a real separation because nobody needed your face to remember you by. And all along the way you had the best of company—others, we others, just like you. When you cried, I did too. When we fought, I was afraid you would break your fingernails or split a seam at the armhole of your jacket. And you made me laugh so hard the sound of it disappeared—returned, I guess, to its beginning when laughter and tears were sisters too.

There is movement in the shadow of a sun that is old now. There, just there. Coming from the rim of the world. A disturbing disturbance that is not a hawk nor stormy weather, but a dark woman, of all things. My sister, my me—rustling, like life.

1985

CHERRÍE MORAGA

La Güera

It requires something more than personal experience to gain
a philosophy or point of view from any specific event. It is the quality
of our response to the event and our capacity to enter into the lives of
others that help us to make their lives and experiences our own.
EMMA GOLDMAN[1]

I am the very well-educated daughter of a woman who, by the standards in this country, would be considered largely illiterate. My mother was born in Santa Paula, Southern California, at a time when much of the central valley there was still farm land. Nearly thirty-five years later, in 1948, she was the only daughter of six to marry an anglo, my father.

I remember all of my mother's stories, probably much better than she realizes. She is a fine storyteller, recalling every event of her life with the vividness of the present, noting each detail right down to the cut and color of her dress. I remember stories of her being pulled out of school at the ages of five, seven, nine, and eleven to work in the fields, along with her brothers and sisters; stories of her father drinking away whatever small

---

[1] Alix Kates Shulman, "Was My Life Worth Living?" *Red Emma Speaks* (New York: Random House, 1972), p. 388.

profit she was able to make for the family; of her going the long way home to avoid meeting him on the street, staggering toward the same destination. I remember stories of my mother lying about her age in order to get a job as a hatcheck girl at Agua Caliente Racetrack in Tijuana. At fourteen, she was the main support of the family. I can still see her walking home alone at 3 A.M., only to turn all of her salary and tips over to her mother, who was pregnant again.

The stories continue through the war years and on: walnut-cracking factories, the Voit Rubber factory, and then the computer boom. I remember my mother doing piecework for the electronics plant in our neighborhood. In the late evening, she would sit in front of the T.V. set, wrapping copper wires into the backs of circuit boards, talking about "keeping up with the younger girls." By that time, she was already in her mid-fifties.

Meanwhile, I was college-prep in school. After classes, I would go with my mother to fill out job applications for her, or write checks for her at the supermarket. We would have the scenario all worked out ahead of time. My mother would sign the check before we'd get to the store. Then, as we'd approach the checkstand, she would say—within earshot of the cashier—"Oh honey, you go 'head and make out the check," as if she couldn't be bothered with such an insignificant detail. No one asked any questions.

I was educated, and wore it with a keen sense of pride and satisfaction, my head propped up with the knowledge, from my mother, that my life would be easier than hers. I was educated; but more than this, I was "la güera": fair-skinned. Born with the features of my Chicana mother, but the skin of my Anglo father, I had it made.

No one ever quite told me this (that light was right), but I knew that being light was something valued in my family (who were all Chicano, with the exception of my father). In fact, everything about my upbringing (at least what occurred on a conscious level) attempted to bleach me of what color I did have. Although my mother was fluent in it, I was never taught much Spanish at home. I picked up what I did learn from school and from over-heard snatches of conversation among my relatives and mother. She often called other lower-income Mexicans "braceros," or "wet-backs," referring to herself and her family as "a different class of people." And yet, the real story was that my family, too, had been poor (some still are) and farmworkers. My mother can remember this in her blood as if it were yesterday. But this is something she would like to forget (and rightfully), for to her, on a basic economic level, being Chicana meant being "less." It was through my mother's desire to protect her children from poverty and illiteracy that we became "anglocized"; the more effectively we could pass in the white world, the better guaranteed our future.

From all of this, I experience, daily, a huge disparity between what I was born into and what I was to grow up to become. Because, (as Goldman suggests) these stories my mother told me crept under my "güera" skin. I had no choice but to enter into the life of my mother. *I had no choice.* I took her life into my heart, but managed to keep a lid on it as long as I feigned being the happy, upwardly mobile heterosexual.

When I finally lifted the lid to my lesbianism, a profound connection with my mother reawakened in me. It wasn't until I acknowledged and confronted my own lesbianism in the flesh, that my heartfelt identification with and empathy for my mother's oppression—due to being poor, uneducated, and Chicana—was realized. My lesbianism is the avenue through which I have learned the most about silence and oppression, and it continues to be the most tactile reminder to me that we are not free human beings.

You see, one follows the other. I had known for years that I was a lesbian, had felt it in my bones, had ached with the knowledge, gone crazed with the knowledge, wallowed in the silence of it. Silence *is* like starvation. Don't be fooled. It's nothing short of that, and felt most sharply when one has had a full belly most of her life. When we are not physically starving, we have the luxury to realize psychic and emotional starvation. It is from this starvation that other starvations can be recognized—if one is willing to take the risk of making the connection—if one is willing to be responsible to the result of the connection. For me, the connection is an inevitable one.

What I am saying is that the joys of looking like a white girl ain't so great since I realized I could be beaten on the street for being a dyke. If my sister's being beaten because she's Black, it's pretty much the same principle. We're both getting beaten any way you look at it. The connection is blatant; and in the case of my own family, the difference in the privileges attached to looking white instead of brown are merely a generation apart.

In this country, lesbianism is a poverty—as is being brown, as is being a woman, as is being just plain poor. The danger lies in ranking the oppressions. *The danger lies in failing to acknowledge the specificity of the oppression.* The danger lies in attempting to deal with oppression purely from a theoretical base. Without an emotional, heartfelt grappling with the source of our own oppression, without naming the enemy within ourselves and outside of us, no authentic, nonhierarchical connection among oppressed groups can take place.

When the going gets rough, will we abandon our so-called comrades in a flurry of racist/heterosexist/what-have-you panic? To whose camp, then, should the lesbian of color retreat? Her very presence violates the ranking and abstraction of oppression. Do we merely live hand to mouth? Do we merely struggle with the "ism" that's sitting on top of our own heads?

The answer is: yes, I think first we do; and we must do so thoroughly and deeply. But to fail to move out from there will only isolate us in our own oppression—will only insulate, rather than radicalize us.

To illustrate: a gay male friend of mine once confided to me that he continued to feel that, on some level, I didn't trust him because he was male; that he felt, really, if it ever came down to a "battle of the sexes," I might kill him. I admitted that I might very well. He wanted to understand the source of my distrust. I responded, "You're not a woman. Be a woman for a day. Imagine being a woman." He confessed that the thought terrified him because, to him, being a woman meant being raped by men. He *had* felt raped by men; he wanted to forget what that meant. What grew from that discussion was the realization that in order for him to create an authentic alliance with me, he must deal with the primary source of his own sense of oppression. He must, first, emotionally come to terms with what it feels like to be a victim. If he—or anyone—were to truly do this, it would be impossible to discount the oppression of others, except by again forgetting how we have been hurt.

And yet, oppressed groups are forgetting all the time. There are instances of this in the rising Black middle class, and certainly an obvious trend of such "unconsciousness" among white gay men. Because to remember may mean giving up whatever privileges we have managed to squeeze out of this society by virtue of our gender, race, class, or sexuality.

Within the women's movement, the connections among women of different backgrounds and sexual orientations have been fragile, at best. I think this phenomenon is indicative of our failure to seriously address ourselves to some very frightening questions: How have I internalized my own oppression? How have I oppressed? Instead, we have let rhetoric do the job of poetry. Even the word "oppression" has lost its power. We need a new language, better words that can more closely describe women's fear of and resistance to one another; words that will not always come out sounding like dogma.

What prompted me in the first place to work on an anthology by radical women of color was a deep sense that I had a valuable insight to contribute, by virtue of my birthright and background. And yet, I don't really understand first-hand what it feels like being shitted on for being brown. I understand much more about the joys of it—being Chicana and having family are synonymous for me. What I know about loving, singing, crying, telling stories, speaking with my heart and hands, even having a sense of my own soul comes from the love of my mother, aunts, cousins . . .

But at the age of twenty-seven, it is frightening to acknowledge that I have internalized a racism and classism, where the object of oppression is not only someone outside of my skin, but the someone inside my skin. In fact, to a large degree, the real battle with such oppression, for all of us, begins under the skin. I have had to confront the fact that much of what I value about being Chicana, about my family, has been subverted by anglo culture and my own cooperation with it. This realization did not occur to me overnight. For example, it wasn't until long after my graduation from the private college I'd attended in Los Angeles that I realized the major reason for my total alienation from and fear of my classmates was rooted in class and culture. CLICK.

Three years after graduation, in an apple-orchard in Sonoma, a friend of mine (who comes from an Italian Irish working-class family) says to me, "Cherríe, no wonder you felt like such a nut in school. Most of the people there were white and rich." It was true. All along I had felt the difference, but not until I had put the words "class" and "color" to the experience, did my feelings make any sense. For years, I had berated myself for not being as "free" as my classmates. I completely bought that they simply had more guts than I did—to rebel against their parents and run around the country hitch-hiking, reading books, and studying "art." They had enough privilege to be atheists, for chrissake. There was no one around filling in the disparity for me between their parents, who were Hollywood filmmakers, and my parents, who wouldn't know the name of a filmmaker if their lives depended on it (and precisely because their lives didn't depend on it, they couldn't be bothered). But I knew nothing about "privilege" then. White was right. Period. I could pass. If I got educated enough, there would never be any telling.

Three years after that, another CLICK. In a letter to Barbara Smith, I wrote:

> I went to a concert where Ntosake Shange was reading. There, everything exploded for me. She was speaking a language that I knew—in the deepest parts of me—existed, and that I had ignored in my own feminist studies and even in my own writing. What Ntosake caught in me is the realization that in my development as a poet, I have, in many ways, denied the voice of my brown mother—the brown in me. I have acclimated to the sound of a white language which, as my father represents it, does not speak to the emotions in my poems—emotions which stem from the love of my mother.
>
> The reading was agitating. Made me uncomfortable. Threw me into a week-long terror of how deeply I was affected. I felt that I had to start all over again. That I turned only to the perceptions of white middle-class women to speak for me and all women. I am shocked by my own ignorance.

Sitting in that auditorium chair was the first time I had realized to the core of me that for years I had disowned the language I knew best—ignored the words and rhythms that were the closest to me. The sounds of my mother and aunts gossiping—half in English, half in Spanish—while drinking cerveza in the kitchen. And the hands—I had cut off the hands in my poems. But not in conversation; still the hands could not be kept down. Still they insisted on moving.

The reading had forced me to remember that I knew things from my roots. But to remember puts me up against what I don't know. Shange's reading agitated me because she spoke with power about a world that is both alien and common to me: "the capacity to enter into the lives of others." But you can't just take the goods and run. I knew that then, sitting in the Oakland auditorium (as I know in my poetry), that the only thing worth writing about is what seems to be unknown and, therefore, fearful.

The "unknown" is often depicted in racist literature as the "darkness" within a person. Similarly, sexist writers will refer to fear in the form of the vagina, calling it "the orifice of death." In contrast, it is a pleasure to read works such as Maxine Hong Kingston's *Woman Warrior*, where fear and alienation are described as "the white ghosts." And yet, the bulk of literature in this country reinforces the myth that what is dark and female is evil. Consequently, each of us—whether dark, female, or both—has in some way *internalized* this oppressive imagery. What the oppressor often succeeds in doing is simply *externalizing* his fears, projecting them into the bodies of women, Asians, gays, disabled folks, whoever seems most "other."

> *call me*
> *roach and presumptuous*
> *nightmare on your white pillow*
> *your itch to destroy*
> *the indestructible*
> *part of yourself*

AUDRE LORDE[2]

But it is not really difference the oppressor fears so much as similarity. He fears he will discover in himself the same aches, the same longings as those of the people he has shitted on. He fears the immobilization threatened by his own incipient guilt. He fears he will have to change his life once he has seen himself in the bodies of the people he has called different. He fears the hatred, anger, the vengeance of those he has hurt.

This is the oppressor's nightmare, but it is not exclusive to him. We women have a similar nightmare, for each of us in some way has been both oppressed and the oppressor. We are afraid to look at how we have failed each other. We are afraid to see how we have taken the values of our oppressor into our hearts and turned them against ourselves and one another. We are afraid to admit how deeply "the man's" words have been ingrained in us.

To assess the damage is a dangerous act. I think of how, even as a feminist lesbian, I have so wanted to ignore my own homophobia, my own hatred of myself for being queer. I have not wanted to admit that my deepest personal sense of myself has not quite "caught up" with my "woman-

---

[2] From "The Brown Menace or Poem to the Survival of Roaches," *The New York Head Shop and Museum* (Detroit: Broadside, 1974), p. 48.

identified" politics. I have been afraid to criticize lesbian writers who choose to "skip over" these issues in the name of feminism. In 1979, we talk of "old gay" and "butch and femme" roles as if they were ancient history. We toss them aside as merely patriarchal notions. And yet, the truth of the matter is that I have sometimes taken society's fear and hatred of lesbians to bed with me. I have sometimes hated my lover for loving me. I have sometimes felt "not woman enough" for her. I have sometimes felt "not man enough." For a lesbian trying to survive in a heterosexist society, there is no easy way around these emotions. Similarly, in a white-dominated world, there is little getting around racism and our own internalization of it. It's always there, embodied in some one we least expect to rub up against.

When we do rub up against this person, *there* then is the challenge. *There* then is the opportunity to look at the nightmare within us. But we usually shrink from such a challenge.

Time and time again, I have observed that the usual response among white women's groups when the "racism issue" comes up is to deny the difference. I have heard comments like, "Well, we're open to *all* women; why don't they (women of color) come? You can only do so much . . ." But there is seldom any analysis of how the very nature and structure of the group itself may be founded on racist or classist assumptions. More importantly, so often the women seem to feel no loss, no lack, no absence when women of color are not involved; therefore, there is little desire to change the situation. This has hurt me deeply. I have come to believe that the only reason women of a privileged class will dare to look at *how* it is that *they* oppress, is when they've come to know the meaning of their own oppression. And understand that the oppression of others hurts them personally.

The other side of the story is that women of color and working-class women often shrink from challenging white middle-class women. It is much easier to rank oppressions and set up a hierarchy, rather than take responsibility for changing our own lives. We have failed to demand that white women, particularly those who claim to be speaking for all women, be accountable for their racism.

The dialogue has simply not gone deep enough.

I have many times questioned my right to even work on an anthology which is to be written "exclusively by Third World women." I have had to look critically at my claim to color, at a time when, among white feminist ranks, it is a "politically correct" (and sometimes peripherally advanta-geous) assertion to make. I must acknowledge the fact that, physically, I have had a *choice* about making that claim, in contrast to women who have not had such a choice, and have been abused for their color. I must reckon with the fact that for most of my life, by virtue of the very fact that I am white-looking, I identified with and aspired toward white values, and that I rode the wave of that Southern Californian privilege as far as conscience would let me.

Well, now I feel both bleached and beached. I feel angry about this— the years when I refused to recognize privilege, both when it worked against me, and when I worked it, ignorantly, at the expense of others. These are not settled issues. That is why this work feels so risky to me. It continues to be discovery. It has brought me into contact with women who invariably know a hell of a lot more than I do about racism, as experienced in the flesh, as revealed in the flesh of their writing.

I think: what is my responsibility to my roots—both white and brown, Spanish-speaking and English? I am a woman with a foot in both worlds; and I refuse the split. I feel the necessity for dialogue. Sometimes I feel it urgently.

But one voice is not enough, nor two, although this is where dialogue begins. It is essential that radical feminists confront their fear of and resis-tance to each other, because without this, there *will* be no bread on the table. Simply, we will not survive. If we could make this connection in our heart of hearts, that if we are serious about a revolution—better—if we seriously believe there should be joy in our lives (real joy, not just "good times"), then we need one another. We women need each other. Because my/your solitary, self-asserting "go-for-the-throat-of-fear" power is not enough. The real power, as you and I well know, is collective. I can't afford to be afraid of you, nor you of me. If it takes head-on collisions, let's do it: this polite timidity is killing us.

As Lorde suggests in the passage I cited earlier, it is in looking to the nightmare that the dream is found. There, the survivor emerges to insist on a future, a vision, yes, born out of what is dark and female. The feminist movement must be a movement of such survivors, a movement with a future.

1983

ADRIENNE RICH

Split at the Root

An Essay on Jewish Identity

For about fifteen minutes I have been sitting chin in hand in front of the typewriter, staring out at the snow. Trying to be honest with myself, trying to figure out why writing this seems to be so dangerous an act, filled with fear and shame, and why it seems so necessary. It comes to me that in order to write this I have to be willing to do two things: I have to claim my father, for I have my Jewishness from him and not from my gentile mother; and I have to break his silence, his taboos; in order to claim him I have in a sense to expose him.

And there is, of course, the third thing: I have to face the sources and the flickering presence of my own ambivalence as a Jew; the daily, mundane anti-Semitisms of my entire life.

These are stories I have never tried to tell before. Why now? Why, I asked myself sometime last year, does this question of Jewish identity float so impalpably, so ungraspably around me, a cloud I can't quite see the outlines of, which feels to me to be without definition?

And yet I've been on the track of this longer than I think.

In a long poem written in 1960, when I was thirty-one years old, I described myself as "Split at the root, neither Gentile nor Jew,/Yankee nor Rebel."[1] I was still trying to have it both ways: to be neither/nor, trying to live (with my Jewish husband and three children more Jewish in ancestry than I) in the predominantly gentile Yankee academic world of Cambridge, Massachusetts.

But this begins, for me, in Baltimore, where I was born in my father's workplace, a hospital in the Black ghetto, whose lobby contained an immense white marble statue of Christ.

My father was then a young teacher and researcher in the department of pathology at the Johns Hopkins Medical School, one of the very few Jews to attend or teach at that institution. He was from Birmingham, Alabama; his father, Samuel, was Ashkenazic, an immigrant from Austria-Hungary and his mother, Hattie Rice, a Sephardic Jew from Vicksburg, Mississippi. My grandfather had had a shoe store in Birmingham, which did well enough to allow him to retire comfortably and to leave my grandmother income on his death. The only souvenirs of my grandfather, Samuel Rich, were his ivory flute, which lay on our living-room mantel and was not to be played with; his thin gold pocket watch, which my father wore; and his Hebrew prayer book, which I discovered among my father's books in the course of reading my way through his library. In this prayer book there was a newspaper clipping about my grandparents' wedding, which took place in a synagogue.

My father, Arnold, was sent in adolescence to a military school in the North Carolina mountains, a place for training white southern Christian gentlemen. I suspect that there were few, if any, other Jewish boys at Colonel Bingham's, or at "Mr. Jefferson's university" in Charlottesville, where he studied as an undergraduate. With whatever conscious forethought, Samuel and Hattie sent their son into the dominant southern WASP culture to become an "exception," to enter the professional class. Never, in describing these experiences, did he speak of having suffered—from loneliness, cultural alienation, or outsiderhood. Never did I hear him use the word *anti-Semitism*.

It was only in college, when I read a poem by Karl Shapiro beginning "To hate the Negro and avoid the Jew / is the curricu-

---

[1] Adrienne Rich, "Readings of History," in *Snapshots of a Daughter-in-Law* (New York: W. W. Norton, 1967), pp. 36–40.

lum," that it flashed on me that there was an untold side to my father's story of his student years. He looked recognizably Jewish, was short and slender in build with dark wiry hair and deep-set eyes, high forehead and curved nose.

My mother is a gentile. In Jewish law I cannot count myself a Jew. If it is true that "we think back through our mothers if we are women" (Virginia Woolf)—and I myself have affirmed this—then even according to lesbian theory, I cannot (or need not?) count myself a Jew.

The white southern Protestant woman, the gentile, has always been there for me to peel back into. That's a whole piece of history in itself, for my gentile grandmother and my mother were also frustrated artists and intellectuals, a lost writer and a lost composer between them. Readers and annotators of books, note takers, my mother a good pianist still, in her eighties. But there was also the obsession with ancestry, with "background," the southern talk of family, not as people you would necessarily know and depend on, but as heritage, the guarantee of "good breeding." There was the inveterate romantic heterosexual fantasy, the mother telling the daughter how to attract men (my mother often used the word "fascinate"); the assumption that relations between the sexes could only be romantic, that it was in the woman's interests to cultivate "mystery," conceal her actual feelings. Survival tactics of a kind, I think today, knowing what I know about the white woman's sexual role in the southern racist scenario. Heterosexuality as protection, but also drawing white women deeper into collusion with white men.

It would be easy to push away and deny the gentile in me—that white southern woman, that social christian. At different times in my life I have wanted to push away one or the other burden of inheritance, to say merely *I am a woman; I am a lesbian.* If I call myself a Jewish lesbian, do I thereby try to shed some of my southern gentile white woman's culpability? If I call myself only through my mother, is it because I pass more easily through a world where being a lesbian often seems like outsiderhood enough?

According to Nazi logic, my two Jewish grandparents would have made me a *Mischling, first-degree*—nonexempt from the Final Solution.

The social world in which I grew up was christian virtually without needing to say so—christian imagery, music, language, symbols, assumptions everywhere. It was also a genteel, white, middle-class world in which "common" was a term of deep opprobrium. "Common" white people might speak of "niggers"; *we* were taught never to use that word—*we* said "Negroes" (even as we accepted segregation, the eating taboo, the assumption that Black people were simply of a separate species). Our language was more polite, distinguishing us from the "rednecks" or the lynch-mob mentality. But so charged with negative meaning was even the word "Negro" that as children we were taught never to use it in front of Black people. We were taught that any mention of skin color in the presence of colored people was treacherous, forbidden ground. In a parallel way, the word "Jew" was not used by polite gentiles. I sometimes heard my best friend's father, a Presbyterian minister, allude to "the Hebrew people" or "people of the Jewish faith." The world of acceptable folk was white, gentile (christian, really), and had "ideals" (which colored people, white "common" people, were not supposed to have). "Ideals" and "manners" included not hurting someone's feelings by calling her or him a Negro or a Jew—naming the hated identity. This is the mental framework of the 1930s and 1940s in which I was raised.

(Writing this, I feel dimly like the betrayer: of my father, who did not speak the word; of my mother, who must have trained me in the messages; of my caste and class; of my whiteness itself.)

Two memories: I am in a play reading at school of *The Merchant of Venice.* Whatever Jewish law says, I am quite sure I was *seen* as Jewish (with a reassuringly gentile mother) in that double vision that bigotry allows. I am the only Jewish girl in the class, and I am playing Portia. As always, I read my part aloud for my father the night before, and he tells me to convey, with my voice, more scorn and contempt with the word "Jew": "Therefore, Jew . . ." I have to say the word out, and say it loudly. I was encouraged to pretend to be a non-Jewish child acting a non-Jewish character who has to speak the word "Jew" emphatically. Such a child would not have had trouble with the part. But *I* must have had trouble with the part, if only because the word itself was really taboo. I can see that there was a kind of terrible, bitter bravado about my father's way of handling this. And who would not dissociate from Shylock in order to identify with Portia? As a Jewish child who was also a female, I loved Portia—and, like every other Shakespearean heroine, she proved a treacherous role model.

A year or so later I am in another play, *The School for Scandal,* in which a notorious spendthrift is described as having "many excellent friends . . . among the Jews." In neither case was anything explained, either to me or to the class at large, about this scorn for Jews and the disgust surrounding Jews and money. Money, when Jews wanted it, had it, or lent it to others, seemed to take on a peculiar nastiness; Jews and money had some peculiar and unspeakable relation.

At this same school—in which we had Episcopalian hymns and prayers, and read aloud through the Bible morning after morning—I gained the impression that Jews were in the Bible and mentioned in English literature, that they had been persecuted centuries ago by the wicked Inquisition, but that they seemed not to exist in everyday life. These were the 1940s, and we were told a great deal about the Battle of Britain, the noble French Resistance fighters, the brave, starving Dutch—but I did not learn of the resistance of the Warsaw ghetto until I left home.

I was sent to the Episcopal church, baptized and confirmed, and attended it for about five years, though without belief. That religion seemed to have little to do with belief or commitment; it was liturgy that mattered, not spiritual passion. Neither of my parents ever entered that church, and my father would not enter *any* church for any reason—wedding or funeral. Nor did I enter a synagogue until I left Baltimore. When I came home from church, for a while, my father insisted on reading aloud to me from Thomas Paine's *The Age of Reason*—a diatribe against institutional religion. Thus, he explained, I would have a balanced view of these things, a choice. He—they—did not give me the choice to be a Jew. My mother explained to me when I was filling out forms for college that if any question was asked about "religion," I should put down "Episcopalian" rather than "none"—to seem to have no religion was, she implied, dangerous.

But it was white social christianity, rather than any particular christian sect, that the world was founded on. The very word *Christian* was used as a synonym for virtuous, just, peace-loving, generous, etc., etc.[2] The norm was christian: "religion: none" was indeed not acceptable. Anti-Semitism was so intrinsic as not to have a name. I don't recall exactly being taught that the Jews killed Jesus—"Christ killer" seems too strong a term for the bland Episcopal vocabulary—but certainly we got the impression that the Jews had been caught out in a terrible mistake, failing to recognize the true Messiah, and were thereby less advanced in moral and spiritual

---

[2] In a similar way the phrase "That's white of you" implied that you were behaving with the superior decency and morality expected of white but not of Black people.

sensibility. The Jews had actually allowed *moneylenders in the Temple* (again, the unexplained obsession with Jews and money). They were of the past, archaic, primitive, as older (and darker) cultures are supposed to be primitive; christianity was lightness, fairness, peace on earth, and combined the feminine appeal of "The meek shall inherit the earth" with the masculine stride of "Onward, Christian Soldiers."

Sometime in 1946, while still in high school, I read in the newspaper that a theater in Baltimore was showing films of the Allied liberation of the Nazi concentration camps. Alone, I went downtown after school one afternoon and watched the stark, blurry, but unmistakable newsreels. When I try to go back and touch the pulse of that girl of sixteen, growing up in many ways so precocious and so ignorant, I am overwhelmed by a memory of despair, a sense of inevitability more enveloping than any I had ever known. Anne Frank's diary and many other personal narratives of the Holocaust were still unknown or unwritten. But it came to me that every one of those piles of corpses, mountains of shoes and clothing had contained, simply, individuals, who had believed, as I now believed of myself, that they were intended to live out a life of some kind of meaning, that the world possessed some kind of sense and order; yet *this* had happened to them. And I, who believed my life was intended to be so interesting and meaningful, was connected to those dead by something— not just mortality but a taboo name, a hated identity. Or was I—did I really have to be? Writing this now, I feel belated rage that I was so impoverished by the family and social worlds I lived in, that I had to try to figure out by myself what this did indeed mean for me. That I had never been taught about resistance, only about passing. That I had no language for anti-Semitism itself.

When I went home and told my parents where I had been, they were not pleased. I felt accused of being morbidly curious, not healthy, sniffing around death for the thrill of it. And since, at sixteen, I was often not sure of the sources of my feelings or of my motives for doing what I did, I probably accused myself as well. One thing was clear: there was nobody in my world with whom I could discuss those films. Probably at the same time, I was reading accounts of the camps in magazines and newspapers; what I remember were the films and having questions that I could not even phrase, such as *Are those men and women "them" or "us"?*

To be able to ask even the child's astonished question *Why do they hate us so?* means knowing how to say "we." The guilt of not knowing, the guilt of perhaps having betrayed my parents or even those victims, those survivors, through mere curiosity—these also froze in me for years the impulse to find out more about the Holocaust.

1947: I left Baltimore to go to college in Cambridge, Massachusetts, left (I thought) the backward, enervating South for the intellectual, vital North. New England also had for me some vibration of higher moral rectitude, of moral passion even, with its seventeenth-century Puritan self-scrutiny, its nineteenth-century literary "flowering," its abolitionist righteousness, Colonel Shaw and his Black Civil War regiment depicted in granite on Boston Common. At the same time, I found myself, at Radcliffe, among Jewish women. I used to sit for hours over coffee with what I thought of as the "real" Jewish students, who told me about middle-class Jewish culture in America. I described my background—for the first time to strangers—and they took me on, some with amusement at my illiteracy, some arguing that I could never marry into a strict Jewish family, some convinced I didn't "look Jewish," others that I did. I learned the names of holidays and foods, which surnames are Jewish and which are "changed names"; about girls who had had their noses "fixed," their hair straightened. For these young Jewish women, students in the late 1940s, it was acceptable, perhaps even necessary, to strive to look as gentile as possible; but they stuck proudly to being Jewish, expected to marry a Jew, have children, keep the holidays, carry on the culture.

I felt I was testing a forbidden current, that there was danger in these revelations. I bought a reproduction of a Chagall portrait of a rabbi in striped prayer shawl and hung it on the wall of my room. I was admittedly young and trying to educate myself, but I was also doing something that *is* dangerous: I was flirting with identity.

One day that year I was in a small shop where I had bought a dress with a too-long skirt. The shop employed a seamstress who did alterations, and she came in to pin up the skirt on me. I am sure that she was a recent immigrant, a survivor. I remember a short, dark woman wearing heavy glasses, with an accent so foreign I could not understand her words. Something about her presence was very powerful and disturbing to me. After marking and pinning up the skirt, she sat back on her knees, looked up at me, and asked in a hurried whisper: "You Jewish?" Eighteen years of training in assimilation sprang into the reflex by which I shook my head, rejecting her, and muttered, "No."

What was I actually saying "no" to? She was poor, older, struggling with a foreign tongue, anxious; she had escaped the death that had been intended for her, but I had no imagination of her possible courage and foresight, her resistance—I did not see in her a heroine who had perhaps saved many lives, including her own. I saw the frightened immigrant, the seamstress hemming the skirts of college girls, the wandering Jew. But I was an American college girl having her skirt hemmed. And I was frightened myself, I think, because she had recognized me ("It takes one to know one," my friend Edie at Radcliffe had said) even if I refused to recognize myself or her, even if her recognition was sharpened by loneliness or the need to feel safe with me.

But why should she have felt safe with me? I myself was living with a false sense of safety.

There are betrayals in my life that I have known at the very moment were betrayals: this was one of them. There are other betrayals committed so repeatedly, so mundanely, that they leave no memory trace behind, only a growing residue of misery, of dull, accreted self-hatred. Often these take the form not of words but of silence. Silence before the joke at which everyone is laughing: the anti-woman joke, the racist joke, the anti-Semitic joke. Silence and then amnesia. Blocking it out when the oppressor's language starts coming from the lips of one we admire, whose courage and eloquence have touched us: *She didn't really mean that; he didn't really say that.* But the accretions build up out of sight, like scale inside a kettle.

1948: I come home from my freshman year at college, flaming with new insights, new information. I am the daughter who has gone out into the world, to the pinnacle of intellectual prestige, Harvard, fulfilling my father's hopes for me, but also exposed to dangerous influences. I have already been reproved for attending a rally for Henry Wallace and the Progressive party. I challenge my father: "Why haven't you told me that I am Jewish? Why do you never talk about being a Jew?" He answers measuredly, "You know that I have never denied that I am a Jew. But it's not important to me. I am a scientist, a deist. I have no use for organized religion. I choose to live in a world of many kinds of people.

There are Jews I admire and others whom I despise. I am a person, not simply a Jew." The words are as I remember them, not perhaps exactly as spoken. But that was the message. And it contained enough truth—as all denial drugs itself on partial truth—so that it remained for the time being unanswerable, leaving me high and dry, split at the root, gasping for clarity, for air.

At that time Arnold Rich was living in suspension, waiting to be appointed to the professorship of pathology at Johns Hopkins. The appointment was delayed for years, no Jew ever having held a professional chair in that medical school. And he wanted it badly. It must have been a very bitter time for him, since he had believed so greatly in the redeeming power of excellence, of being the most brilliant, inspired man for the job. With enough excellence, you could presumably make it stop mattering that you were Jewish; you could become the *only* Jew in the gentile world, a Jew so "civilized," so far from "common," so attractively combining southern gentility with European cultural values that no one would ever confuse you with the raw, "pushy" Jews of New York, the "loud, hysterical" refugees from eastern Europe, the "overdressed" Jews of the urban South.

We—my sister, mother, and I—were constantly urged to speak quietly in public, to dress without ostentation, to repress all vividness or spontaneity, to assimilate with a world which might see us as too flamboyant. I suppose that my mother, pure gentile though she was, could be seen as acting "common" or "Jewish" if she laughed too loudly or spoke aggressively. My father's mother, who lived with us half the year, was a model of circumspect behavior, dressed in dark blue or lavender, retiring in company, ladylike to an extreme, wearing no jewelry except a good gold chain, a narrow brooch, or a string of pearls. A few times, within the family, I saw her anger flare, felt the passion she was repressing. But when Arnold took us out to a restaurant or on a trip, the Rich women were always tuned down to some WASP level my father believed, surely, would protect us all— maybe also make us unrecognizable to the "real Jews" who wanted to seize us, drag us back to the *shtetl*, the ghetto, in its many manifestations.

For, yes, that *was* a message—that some Jews would be after you, once they "knew," to rejoin them, to re-enter a world that was messy, noisy, unpredictable, maybe poor—"even though," as my mother once wrote me, criticizing my largely Jewish choice of friends in college, "some of them will be the most brilliant, fascinating people you'll ever meet." I won-

der if that isn't one message of assimilation—of America—that the un-
lucky or the unachieving want to pull you backward, that to identify with
them is to court downward mobility, lose the precious chance of passing,
of token existence. There was always within this sense of Jewish identity a
strong class discrimination. Jews might be "fascinating" as individuals but
came with huge unruly families who "poured chicken soup over everyone's
head" (in the phrase of a white southern male poet). Anti-Semitism could
thus be justified by the bad behavior of certain Jews; and if you did not
effectively deny family and community, there would always be a remote
cousin claiming kinship with you who was the "wrong kind" of Jew.

*I have always believed his attitude toward other Jews depended on who
they were. . . . It was my impression that Jews of this background looked
down on Eastern European Jews, including Polish Jews and Russian Jews,
who generally were not as well educated.* This from a letter written to me
recently by a gentile who had worked in my father's department, whom I
had asked about anti-Semitism there and in particular regarding my father.
This informant also wrote me that it was hard to perceive anti-Semitism in
Baltimore because the racism made so much more intense an impression:
*I would almost have to think that blacks went to a different heaven than the
whites, because the bodies were kept in a separate morgue, and some white
persons did not even want blood transfusions from black donors.* My father's
mind was predictably racist and misogynist; yet as a medical student he
noted in his journal that southern male chivalry stopped at the point of any
white man in a streetcar giving his seat to an old, weary Black woman
standing in the aisle. Was this a Jewish insight—an outsider's insight, even
though the outsider was striving to be on the inside?

Because what isn't named is often more permeating than what is, I
believe that my father's Jewishness profoundly shaped my own identity and
our family existence. They were shaped both by external anti-Semitism
and my father's self-hatred, and by his Jewish pride. What Arnold did, I
think, was call his Jewish pride something else: achievement, aspiration,
genius, idealism. Whatever was unacceptable got left back under the ru-
bric of Jewishness or the "wrong kind" of Jews—uneducated, aggressive,
loud. The message I got was that we were really superior: nobody else's father had collected so many books, had traveled so far, knew so many languages. Baltimore was a musical city, but for the most part, in the families
of my school friends, culture was for women. My father was an amateur

musician, read poetry, adored encyclopedic knowledge. He prowled and pounced over my school papers, insisting I use "grown-up" sources; he criticized my poems for faulty technique and gave me books on rhyme and meter and form. His investment in my intellect and talent was egotistical, tyrannical, opinionated, and terribly wearing. He taught me, nevertheless, to believe in hard work, to mistrust easy inspiration, to write and rewrite; to feel that I *was* a person of the book, even though a woman; to take ideas seriously. He made me feel, at a very young age, the power of language and that I could share in it.

The Riches were proud, but we also had to be very careful. Our behavior had to be more impeccable than other people's. Strangers were not to be trusted, nor even friends; family issues must never go beyond the family; the world was full of potential slanderers, betrayers, *people who could not understand*. Even within the family, I realize that I never in my whole life knew what my father was really feeling. Yet he spoke—monologued—with driving intensity. You could grow up in such a house mesmerized by the local electricity, the crucial meanings assumed by the merest things. This used to seem to me a sign that we were all living on some high emotional plane. It was a difficult force field for a favored daughter to disengage from.

Easy to call that intensity Jewish; and I have no doubt that passion is one of the qualities required for survival over generations of persecution. But what happens when passion is rent from its original base, when the white gentile world is softly saying "Be more like us and you can be almost one of us"? What happens when survival seems to mean closing off one emotional artery after another? His forebears in Europe had been forbidden to travel or expelled from one country after another, had special taxes levied on them if they left the city walls, had been forced to wear special clothes and badges, restricted to the poorest neighborhoods. He had wanted to be a "free spirit," to travel widely, among "all kinds of people." Yet in his prime of life he lived in an increasingly withdrawn world, in his house up on a hill in a neighborhood where Jews were not supposed to be able to buy property, depending almost exclusively on interactions with his wife and daughters to provide emotional connectedness. In his home, he created a private defense system so elaborate that even as he was dying, my mother felt unable to talk freely with his colleagues or others who might have helped her. Of course, she acquiesced in this.

The loneliness of the "only," the token, often doesn't feel like loneliness but like a kind of dead echo chamber. Certain things that ought to don't resonate. Somewhere Beverly Smith writes of women of color "inspiring the behavior" in each other. When there's nobody to "inspire the behavior," act out of the culture, there is an atrophy, a dwindling, which is partly invisible.

I was married in 1953, in the Hillel House at Harvard, under a portrait of Albert Einstein. My parents refused to come. I was marrying a Jew of the "wrong kind" from an Orthodox eastern European background. Brooklyn-born, he had gone to Harvard, changed his name, was both indissolubly connected to his childhood world and terribly ambivalent about it. My father saw this marriage as my having fallen prey to the Jewish family, eastern European division.

Like many women I knew in the fifties living under a then-unquestioned heterosexual imperative, I married in part because I knew no better way to disconnect from my first family. I married a "real Jew" who was himself almost equally divided between a troubled yet ingrained Jewish identity, and the pull toward Yankee approval, assimilation. But at least he was not adrift as a single token in a gentile world. We lived in a world where there was much intermarriage and where a certain "Jewish flavor" was accepted within the dominant gentile culture. People talked glibly of "Jewish self-hatred," but anti-Semitism was rarely identified. It was as if you could have it both ways—identity and assimilation—without having to think about it very much.

I was moved and gratefully amazed by the affection and kindliness my husband's parents showed me, the half *shiksa*. I longed to embrace that family, that new and mysterious Jewish world. It was never a question of conversion—my husband had long since ceased being observant—but of a burning desire to do well, please these new parents, heal the split consciousness in which I had been raised, and, of course, to belong. In the big, sunny apartment on Eastern Parkway, the table would be spread on Saturday afternoons with a white or an embroidered cloth and plates of coffeecake, spongecake, mohncake, cookies for a family gathering where everyone ate and drank—coffee, milk, cake—and later the talk still eddied among the women around the table or in the kitchen, while the men ended up in the living room watching the ball game. I had never known this kind of family, in which mock insults were cheerfully exchanged, secrets whispered in corners among two or three, children and grandchildren boasted about, and the new daughter-in-law openly inspected. I was profoundly attracted by all this, including the punctilious observance of *kashrut*, the symbolism lurking behind daily kitchen tasks. I saw it all as quintessentially and authentically Jewish, and I objectified both the people and the culture. My unexamined anti-Semitism allowed me to do this. But also, I had not yet recognized that as a woman I stood in a particular and unexamined relationship to the Jewish family and to Jewish culture.

There were several years during which I did not see, and barely communicated with, my parents. At the same time, my father's personality haunted my life. Such had been the force of his will in our household that for a long time I felt I would have to pay in some terrible way for having disobeyed him. When finally we were reconciled, and my husband and I and our children began to have some minimal formal contact with my parents, the obsessional power of Arnold's voice or handwriting had given way to a dull sense of useless anger and pain. I wanted him to cherish and approve of me, not as he had when I was a child, but as the woman I was, who had her own mind and had made her own choices. This, I finally realized, was not to be; Arnold demanded absolute loyalty, absolute submission to his will. In my separation from him, in my realization at what price that once-intoxicating approval had been bought, I was learning in concrete ways a great deal about patriarchy, in particular how the "special" woman, the favored daughter, is controlled and rewarded.

Arnold Rich died in 1968 after a long, deteriorating illness; his mind had gone, and he had been losing his sight for years. It was a year of intensifying political awareness for me: the Martin Luther King and Robert Kennedy assassinations, the Columbia strike. But it was not that these events, and the meetings and demonstrations that surrounded them, preempted the time of mourning for my father; I had been mourning a long time for an early, primary, and intense relationship, by no means always benign, but in which I had been ceaselessly made to feel that what I did with my life, the choices I made, the attitudes I held, were of the utmost consequence.

Sometime in my thirties, on visits to Brooklyn, I sat on Eastern Parkway, a baby stroller at my feet—one of many rows of young Jewish women on benches with children in that neighborhood. I used to see the Lubavitcher Hasidim—then beginning to move into the Crown Heights neighborhood—walking out on *Shabbes*, the women in their *shaytls* a little behind the men. My father-in-law pointed them out as rather exotic—too old-country, perhaps, too unassimilated even for his devout yet Americanized sense of Jewish identity. It took many years for me to understand—partly because I understood so little about class in America—how in my own family, and in the very different family of my in-laws, there were degrees and hierarchies of assimilation which looked askance upon each other—and also geographic lines of difference, as between southern Jews and New York Jews, whose manners and customs varied along class as well as regional lines.

I had three sons before I was thirty, and during those years I often felt that to be a Jewish woman, a Jewish mother, was to be perceived in the Jewish family as an entirely physical being, a producer and nourisher of children. The experience of motherhood was eventually to radicalize me. But before that, I was encountering the institution of motherhood most directly in a Jewish cultural version; and I felt rebellious, moody, defensive, unable to sort out what was Jewish from what was simply motherhood or female destiny. (I lived in Cambridge, not Brooklyn; but there, too, restless, educated women sat on benches with baby strollers, half-stunned, not by Jewish cultural expectations, but by the middle-class American social expectations of the 1950s.)

My children were taken irregularly to Seders, to bar mitzvahs, and to special services in their grandfather's temple. Their father lit Hanukkah candles while I stood by, having rememorized each year the English meaning of the Hebrew blessing. We all celebrated a secular, liberal Christmas. I read aloud from books about Esther and the Maccabees and Moses, and also from books about Norse trolls and Chinese grandmothers and Celtic dragon slayers. Their father told stories of his boyhood in Brooklyn, his grandmother in the Bronx who had to be visited by subway every week, of misdeeds in Hebrew school, of being a bright Jewish kid at Boys' High. In the permissive liberalism of academic Cambridge, you could raise your children to be as vaguely or distinctly Jewish as you would, but Christian myth and calendar organized the year. My sons grew up knowing far more about the existence and concrete meaning of Jewish culture than I had. But I don't recall sitting down with them and telling them that millions of people like themselves, many of them children, had been rounded up and murdered in Europe in their parents' lifetime. Nor was I able to tell them that they came in part out of the rich, thousand-year-old Ashkenazic culture of eastern Europe, which the Holocaust destroyed; or that they came from a people whose traditions, religious and secular, included a hatred of oppression and an imperative to pursue justice and care for the stranger—an anti-racist, a socialist, and even sometimes a feminist vision. I could not tell them these things because these things were still too indistinct in my own mind.

The emergence of the Civil Rights movement in the sixties I remember as lifting me out of a sense of personal frustration and hopelessness. Reading James Baldwin's early essays in the fifties had stirred me with a sense that apparently "given" situations like racism could be analyzed and described and that this could lead to action, to change. Racism had been so utter and implicit a fact of my childhood and adolescence, had felt so central among the silences, negations, cruelties, fears, superstitions of my early life, that somewhere among my feelings must have been the hope that if Black people could become free of the immense political and social burdens they were forced to bear, I, too, could become free of all the ghosts and shadows of my childhood, named and unnamed. When "the movement" began, it felt extremely personal to me. And it was often Jews who spoke up for the justice of the cause, Jewish students and civil rights lawyers who traveled South; it was two young Jews who were found murdered with a young Black man in Mississippi: Schwerner, Goodman, Chaney.

Moving to New York in the mid-sixties meant being plunged almost immediately into the debate over community control of public schools, in which Black and Jewish teachers and parents were often on opposite sides of extremely militant barricades. It was easy as a white liberal to deplore and condemn the racism of middle-class Jewish parents or angry Jewish schoolteachers, many of them older women; to displace our own racism onto them; or to feel it as too painful to think about. The struggle for Black civil rights had such clarity about it for me: I knew that segregation was wrong, that unequal opportunity was wrong; I knew that segregation in particular was more than a set of social and legal rules—it meant that even "decent" white people lived in a network of lies and arrogance and moral collusion. In the world of Jewish assimilationist and liberal politics which I knew best, however, things were far less clear to me, and anti-Semitism went almost unmentioned. It was even possible to view concern about anti-Semitism as a reactionary agenda, a monomania of *Commentary* magazine or, later, the Jewish Defense League. Most of the political work I was doing in the late 1960s was on racial issues, in particular as a teacher in the City University during the struggle for open admissions. The white colleagues I thought of as allies were, I think, mostly Jewish. Yet it was easy to see other New York Jews, who had climbed out of poverty and exploitation through the public-school system and the free city colleges, as now trying to block Black and Puerto Rican students trying to do likewise. I didn't understand then that I was living between two strains of Jewish social identity: the Jew as radical visionary and activist who understands oppression firsthand, and the Jew as part of America's devouring plan in which the persecuted, called to assimilation, learn that the price is to engage in persecution.

And, indeed, there *was* intense racism among Jews as well as white gentiles in the City University, part of the bitter history of Jews and Blacks which James Baldwin had described much earlier, in his 1948 essay "The Harlem Ghetto";[3] part of the divide-and-conquer script still being rehearsed by those of us who have the least to gain from it.

By the time I left my marriage, after seventeen years and three children, I had become identified with the Women's Liberation movement. It was an astonishing time to be a woman of my age. In the 1950s, seeking a way to grasp the pain I seemed to be feeling most of the time, to set it in some larger context, I had read all kinds of things; but it was James Baldwin and Simone de Beauvoir who had described the world—though differently—in terms that made the most sense to me. By the end of the sixties there were two political movements—one already meeting severe repression, one just emerging—which addressed those descriptions of the world.

And there was, of course, a third movement, or a movement-within-a-movement: the early lesbian manifestoes, the new visibility and activism of lesbians everywhere. I had known very early on that the women's movement was not going to be a simple walk across an open field; that it would pull on every fiber of my existence; that it would mean going back and

[3] James Baldwin, "The Harlem Ghetto," in *Notes of a Native Son* (Boston: Beacon Press, 1955).

searching the shadows of my consciousness. Reading *The Second Sex* in the 1950s isolation of an academic housewife had felt less dangerous than reading "The Myth of Vaginal Orgasm" or "Woman-identified Woman" in a world where I was in constant debate and discussion with women over every aspect of our lives that we could as yet name. De Beauvoir had placed "The Lesbian" on the margins, and there was little in her book to suggest the power of woman bonding. But the passion of debating ideas with women was an erotic passion for me, and the risking of self with women that was necessary in order to win some truth out of the lies of the past was also erotic. The suppressed lesbian I had been carrying in me since adolescence began to stretch her limbs, and her first full-fledged act was to fall in love with a Jewish woman.

Some time during the early months of that relationship, I dreamed that I was arguing feminist politics with my lover. *Of course,* I said to her in this dream, *if you're going to bring up the Holocaust against me, there's nothing I can do.* If, as I believe, I was both myself and her in this dream, it spoke of the split in my consciousness. I had been, more or less, a Jewish heterosexual woman. But what did it mean to be a Jewish lesbian? What did it mean to feel myself, as I did, both anti-Semite and Jew? And, as a feminist, how was I charting for myself the oppressions within oppression?

The earliest feminist papers on Jewish identity that I read were critiques of the patriarchal and misogynist elements in Judaism, or of the caricaturing of Jewish women in literature by Jewish men. I remember hearing Judith Plaskow give a paper called "Can a Woman Be a Jew?" (Her conclusion was "Yes, but . . .") I was soon after in correspondence with a former student who had emigrated to Israel, was a passionate feminist, and wrote to me at length of the legal and social constraints on women there, the stirrings of contemporary Israeli feminism, and the contradictions she felt in her daily life. With the new politics, activism, literature of a tumultuous feminist movement around me, a movement which claimed universality though it had not yet acknowledged its own racial, class, and ethnic perspectives or its fears of the differences among women, I pushed aside for one last time thinking further about myself as a Jewish woman. I saw Judaism simply as another strand of patriarchy. If asked to choose, I might have said (as my father had said in other language): *I am a woman, not a Jew.* (But, I always added mentally, if Jews had to wear yellow stars again, I, too, would wear one—as if I would have the choice to wear it or not.)

Sometimes I feel I have seen too long from too many disconnected angles: white, Jewish, anti-Semite, racist, anti-racist, once-married, lesbian, middle-class, feminist, exmatriate southerner, *split at the root*—that I will never bring them whole. I would have liked, in this essay, to bring together the meanings of anti-Semitism and racism as I have experienced them and as I believe they intersect in the world beyond my life. But I'm not able to do this yet. I feel the tension as I think, make notes: *If you really look at the one reality, the other will waver and disperse.* Trying in one week to read Angela Davis and Lucy Davidowicz;[4] trying to hold throughout to a feminist, a lesbian, perspective—what does this mean? Nothing has trained me for this. And sometimes I feel inadequate to make any statement as a Jew; I feel the history of denial within me like an injury, a scar. For assimilation has affected *my* perceptions; those early lapses in meaning, those blanks, are with me still. My ignorance can be dangerous to me and to others.

Yet we can't wait for the undamaged to make our connections for us; we can't wait to speak until we are perfectly clear and righteous. There is no purity and, in our lifetimes, no end to this process.

This essay, then, has no conclusions: it is another beginning for me. Not just a way of saying, in 1982 Right Wing America, *I, too, will wear the yellow star.* It's a moving into accountability, enlarging the range of accountability. I know that in the rest of my life, the next half century or so, every aspect of my identity will have to be engaged. The middle-class white girl taught to trade obedience for privilege. The Jewish lesbian raised to be a heterosexual gentile. The woman who first heard oppression named and analyzed in the Black Civil Rights struggle. The woman with three sons, the feminist who hates male violence. The woman limping with a cane, the woman who has stopped bleeding are also accountable. The poet who knows that beautiful language can lie, that the oppressor's language sometimes sounds beautiful. The woman trying, as part of her resistance, to clean up her act.

1982

---

[4] Angela Y. Davis, *Women, Race and Class* (New York: Random House, 1981); Lucy S. Davidowicz, *The War against the Jews 1933–1945* (1975; New York: Bantam, 1979).

Writing from the Darkness

I remember childhood as time in anguish, as a dark time—not darkness in any sense that is stark, bleak, or empty but as a rich space of knowledge, struggle, and awakening. We seemed bound to the earth then, as though like other living things our roots were so deep in the soil of our surroundings there was no way to trace beginnings. We lived in the county, in a space between city and country, a barely occupied space. Houses stood at a distance from one another, few of them beautiful; always a sense of isolation and unbearable loneliness hovered about them. We lived on hilly land, trees and wild honeysuckle hiding the flat spaces where gardens grew. I do not remember darkness there. It was the blackness enveloping earth and sky out in the country at Daddy Jerry's and Mama Willie's house that gave feeling and meaning to darkness. There it seemed textured, as though it were velvet cloth folded in many layers. That darkness had to be confronted as we made our way before bedtime to the outhouse. "No light necessary," Granddaddy would say. "There is light in darkness, you just have to find it." That was early childhood. From then on I was terribly lost in an inner darkness as deep and thick as the blackness of those nights. I could not find my way or see the light there.

I was a child and his words had given me confidence. I believed with him that there was light in darkness waiting to be found. Later unable to find my way, I began to feel uncertain, displaced, estranged even. This was the condition of my spirit when I decided to be a writer, to seek for that light in words. No one understood. Coming from country black folks, seemingly always old, folks with the spirit of the backwoods, odd habits and odd ways, I had no way to share this longing—this ache to write words. In our world there was an intense passionate place for telling stories. It was really some big-time thing to be able to tell a good story, to, as Cousin Bo would say, "call out the hell in words." Writing had no such place. Writing the old people could not do even if they had been lucky enough to learn how. Folks wrote only when they had to; it was an awesome task, a burden. Making lists or writing letters could anguish the spirit. And who would anguish the spirit unnecessarily?

Searching for a space where writing could be understood, I asked for a diary. I remember early on getting the imitation-leather red or green books at holiday times, with "Diary" written on them in bright gold letters, and of course there were those ever-so-tiny gold keys, two of them. Keys which were inevitably lost. Whole diaries gone because I refused to pry them open, not wanting what was private to be accessible. Confessional writing in diaries was acceptable in our family because it was writing that was never meant to be read by anyone. Keeping a daily diary did not mean that I was seriously called to write, that I would ever write for a reading public. This was "safe" writing. It would (or so my parents thought) naturally be forsaken as one grew into womanhood. I shared with them this assumption. Such writing was seen as a necessary stage but only that. It was for me the space for critical reflection, where I struggled to understand myself and the world around me, that crazy world of family and community, that painful world. I could say there what was hurting me, how I felt about things, what I hoped for. I could be angry there with no threat of punishment. I could "talk back." Nothing had to be concealed. I could hold onto myself there.

However much the realm of diary-keeping has been a female experience that has often kept us closeted writers, away from the act of writing as authorship, it has most assuredly been a writing act that intimately connects the art of expressing one's feeling on the written page with the construction of self and identity, with the effort to be fully self-actualized. This precious powerful sense of writing as a healing place where our souls can speak and unfold has been crucial to woman's development of a counterhegemonic experience of creativity within patriarchal culture. Significantly, diary writing has not been traditionally seen by literary scholars as subversive autobiography, as a form of authorship that challenges conventional notions about the primacy of confessional writing as mere documentation (for women most often a record of our sorrows). Yet in the many cases where such writing has enhanced our struggle to be self-defining it emerges as a narrative of resistance, as writing which enables us to experience both self-discovery and self-recovery.

Faced with the radical possibility of self-transformation that confessional writing can evoke, many females cease to write. Certainly, when I was younger I did not respond to the realization that diary writing was a place where I could critically confront the "self" with affirmation. At times diary writing was threatening. For me the confessions written there were testimony, documenting realities I was not always able to face. My response to this sense of threat was to destroy the diaries. That destruction was linked to my fear that growing up was not supposed to be hard and difficult, a time of anguish and torment. Somehow the diaries were another excusing voice declaring that I was not "normal." I destroyed that writing and I wanted to destroy that tormented and struggling self. I did not understand, then, the critical difference between confession as an act of displacement and confession as the beginning stage in a process of self-transformation. Before this understanding, the diary as mirror was a place where that part of myself I could not accept or love could be named, touched, and then destroyed. Such writing was release. It took the terror and pain away—that was all. It was not then a place of reconciliation and reclamation.

None of the many diaries I wrote growing up exist today. They were all destroyed. Years ago when I began a therapeutic process of retrospective self-examination, I really missed this writing and mourned the loss. Since I use journals now as a way to engage in critical self-reflection, confrontation, and challenge, I know that I would be able to know myself differently were I able to read back, to remember with that writing. Those years of sustained diary writing were crucial to my later development as a writer, for it was this realm of confessional writing that enabled me to find a voice. Still there was a frightening tension between the discovery of that voice and the assumption that, though expressed, it would then need to be concealed, contained, hidden, and ultimately destroyed. While I had been given permission to keep diaries, it was writing that my family began to see as dangerous when I began to express ideas considered strange and alien. Diaries provided a space for me to develop an autonomous voice and that meant such writing, once sanctioned, became suspect. It was impressed upon my consciousness that having a voice was dangerous. This was reinforced when my sisters would find and read my diaries, then deliver them to our mother as evidence that I was truly a mad person, an alien, a stranger in their household.

This tension between writing as an expression of my longing to emerge as autonomous creative thinker and the fear that such expression and any other manifestation of independence would mean madness, an end to life, created barriers between me and those written words. I was afraid of their power and yet I needed them. Writing was the only space where I could express myself freely. It was crucial to my fragile sense of well-being. I was often the family scapegoat—persecuted, ridiculed, I was often punished. It was as though I lived in a constant state of siege, subject to unprovoked and unexpected terrorist attacks. I lived in dread. Nothing I did was ever right. That constant experience of estrangement was deeply saddening. I was brokenhearted. Writing was the healing place where I could collect the bits and pieces, where I could put them together again. It was the sanctuary, the safe place. Yet I could not make that writing part of an overall process of self-recovery. I was able to use it constructively only as an outlet for suppressed feeling. Knowledge that the writing could have enabled transformation was blocked by feelings of shame. I was ashamed that I needed this sanctuary in words. Confronting parts of my self there was humiliating. To me that confession was a process of unmasking, stripping the soul. It made me naked and vulnerable. Even though the experience was cleansing and redemptive, it was a process I could not fully affirm or celebrate. Feelings of shame compelled me to destroy what I had written. Diary writing, as a record of confession, brought me face to face with the shadow-self, the one we spend lifetimes avoiding. I was ashamed that this "me" existed. I read my words. They were mirrors. I looked at the self represented there. Destroying the diaries, I destroyed that shadow. There was no trace of her, nothing that could bear witness. I could not embrace that inner darkness, find the light in it. I could not hold that being or love her.

Undoubtedly this process of destroying the diaries, and the self represented there, kept me from attempting suicide. There were times when I felt that death was the only way I could escape that inner darkness. I remember even now how much I longed to be rid of the wounded me, that secret shadow-self. In Lyn Cowan's Jungian discussion of masochism she describes that moment when we learn to "embrace the shadow" as a necessary stage in the psychic journey leading to recovery and the restoration of well-being. She comments: "Jung said the shadow connects an individual to the collective unconscious, and beyond that to animal life at its most primitive level. The shadow is the tunnel, channel, or connector through which one reaches the deepest, most elemental layers of psyche." Confronting that shadow-self can both humiliate and humble. Humiliation in the face of aspects of the self we think are unsound, inappropriate, ugly, or downright nasty, blocks one's ability to see the possibility for transformation that such a facing of one's reality promises.

That sense of profound shame evoked whenever I looked at the shadow-self portrayed in the writing was a barrier. It kept me stuck in the woundedness. Even though acknowledging that self in writing was a necessary anchor enabling me to keep a hold on life, it was not enough. That shame had to be let go before I could fully emerge as a writer because it was there whenever I tried to create, whether the work was confessional or not. When I left home to attend college I carried with me the longing to write. I knew then that I would need to work through these feelings of shame. One of the early journal entries from that time reads:

> Writing, and the hope of writing pulls me back from the edges of despair. I believe insanity and despair are at times one and the same. And I hear the voices of my past telling me that I will go crazy, that I will end up in a mental institution—alone. I remember my oldest sister laughing, telling me that no one would visit me there, that "girl, you ought to stop." Stop thinking. Stop dreaming. Stop trying to experience and understand life. Stop living in the world of the mind. That day I had sat a hot iron on my arm. I was ironing our father's pajamas. They were collectively mocking me. I asked them to leave me alone. I pleaded with them, "Why can't I just be left alone to be me?" I did not want to be molded. I was something. And when the hot iron came down on my arm I did not feel it. I was momentarily carried away, pleading with them. I stood there in the hallway ironing and even when the stinging pain was there I continued to iron. I stood there struggling to hide the pain and sorrow, not wanting to cry, not wanting

them to know how much it hurt. I was trying to be brave. I know now that an anguished heart is never a brave heart. It's like some wounded body part that keeps bleeding, that can't stop itself. Writing eases the anguish. It is my connection. Through it and with it I transcend despair.

Writing, whether confessional prose or poetry, was irrevocably linked in my mind with the effort to maintain well-being. I began writing poetry about the same time that I began keeping diaries. Poetry writing was radically different. Unlike confessional prose, one could use language in writing poetry to mask feelings, to hide the experiential reality leading one to create. Poems on the subject of death and dying did not necessarily make explicit to the reader that I was at times struggling with the issue of whether to stay alive. Poetry writing as creative process was intimately linked with the experience of transcendence. Unlike the diary writing, which became a space where I confronted pain, poetry was the way to move beyond it. I never destroyed poems because I felt there was nothing revealed there about the "me of me."

Then and now I remain a great admirer of Emily Dickinson, often marveling that she as living presence seemed always absent from her poems. To me they do not stand as a record of her experience but more as expressions of what I believe she felt was a fitting and worthy subject for poetry. Her poems are masks, together creating a collective drama where the self remains in the shadows, dark and undiscovered. It is difficult to look behind the poems, to see, to enter those shadows. Poetry writing may have been just that for Dickinson, the making of an enclosure—the poem as wall, a screen shielding her from the shadow-self. Perhaps there was for her no safe place, nowhere that the unnamed could be voiced, remembered, held. Even if it is there in the poems, we as readers cannot necessarily know or find it. What is clear is that writing was for Dickinson a way to keep a hold on life.

Writing that keeps us away from death, from despair, does not necessarily help us to be well. Anne Sexton could confess, "I am trying a flat mask to hold my sanity up . . . my life is falling through a sieve" and then "the thing that seems to be saving me is the poetry." I remember her, Sylvia Plath, and not so well-known black women poets Georgia Douglass Johnson and Clarissa Scott Delany, because they all struggled with dangerous melancholy and killing despair. We know that poetry does not save us, that writing does not always keep us away from death, that the sorrow of wounds that have never healed, excruciating self-doubt, or overwhelming melancholy often crushes the spirit, making it impossible to stay alive. Julia Kristeva speaks about woman's struggle to find and sustain creative voice in the chapter "I Who Want Not To Be," which is part of the introduction to *About Chinese Women*. There she addresses the tension between our longing to "speak as women," to have being that is strong enough to bear the identity *writer*, and the coercive imposition of a feminine identity within patriarchy which opposes such being. Within patriarchy woman has no legitimate voice. Her voice is constructed in either complicity or resistance. If the choice is not radical then we speak only what the patriarchal culture would have us say. If we do not speak as liberators we collapse under the weight of this effort to speak within patriarchal confines or lose ourselves without dying. Kristeva recalls the Russian poet Maria Tsvetaieva, who hanged herself, writing: "I don't want to die. I want not to be." Her words echo my longing to be rid of the shadow-self, the "me of me."

Writing enables us to be more fully alive only if it is not a terrain wherein we leave the self—the shadows behind, escaping. Anne Sexton reiterated again and again in her letters that it was crucial that the writer keep a hold on life by learning to face reality: "I think that writers must try not to avoid knowing what is happening. Everyone has somewhere the ability to mask the events of pain and sorrow. . . . But the creative person must not use this mechanism anymore than they have to in order to keep breathing." A distinction must be made between that writing which enables us to hold onto life even as we are clinging to old hurts and wounds and that writing which offers to us a space where we are able to confront reality in such a way that we live more fully. Such writing is not an anchor that we mistakenly cling to so as not to drown. It is writing that truly rescues, that enables us to reach the shore, to recover.

To become a writer I needed to confront that shadow-self, to learn ways to accept and care for that aspect of me as part of a process of healing and recovery. I longed to create a groundwork of being that could affirm my struggle to be a whole self and my effort to write. To fulfill this longing I had to search for that shadow-self and reclaim it. That search was part of a process of long inward journeying. Much of it took place in writing. I spent more than ten years writing journals, unearthing and restoring memories of that shadow-self, connecting the past with present being. This writing enabled me to look myself over in a new way, without the shame I had experienced earlier. It was no longer an act of displacement. I was not trying to be rid of the shadows, I wanted instead to enter them. That encounter enabled me to learn the self anew in ways that allowed transformation in consciousness and being. Resurrecting the shadow-self, I could finally embrace it, and by so doing come back to myself.

That woundedness which I was once so ashamed to recognize became for me a place of recovery, the dark deeps into which I could enter to find both the source of that pain and the means to heal. Only in fully knowing the wound could I discover ways to attend to it. Writing was a way of knowing. After what seemed like endless years of journal writing about the past, I wrote a memoir of my girlhood. It was indeed the culmination of this effort to accept the past and yet surrender its hold on me. This writing was redemptive. I no longer need to make this journey again and again.

1989

Monday, May 3rd, 1982

Such a peaceful, windless morning here for my seventieth birthday—the sea is pale blue, and although the field is still brown, it is dotted with daffodils at last. It has seemed an endless winter. But now at night the peepers are in full fettle, peeping away. And I was awakened by the cardinal, who is back again with his two wives, and the raucous cries of the male pheasant. I lay there, breathing in spring, listening to the faint susurration of the waves and awfully glad to be alive.

The table is set downstairs, all blue and white, with a tiny bunch of miniature daffodils, blue starflowers, and, glory be, two fritillaries. They always seem unreal with their purple-and-white-checkered bells, and I have never succeeded with a real show of them.

Then at each corner of the square table I have put a miniature rose, two white and two pale yellow, part of a bounty of miniature roses that have come for my birthday and will go along the terrace wall when the nights are not quite so cold. They are from Edythe Haddaway, one of the blessings of the last five years, for she comes when I am away to take care of Tamas and Bramble, feels at peace in this house, she tells me, and makes it peaceful for me to know that she is in residence and all is well at home when I am off on poetry-reading trips.

What is it like to be seventy? If someone else had lived so long and could remember things sixty years ago with great clarity, she would seem very old to me. But I do not feel old at all, not as much a survivor as a person still on her way. I suppose real old age begins when one looks backward rather than forward, but I look forward with joy to the years ahead and especially to the surprises that any day may bring.

In the middle of the night things well up from the past that are not always cause for rejoicing—the unsolved, the painful encounters, the mistakes, the reasons for shame or woe. But all, good or bad, painful or delightful, weave themselves into a rich tapestry, and all give me food for thought, food to grow on.

I am just back from a month of poetry readings, in and out through all of April. At Hartford College in Connecticut I had been asked to talk about old age—"The View From Here," I called the reading—in a series on "The Seasons of Womanhood." In the course of it I said, "This is the best time of my life. I love being old." At that point a voice from the audience asked loudly, "Why is it good to be old?" I answered spontaneously and a little on the defensive, for I sensed incredulity in the questioner, "Because I am more myself than I have ever been. There is less conflict. I am happier, more balanced, and" (I heard myself say rather aggressively) "more powerful." I felt it was rather an odd word, "powerful," but I think it is true. It might have been more accurate to say "I am better able to use my powers." I am surer of what my life is all about, have less self-doubt to conquer, although it has to be admitted that I wrote my new novel *Anger* in an agony of self-doubt most of the year, the hardest subject I have attempted to deal with in a novel since *Mrs. Stevens Hears the Mermaids Singing*. There I was breaking new ground, giving myself away. I was fifty-three and I deliberately made Mrs. Stevens seventy, and now here I am at what then seemed eons away, safely "old."

I have always longed to be old, and that is because all my life I have had such great exemplars of old age, such marvelous models to contemplate. First of all, of course, was Marie Closset (her pen name, Jean Dominique), whom I celebrated in my first novel and with whom I exchanged lives through letters and meetings from my twenty-fifth year until her death. I turn to her bound volumes of poetry this minute and open to the line "Au silence léger des nuits près de la mer," but I am bound to look for and find the long lyric addressed to Poetry, and as I write it here, I hear very clearly her light, grave voice, and we are sitting in her study, side by side:

Poésie! Je t'ai portée à mes lèvres
Comme un caillou frais pour ma soif,
Je t'ai gardée dans ma bouche obscure et sèche
Comme une petite pierre qu'on remasse
Et que l'on mâche avec du sang sur les lèvres!

Poésie, ah! je t'ai donné l'Amour,
L'Amour avec sa face comme une aube d'argent
Sur la mer,—et mon âme, avec la mer dedans,
Et la tempête avec le ciel du petit jour
Livide et frais comme un coquillage luisant.

How happy Jean-Do would be to know that at seventy I live by the sea, and all those images are newly minted for me today "like a cool pebble for my thirst," "and my soul with the sea in it, and the tempest at dawn, pale and fresh as a shining shell." (But where is the music in English?)

Then Lugné-Poë, my father in the theater, was a constant challenger and giver of courage during the theater years. I see his immense devouring smile and remember my pet name for him, "mon éléphant." So he always signed his letters with an elephant head and a long trunk waving triumphantly at the end of a page.

Basil de Selincourt, my father in poetry, fierce as a hawk (and he looked rather like a hawk), wrote the first really good review I ever had (in the London *Observer* on *Encounter in April*, my first book of poems) and that was before we became friends. He taught me many things, not least how to garden into very old age by working at an extremely slow tempo—but I never did really learn it. That is still to come when, like Basil, I hope to put in a vegetable garden in my late eighties.

Then there is Eva Le Gallienne, who was only thirty when I first knew her as the star and creator of the Civic Repertory Theatre, and who has again triumphed in her eighties and shown a whole new generation what great acting is. She is proof that one can be eighty-three and still young. She too is a great gardener, so perhaps a good old age has to do with being still a friend of the earth.

I think also of Camille Mayran, who has written a magnificent book in her nineties, *Portrait de Ma Mère en Son Grand Âge.* She tells me that now, well over ninety, she sees no change in herself except for a "slight slowing down." She is all soul and mind, not a gardener at all! So one cannot generalize. But Eleanor Blair has just telephoned to wish me a happy birthday, as I write, and she says her garden is flourishing. Her voice sounded so young on the phone!

Perhaps the answer is not detachment as I used to believe but rather to be deeply involved in something, is to be attached. I am attached in a thousand ways—and one of them compels me now to leave this airy room high up in the house to go down and get ready for my guests.

1984

PART THREE

Breaking the Silence

Women Confront Oppression and Violence

One day I'll huff and puff and blow the lid off

this can of spinach. Choice will leap

off the shelf and sink into my arms.

SHANA PENN

SUSAN FALUDI

Speak for Yourself

I am at the boiling point! If I do not find some day the use of

my tongue . . . I shall die of an intellectual repression,

a woman's rights convulsion.

ELIZABETH CADY STANTON,

IN A LETTER TO SUSAN B. ANTHONY

"Oh, and then you'll be giving that speech at the Smithsonian Tuesday on the status of American women," my publisher's publicist reminded me as she rattled off the list of "appearances" for the week. "What?" I choked out. "I thought that was *at least* another month away." But the speech was distant only in my wishful consciousness, which pushed all such events into a mythical future when I would no longer lunge for smelling salts at the mention of public speaking.

For the author of what was widely termed an "angry" and "forceful" book, I exhibit a timorous verbal demeanor that belies my barracuda blurbs. My fingers may belt out my views when I'm stationed before the computer, but stick a microphone in front of me and I'm a Victorian lady with the vapors. Like many female writers with strong convictions but weak stomachs for direct confrontation, I write so forcefully precisely because I speak so tentatively. One form of self-expression has overcompensated for the weakness of the other, like a blind person who develops a hypersensitive ear.

"Isn't it wonderful that so many people want to hear what you have to say about women's rights?" the publicist prodded. I grimaced. "About as wonderful as walking down the street with no clothes on." Yes, I wanted people to hear what I had to say. Yes, I wanted to warn women of the backlash to our modest gains. But couldn't they just read what I wrote? Couldn't I just speak softly and carry a big book?

It has taken me a while to realize that my publicist is right. It's *not* the same—for my audience or for me. Public speech can be a horror for the shy person, but it can also be the ultimate act of liberation. For me, it became the moment where the public and the personal truly met.

For many years, I believed the imbalance between my incensed writing and my atrophied vocal cords suited me just fine. After a few abysmal auditions for school plays—my one role was Nana the dog in "Peter Pan," not, needless to say, a speaking role—I retired my acting aspirations and retreated to the school newspaper, a forum where I could bluster at injustices large and small without public embarrassment. My friend Barbara and I co-edited the high school paper (titled, interestingly, The Voice), fearlessly castigating all scoundrels from our closet-size office. But we kept our eyes glued to the floor during class discussion. Partly this was shyness, a genderless condition. But it was a condition reinforced by daily gendered reminders—we saw what happened to the girls who argued in class. The boys called them "bitches," and they sat home Saturday nights. Popular girls raised their voices only at pep squad.

While both sexes fear public speaking (pollsters tell us it's the public's greatest fear, rivaling even death), women—particularly women challenging the status quo—seem to be more afraid, and with good reason. We *do* have more at stake. Men risk a loss of face; women a loss of femininity. Men are chagrined if they blunder at the podium; women face humiliation either way. If we come across as commanding, our womanhood is called into question. If we reveal emotion, we are too hormonally driven to be taken seriously.

I had my own taste of this double standard while making the rounds of radio and television talk shows for a book tour. When I disputed a point with a man, male listeners would often phone in to say they found my behavior "offensive," or even "unattractive." And then there were my own internalized "feminine" voices: Don't interrupt, be agreeable, keep the volume down. "We're going to have to record that again," a weary radio producer said, rewinding the tape for the fifth time. "Your words are angry, but it's not coming through in your voice."

In replacing lacerating speech with a literary scalpel, I had adopted a well-worn female strategy, used most famously by Victorian female reformers protesting slavery and women's lowly status. "I want to be doing something with the pen, since no other means of action in politics are in a woman's power," Harriet Martineau, the British journalist, wrote in 1832. But while their literature makes compelling reading, the suffrage movement didn't get under way until women took a public stand from the platform of the Seneca Falls Women's Rights Convention. And while Betty Friedan's 1963 *The Feminine Mystique* raised the consciousness of millions of women, the contemporary women's movement only began to affect social policy when Friedan and other feminists started addressing the public.

Public speech is a more powerful stimulus because it is more dangerous for the speaker. An almost physical act, it demands projecting one's voice, hurling it against the public ear. Writing, on the other hand, occurs at one remove. The writer asserts herself from behind the veil of the printed page.

The dreaded evening of the Smithsonian speech finally arrived. I stood knock-kneed and green-gilled before three hundred people. Was it too late to plead a severe case of laryngitis? I am Woman, Hear Me Whisper.

I cleared my throat and, to my shock, a hush fell over the room. People were listening—with an intensity that strangely emboldened me. It was as if their attentive silence allowed me to make contact with my own muffled self. I began to speak. A stinging point induced a ripple of agreement. I told a joke and they laughed. My voice got surer, my delivery rising. A charge passed between me and the audience, uniting and igniting us both. That internal "boiling point" that Elizabeth Cady Stanton described was no longer under "intellectual repression." And its heat, I discovered, could set many kettles to whistling.

Afterward, it struck me that in some essential way I hadn't really proved myself a feminist until now. Until you translate personal words on a page into public connections with other people, you aren't really part of a political movement. I hadn't declared my independence until I was willing to declare it out loud. I knew public speaking was important to reform public life—but I hadn't realized the transformative effect it could have on the speaker herself. Women need to be heard not just to change the world, but to change themselves.

I can't say that this epiphany has made me any less anxious when approaching the lectern. But it has made me more determined to speak in spite of the jitters—and more hopeful that other women will do the same. Toward that end, I'd like to make a modest proposal for the next stage of the women's movement. A new method of consciousness-raising: Feminist Toastmasters.

1992

PATRICIA J. WILLIAMS

On Being
the Object of Property

ON BEING INVISIBLE
Reflections

For some time I have been writing about my
great-great-grandmother. I have considered the significance of her history
and that of slavery from a variety of viewpoints on a variety of occasions: in
every speech, in every conversation, even in my commercial transactions
class. I have talked so much about her that I finally had to ask myself what
it was I was looking for in this dogged pursuit of family history. Was I being
merely indulgent, looking for roots in the pursuit of some genetic heraldry,
seeking the inheritance of being special, different, unique in all that pri-
mogeniture hath wrought?

I decided that my search was based in the utility of such a quest, not
mere indulgence, but a recapturing of that which had escaped historical
scrutiny, which had been overlooked and underseen. I, like so many
blacks, have been trying to pin myself down in history, place myself in the
stream of time as significant, evolved, present in the past, continuing into
the future. To be without documentation is too unsustaining, too spontaneously ahistorical, too dangerously malleable in the hands of those who
would rewrite not merely the past but my future as well. So I have been
picking through the ruins for my roots.

What I know of my mother's side of the family begins with my great-great-grandmother. Her name was Sophie and she lived in Tennessee. In 1850, she was about twelve years old. I know that she was purchased when she was eleven by a white lawyer named Austin Miller and was immediately impregnated by him. She gave birth to my great-grandmother Mary, who was taken away from her to be raised as a house servant.[1] I know nothing more of Sophie (she was, after all, a black single mother—in today's terms—suffering the anonymity of yet another statistical teenage pregnancy). While I don't remember what I was told about Austin Miller before I decided to go to law school, I do remember that just before my first day of class, my mother said, in a voice full of secretive reassurance, "The Millers were lawyers, so you have it in your blood."[2]

When my mother told me that I had nothing to fear in law school, that law was "in my blood," she meant it in a very complex sense. First and foremost, she meant it defiantly; she meant that no one should make me feel inferior because someone else's father was a judge. She wanted me to reclaim that part of my heritage from which I had been disinherited, and she wanted me to use it as a source of strength and self-confidence. At the same time, she was asking me to claim a part of myself that was the dispossessor of another part of myself; she was asking me to deny that disenfranchised little black girl of myself that felt powerless, vulnerable and, moreover, rightly felt so.

In somewhat the same vein, Mother was asking me not to look to her as a role model. She was devaluing that part of herself that was not Harvard and refocusing my vision to that part of herself that was hard-edged, proficient, and Western. She hid the lonely, black, defiled-female part of herself and pushed me forward as the projection of a competent self, a cool rather than despairing self, a masculine rather than a feminine self.

I took this secret of my blood into the Harvard milieu with both the pride and the shame with which my mother had passed it along to me. I found myself in the situation described by Marguerite Duras, in her novel *The Lover*: "We're united in a fundamental shame at having to live. It's here

[1] For a more detailed account of the family history to this point, see Patricia Williams, "Grandmother Sophie," *Harvard Blackletter* 3 (1986): 79.
[2] Patricia Williams, "Alchemical Notes: Reconstructing Ideals from Deconstructed Rights," *Harvard Civil Rights–Civil Liberties Law Review* 22 (1987): 418.

we are at the heart of our common fate, the fact that [we] are our mother's children, the children of a candid creature murdered by society. We're on the side of society which has reduced her to despair. Because of what's been done to our mother, so amiable, so trusting, we hate life, we hate ourselves."[3]

Reclaiming that from which one has been disinherited is a good thing. Self-possession in the full sense of that expression is the companion to self-knowledge. Yet claiming for myself a heritage the weft of whose genesis is my own disinheritance is a profoundly troubling paradox.

Images

A friend of mine practices law in rural Florida. His office is in Belle Glade, an extremely depressed area where the sugar industry reigns supreme, where blacks live pretty much as they did in slavery times, in dormitories called slave ships. They are penniless and illiterate and have both a high birth rate and a high death rate.

My friend told me about a client of his, a fifteen-year-old young woman pregnant with her third child, who came seeking advice because her mother had advised a hysterectomy—not even a tubal ligation—as a means of birth control. The young woman's mother, in turn, had been advised of the propriety of such a course in her own case by a white doctor some years before. Listening to this, I was reminded of a case I worked on when I was working for the Western Center on Law and Poverty about eight years ago. Ten black Hispanic women had been sterilized by the University of Southern California–Los Angeles County General Medical Center, allegedly without proper consent, and in most instances without even their knowledge.[4] Most of them found out what had been done to them upon inquiry, after a much-publicized news story in which an intern charged that the chief of obstetrics at the hospital pursued a policy of recommending Caesarian delivery and simultaneous sterilization for any pregnant woman with three or more children and who was on welfare. In the course of researching the appeal in that case, I remember learning that one-

[3] Marguerite Duras, *The Lover* (New York: Harper and Row, 1985), p. 55.
[4] *Madrigal v. Quilligan*, U.S. Court of Appeals, 9th Circuit, Docket no. 78-3187, October 1979.

quarter of all Navajo women of childbearing age—literally all those of childbearing age ever admitted to a hospital—have been sterilized.[5]

Vision

Reflecting on my roots makes me think again and again of the young woman in Belle Glade, Florida. She told the story of her impending sterilization, according to my friend, while keeping her eyes on the ground at all times. My friend, who is white, asked why she wouldn't look up, speak with him eye to eye. The young woman answered that she didn't like white people seeing inside her.

My friend's story made me think of my own childhood and adolescence: my parents were always telling me to look up at the world; to look straight at people, particularly white people; not to let them stare me down; to hold my ground; to insist on the right to my presence no matter what. They told me that in this culture you have to look people in the eye because that's how you tell them you're their equal. My friend's story also reminded me how very difficult I had found that looking-back to be. What was hardest was not just that white people saw me, as my friend's client put it, but that they looked through me, that they treated me as though I were transparent.

By itself, seeing into me would be to see my substance, my anger, my vulnerability, and my wild raging despair—and that alone is hard enough to show, to share. But to uncover it and to have it devalued by ignore-ance,

---

[5]This was the testimony of one of the witnesses. It is hard to find official confirmation for this or any other sterilization statistic involving Native American women. Official statistics kept by the U.S. Public Health Service, through the Centers for Disease Control in Atlanta, come from data gathered by the National Hospital Discharge Survey, which covers neither federal hospitals nor penitentiaries. Services to Native American women living on reservations are provided almost exclusively by federal hospitals. In addition, the U.S. Public Health Service breaks down its information into only three categories: "White," "Black," and "Other." Nevertheless, in 1988, the Women of All Red Nations Collective of Minneapolis, Minnesota, distributed a fact sheet entitled "Sterilization Studies of Native American Women," which claimed that as many as 50 percent of all Native American women of childbearing age have been sterilized. According to "Surgical Sterilization Surveillance: Tubal Sterilization and Hysterectomy in Women Aged 15–44, 1979–1980," issued by the Centers for Disease Control in 1983, "In 1980, the tubal sterilization rate for black women . . . was 45 percent greater than that for white women" (7). Furthermore, a study released in 1984 by the Division of Reproductive Health of the Center for Health Promotion and Education (one of the Centers for Disease Control) found that, as of 1982, 48.8 percent of Puerto Rican women between the ages of 15 and 44 had been sterilized.

to hold it up bravely in the organ of my eyes and to have it greeted by an impassive stare that passes right through all that which is me, an impassive stare that moves on and attaches itself to my left earlobe or to the dust caught in the rusty vertical geysers of my wiry hair or to the breadth of my freckled brown nose—this is deeply humiliating. It re-wounds, relives the early childhood anguish of uncensored seeing, the fullness of vision that is the permanent turning-away point for most blacks.

The cold game of equality-staring makes me feel like a thin sheet of glass: white people see all the worlds beyond me but not me. They come trotting at me with force and speed; they do not see me. I could force my presence, the real me contained in those eyes, upon them, but I would be smashed in the process. If I deflect, if I move out of the way, they will never know I existed.

Marguerite Duras, again in *The Lover*, places the heroine in relation to her family. "Every day we try to kill one another, to kill. Not only do we not talk to one another, we don't even look at one another. When you're being looked at you can't look. To look is to feel curious, to be interested, to lower yourself."[6]

To look is also to make myself vulnerable; yet not to look is to neutralize the part of myself which is vulnerable. I look in order to see, and so I must look. Without that directness of vision, I am afraid I will will my own blindness, disinherit my own creativity, and sterilize my own perspective of its embattled, passionate insight.

ON LIFE AND DEATH
Sighing into space

There are moments in my life when I feel as though a part of me is missing. There are days when I feel so invisible that I can't remember what day of the week it is, when I feel so manipulated that I can't remember my own name, when I feel so lost and angry that I can't speak a civil word to the people who love me best. Those are the times when I catch sight of my reflection in store windows and am surprised to see a whole person looking back. Those are the times when my skin be-

---

[6] Duras, p. 54.

comes gummy as clay and my nose slides around on my face and my eyes drip down to my chin. I have to close my eyes at such times and remember myself, draw an internal picture that is smooth and whole; when all else fails, I reach for a mirror and stare myself down until the features reassemble themselves like lost sheep.

Two years ago, my godmother Marjorie suffered a massive stroke. As she lay dying, I would come to the hospital to give her meals. My feeding her who had so often fed me became a complex ritual of mirroring and self-assembly. The physical act of holding the spoon to her lips was not only a rite of nurture and of sacrifice, it was the return of a gift. It was a quiet bowing to the passage of time and the doubling back of all things. The quiet woman who listened to my woes about work and school required now that I bend my head down close to her and listen for mouthed word fragments, sentence crumbs. I bent down to give meaning to her silence, her wandering search for words.

She would eat what I brought to the hospital with relish; she would reject what I brought with a turn of her head. I brought fruit and yogurt, ice cream and vegetable juice. Slowly, over time, she stopped swallowing. The mashed potatoes would sit in her mouth like cotton, the pudding would slip to her chin in slow sad streams. When she lost not only her speech but the power to ingest, they put a tube into her nose and down to her stomach, and I lost even that medium by which to communicate. No longer was there the odd but reassuring communion over taste. No longer was there some echo of comfort in being able to nurture one who nurtured me.

This increment of decay was like a little newborn death. With the tube, she stared up at me with imploring eyes, and I tried to guess what it was that she would like. I read to her aimlessly and in desperation. We entertained each other with the strange embarrassed flickering of our eyes. I told her stories to fill the emptiness, the loneliness, of the white-walled hospital room.

I told her stories about who I had become, about how I had grown up to know all about exchange systems, and theories of contract, and monetary fictions. I spun tales about blue-sky laws and promissory estoppel, the wispy-feathered complexity of undue influence and dark-hearted theories of unconscionability. I told her about market norms and gift economy and the thin razor's edge of the bartering ethic. Once upon a time, I rambled, some neighbors of mine included me in their circle of barter. They were in the habit of exchanging eggs and driving lessons, hand-knit sweaters and computer programming, plumbing and calligraphy. I accepted the generosity of their inclusion with gratitude. At first, I felt that, as a lawyer, I was worthless, that I had no barterable skills and nothing to contribute. What I came to realize with time, however, was that my value to the group was not calculated by the physical items I brought to it. These people included me because they wanted me to be part of their circle, they valued my participation apart from the material things I could offer. So I gave of myself to them, and they gave me fruit cakes and dandelion wine and smoked salmon, and in their giving, their goods became provisions. Cradled in this community whose currency was a relational ethic, my stock in myself soared. My value depended on the glorious intangibility, the eloquent invisibility of my just being *part* of the collective; and in direct response I grew spacious and happy and gentle.

My gentle godmother. The fragility of life; the cold mortuary shelf.

ON CANDOR
Me

I have never been able to determine my horoscope with any degree of accuracy. Born at Boston's now-defunct Lying-In Hospital, I am a Virgo, despite a quite poetic soul. Knowledge of the *hour* of my birth, however, would determine not just my sun sign but my moons and all the more intimate specificities of my destiny. Once upon a time, I sent for my birth certificate, which was retrieved from the oblivion of Massachusetts microfiche. Said document revealed that an infant named Patricia Joyce, born of parents named Williams, was delivered into the world "colored." Since no one thought to put down the hour of my birth, I suppose that I will never know my true fate.

In the meantime, I read what text there is of me.

My name, Patricia, means patrician. Patricias are noble, lofty, elite, exclusively educated, and well mannered despite themselves. I was on the cusp of being Pamela, but my parents knew that such a me would require lawns, estates, and hunting dogs too.

I am also a Williams. Of William, whoever he was: an anonymous white man who owned my father's people and from whom some escaped. That rupture is marked by the dark-mooned mystery of utter silence.

Williams is the second most common surname in the United States; Patricia is *the* most common prename among women born in 1951, the year of my birth.

Them

In the law, rights are islands of empowerment. To be un-righted is to be disempowered, and the line between rights and no rights is most often the line between dominators and the oppressed. Rights contain images of power, and manipulating those images, either visually or linguistically, is central in the making and maintenance of rights. In principle, therefore, the more dizzyingly diverse the images that are propagated, the more empowered we will be as a society.

In reality, it was a lovely polar bear afternoon. The gentle force of the earth. A wide wilderness of islands. A conspiracy of polar bears lost in timeless forgetting. A gentleness of polar bears, a fruitfulness of polar bears, a silent black-eyed interest of polar bears, a bristled expectancy of polar bears. With the wisdom of innocence, a child threw stones at the polar bears. Hungry, they rose from their nests, inquisitive, dark-souled, patient with foreboding, fearful in tremendous awakening. The instinctual ferocity of the hunter reflected upon the hunted. Then, proud teeth and warrior claws took innocence for wilderness and raging insubstantiality for tender rabbit breath.

In the newspapers the next day, it was reported that two polar bears in the Brooklyn Zoo mauled to death an eleven-year-old boy who had entered their cage to swim in the moat. The police were called and the bears were killed.[7]

In the public debate that ensued, many levels of meaning emerged. The rhetoric firmly established that the bears were innocent, naturally territorial, unfairly imprisoned, and guilty. The dead child (born into the urban jungle of a black, welfare mother and a Hispanic alcoholic father who had died literally in the gutter only six weeks before) was held to a similarly

---

[7]J. Barron, "Polar Bears Kill a Child at Prospect Park Zoo," *New York Times* (May 20, 1987), sec. A.

stern standard. The police were captured, in a widely disseminated photograph,[8] shooting helplessly, desperately, into the cage, through three levels of bars, at a pieta of bears; since this image, conveying much pathos, came nevertheless not in time to save the child, it was generally felt that the bears had died in vain.[9]

In the egalitarianism of exile, pluralists rose up as of one body, with a call to buy more bears, control juvenile delinquency, eliminate all zoos, and confine future police.[10]

In the plenary session of the national meeting of the Law and Society Association, the keynote speaker unpacked the whole incident as a veritable laboratory of emergent rights discourse. Just seeing that these complex levels of meaning exist, she exulted, should advance rights discourse significantly.[11]

At the funeral of the child, the presiding priest pronounced the death of Juan Perez not in vain, since he was saved from growing into "a lifetime of crime." Juan's Hispanic-welfare-black-widow-of-an-alcoholic mother decided then and there to sue.

The universe between

How I ended up at Dartmouth College for the summer is too long a story to tell. Anyway, there I was, sharing the town of Hanover, New Hampshire, with about two hundred prepubescent males enrolled in Dartmouth's summer basketball camp, an all-white, very expensive, affirmative action program for the street-deprived.

One fragrant evening, I was walking down East Wheelock Street when I encountered about a hundred of these adolescents, fresh from the courts, wet, lanky, big-footed, with fuzzy yellow crew cuts, loping toward Thayer Hall and food. In platoons of twenty-five or so, they descended upon me, jostling me, smacking me, and pushing me from the sidewalk

---

[8] *New York Post* (May 22, 1987), p. 1.

[9] J. Barron, "Officials Weigh Tighter Security at Zoos in Parks," *New York Times* (May 22, 1987), sec. B.

[10] Ibid.

[11] Patricia Williams, "The Meaning of Rights" (address to the annual meeting of the Law and Society Association, Washington, D.C., June 6, 1987).

into the gutter. In a thoughtless instant, I snatched off my brown silk head-rag, my flag of African femininity and propriety, my sign of meek and sup-plicatory place and presentation. I released the armored rage of my short nappy hair (the scalp gleaming bare between the angry wire spikes) and hissed: "Don't I exist for you?! See Me! And deflect, godammit!" (The quaint professionalism of my formal English never allowed the rage in my head to rise so high as to overflow the edges of my text.)

They gave me wide berth. They clearly had no idea, however, that I was talking to them or about them. They skirted me sheepishly, suddenly polite, because they did know, when a crazed black person comes crashing into one's field of vision, that it is impolite to laugh. I stood tall and spoke loudly into their ranks: "I have my rights!" The Dartmouth Summer Bas-ketball Camp raised its collective eyebrows and exhaled, with a certain tested nobility of exhaustion and solidarity.

I pursued my way, manumitted back into silence. I put distance be-tween them and me, gave myself over to polar bear musings. I allowed my-self to be watched over by bear spirits. Clean white wind and strong bear smells. The shadowed amnesia; the absence of being; the presence of polar bears. White wilderness of icy meateaters heavy with remembrance; leaden with undoing; shaggy with the effort of hunting for silence; frozen in a web of intention and intuition. A lunacy of polar bears. A history of polar bears. A pride of polar bears. A consistency of polar bears. In those meandering pastel polar bear moments, I found cool fragments of white-fur invisibility. Solid, black-gummed, intent, observant. Hungry and pa-tient, impassive and exquisitely timed. The brilliant bursts of exclusive ter-ritoriality. A complexity of messages implied in our being.

1988

JANE SLAUGHTER

A Beaut of a Shiner

I have had a black eye for a week now; it's fading and I'm sorry to see it go. People are fascinated by shiners in a way other injuries can't match: Did you ever hear anyone call a broken arm or a bloody nose "a beaut"? Maybe it's got something to do with the pretty colors—mine started out with a pale green under the brow and dark purple for eyeliner and evolved into shades of lavender and magenta.

But that's not the main fascination. When a woman has a black eye, it is assumed that her husband or lover is responsible. I have two disinterested witnesses to the fact that I got mine by walking into a street sign at the corner of Michigan Avenue and Florida in southwest Detroit. So why are you all smirking and saying, "Oh, sure"? Okay, so my witnesses have left the country, and I neglected to get affidavits. I didn't know I was going to need them.

I'm reasonably confident that wife-beating is less common among the people I see regularly than it is in the general population. My friends of both sexes call themselves feminists; the women aren't financially dependent on their men. All of them think a poke in the eye is politically incorrect. And yet the most common reaction of my friends and co-workers to the state of my face is—no comment.

Someone you know walks in with a black eye and you don't say anything? If your male buddy shows up with a shiner, don't you ask what happened?

One girlfriend admitted, after I raised the subject, "I didn't want to say anything. I thought, 'Peter wouldn't hit her, would he?' But I didn't want to embarrass you so I kept my mouth shut." A male friend said, "I wanted to ask you, but there were too many people around." Another girl-friend said, "I figured if you wanted me to know how you got it, you'd tell me."

Offhand, I can think of three ways to acquire a black eye: a fight with a friend, a fight with a stranger, or an incident of klutz. Detroit is not a low-crime town, and I have been known to be a klutz, but all the kidding I got presumed the first option. "You can come up with a better story than *that*," was all I heard. And I hadn't even claimed to have bumped into a door.

A friend who works in an axle plant tells me that if I worked there, there's no way on earth I could convince my fellow workers that my old man hadn't knocked me around. The ragging would be nonstop, and its gist would be, "You must have really messed up this time." Nobody would be outraged. A shiner would be "kind of normal."

The universal assumption and my resulting defensiveness were so strong that sometimes I believed I really did have a guilty secret. (Notice that *I* would be the guilty one here.) When I repeated the tale of me and the street sign to those who did ask, I found it hard to make eye-contact; an embarrassed grin would steal across my face. If I elaborated, I felt like the lady who doth protest too much.

At the dentist and the oral surgeon, it was worse. The female assistants refrained from comment. And the surgeon, his eyes sliding away, reassured me, "I'm sure it wasn't your fault, whatever happened."

I believe the joking is our way of dealing with our culture's preoccupation with sex, violence, and the combination thereof. If you haven't been battered, you can make a joke of it and avoid admitting how nasty it is in real life.

Women explain innocent cuts and bruises with a catch-phrase: "My other lover's been beating me." Men and women both use language that disguises brutality and makes it sound almost playful. "Knock her around, give her a poke."

When I told one friend how people had been reacting to my black eye, she thought it was preposterous. "But you'd be the last person to let that happen to you," she said.

Well, thank you. But the unfunny truth is that it can happen to any woman once.

Meanwhile, my sweetheart says *his* feelings are hurt—that our friends would think for a moment that he hit me.

But he knew it would happen. His first thought, as I bounced off the street sign, was, "Now the rumors are going to fly." Just as my first words were, "Now your reputation is shot."

I'm convinced that people's reactions and assumptions are independent of the two individuals involved and are, instead, an indication of just where relations between the sexes lie in 1987, twenty years after the second wave of feminism began.

But I'm still defensive. Come to Detroit and I'll show you that bent street sign. I just hope Mayor Young hasn't gotten around to fixing it.

1987

Give and Take

I haven't seen my parents in more than three years. But the last time I visited them I remember hugging my father goodbye at the airport gate. I tried to avoid his lips, but ended up getting a sloppy wet kiss, tongue and all. My mother was standing next to him. I wondered if she knew he kissed his adult daughters that way.

And I wondered if she knew what else he'd forced into my mouth when it was barely big enough to suck three fingers. For a long time I was sure she couldn't have known. If she'd known, she would have stopped him. She would have kicked him out of the house. Three years ago, when I told her my father had molested me at home and at church, regular as his Sunday sermon, she assured me she didn't know. She quickly added, "If it were my father I'd never forgive him," then, without pause, "You've got to forgive your father," and finally, "My husband would never do that."

Daughter, mother, wife—the three parts of her spinning like a gyroscope. I see her girlhood at the center, never touching the outer rings of her adult life. If my mother had remembered her own girlhood, could she have saved me? Would she have made my father stop?

Every Saturday night my mother typed my father's sermons. I remember lying in bed hearing the metal type bars strike the platen and the bell preceding each carriage return. I wondered how many bells before my father would enter my room. I'd lie awake pretending to sleep, praying the bells would stop ringing soon. When my mother stopped typing in the downstairs kitchen, my father stopped what he was doing to me.

Three years ago, when my mother assured me she didn't know about the incest, I believed her. And somehow the memory of her typing my father's sermons downstairs, while he was molesting me upstairs, validated her statement. However, my mother eventually chose not to know about the incest again. She told my therapist, "I have no reason not to believe my daughter, but if I believe her I'll have to leave my husband, and I can't live without him." A door that had opened a crack between my mother and me closed for good.

Since then I've remembered the time my mother discovered my father and me in her bed. I must have been two and a half, because she was pregnant with my sister. I remember her screaming: "Go! Just get out!" not to my father, but to me. I don't remember much after that, except that I heard the door slam and remember being on the other side of it.

When my mother was close to delivery, she sent me away for two weeks while she went to the hospital to have my sister. My two older brothers stayed home. "You're too much for your father to handle," she told me. Maybe it was the only truly protective thing my mother ever did for me. But in my two-and-a-half-year-old mind I must have thought I'd been sent away for being a bad girl. When I returned, I discovered a good baby girl had replaced me.

I hadn't asked for a sister. Yet she turned out to be the best gift my parents ever gave me. I hadn't asked for bikini underwear, either. Not now, and not for all those Christmases and birthdays when my father would brag, "I picked out the black ones."

What I had asked for in a letter last year were a few cherished items my parents possessed, which I thought I might never see again: a blue-and-white flowered teacup my mother reserved for me whenever I visited, a cassette tape of a chamber-music concert I performed the week after I told my mother about the incest, a photograph of myself with John Williams at my debut as a pianist with the Boston Pops and, most important, a silver hand mirror that belonged to my grandmother. She lived with us every summer until she died when I was thirteen. I felt safe and protected when she was around. My father behaved when his mother was in the house. But best of all, she loved me. She let me play with the silver mirror that always sat on her dresser. I'd look into it and long to be someone else—anyone else—and for a few precious moments I was.

My parents sent everything I asked for except the mirror, and in its place sent the last thing I ever wanted from them.

Sometimes my mother sends my sister underwear too, but they are the waist-high variety, and mostly white. My sister was the only one of the four of us my mother protected. One year my sister and I held up our gifts under the Christmas tree—my scanty lace bikinis, her high-waisted briefs. My sister sighed. She said our mother had always told her I was the more attractive daughter, and bought her dowdy underwear to remind her of her fate. In fact, my sister is beautiful. I didn't tell her then, but I wonder if her underwear was really sent to remind her of the fate she'd missed, the fate our mother protected her from.

The day after I opened the latest lingerie gift from our parents, I called my sister to ask her advice. She's usually very practical in such matters. "Take them back to a department store and pocket the money, or buy something nice for yourself," she said. I thanked her and thought about what I might buy with the money. High-waisted white cotton briefs? Long johns for cold winter nights? Something soft and feminine I picked out for myself? Nothing felt right. And the thought of handing high-cut lace bikini underwear to the woman wearing half-glasses behind the lingerie counter made me sick. Surely she would know they came from another store. Would she know they came from my parents?

Instead, I took them to my incest survivors' group. One woman was envious. "Hard evidence," she said. Another wanted to tear them up. I almost let her. A third woman suggested I return them, not to the store, but to their rightful owners. "The money will be tainted," she said. "Get rid of them." I sat there stunned for a moment, then looked down at the lacy heap in my lap. Throughout all the painful Christmases and birthdays of my life, I'd never thought once of returning a gift to the giver.

Three years ago, after telling my mother about the incest, I wrote to my father: "I know what you did to me and I can't pretend it didn't happen anymore." Six months later, I received a letter from my father imploring me to begin a new chapter.

I have. I told my parents I would no longer remain silent about the incest. I told them I would no longer accept lingerie gifts from the father who molested me and the mother who ignored my pleas for help.

Five women helped me reseal the package. Five women walked me to the mailbox. When I let the package slide off my fingers and down the black hole, five women cried out, laughed, and hugged me.

That's a gift I'll keep forever.

1993

Death of Popeye

He doesn't go away. His movements make me dizzy. The circular rhythms grow hypnotic and weaken the grip of my muscles. They shake me loose, unanchor me. My will to be concealed unravels.

I am three-and-a-half years old. Trapped beneath hungry gyrations. Suddenly I am wise beyond my years, beyond my choice to kick. I am frightened. Should I forget?

I know this boy. A neighborhood teenager. Oily complexion. He never played with the other kids on the block. I hear my mother remind me, "Be nice to the baby-sitter."

Wet, mute lips lick my nape. Fog sweeps down my neck. His weight crushes my spine. I am pushed into the crisp, white sheets, forced through the springs and cotton fluff of the mattress, squashed between bed and floor. Nerve endings retreat from the interior walls of my skin to dodge his touch. I slither and slide across muscle, tissue, pumping blood. Where am I going? A crack or hole, I must escape.

Earlier that night he followed me around the house and watched me play my favorite game: Popeye Shipwrecked on a Desert Island. In the living room I find shelter from a storm under the

188

glass coffee table. I crawl on hands and knees between green paisley chairs and floor lamps, and scour the island for spinach. Spinach will give me strength to rebuild my boat. Climbing a hillside covered with poppies and dandelions, up the steps from the foyer to the second floor, I spot leafy greens. Noisily I munch my fill, then stand erect, facing west, to await transformation from sailorman to Superman. My body begins to swell, veins pop out, thighs throb. Muscles of a weight lifter ripple through my blouse and shorts. I explode into superhuman dimensions and torpedo through the house, unleashing a whirlwind that magically repairs my boat. Seconds later, I set sail from the top of the staircase. The ocean waves are choppy. I bump down the steps on my behind. Home to Olive Oyl.

The entire evening I play and he watches. Occasionally I feel his eyes on my body. "Want to play?" I ask. He shakes his head no. My brother Andy would have raced me up the stairs to gobble down the spinach. He would have held me and reassured me, told me not to be afraid during the storm. This boy just watches. He hardly speaks at all. Eventually I exhaust myself, and he tells me it is time for bed. Later that night he wakes me to his own game.

He doesn't have a sister. He doesn't know how to play. I hide under a pillow and crawl into a clenched fist. A coward, feigning sleep. In the silence of his motions, I wait for him to leave my body, my bedroom, my space. Not once do I speak. Nor do I open my eyes. I am abandoned to a task I never asked for.

I wake up burdened. Bruised with memory, the weight of his body, the silence of my room. It is Sunday morning. Everyone is home. I hear my brothers rolling around on the living room floor. Down the hallway, the television is playing in my parents' bedroom.

I could be watching Popeye.

Rising from my bed, I inch down the hallway to my parents' bedroom. Reaching through shadows, I gather my will into knuckles that tap at their door.

My parents are reading the Sunday paper. I shuffle about awkwardly. The gray-blue carpet swallows my knees. I am treading in gray-blue carpet. My voice is a scant flutter of light across shadows.

"Mommy, Daddy, I don't like the baby-sitter. He hurt me."

My father raises his eyebrows and for one brief moment looks at me. He clears his throat and continues to read the paper. My mother glances at him, then leans toward me. Her newspaper section collapses between us.

"What did he do to you?" she asks.

"He hugged me," I mumble from the foot of the bed.

Her eyes tug at me. My throat caves in. Why doesn't she hold me? Why doesn't he say something?

My father swallows his breath and flips through the pages. His legs press into the bedding. My mother looks at my father.

"Don't worry," she says. "We won't let him baby-sit again." I hear her tell me to run downstairs and play with my brothers.

I retreat to the doorway. My mother and father return to reading. Emptied ice cream bowls are stacked on the night table. Bathrobes are draped over a gray stuffed chair. My father yawns. My mother sighs. The bedroom starts to fade. Tears blur my vision, remain planted in my eyes. I am scared to hold myself.

I descend the hallway stairs one by one past last night's hill of spinach. I return, a castaway, to my desert island. My brothers are wrestling in the living room. Their heads bob up from the floor behind the sofa. Grinning monkeys. They taunt me to join them. I smile weakly. If I play with them, I'll wind up with a busted lip or bruised behind. Not today. I am Olive Oyl, stuck in an empty can of spinach. No one knows that I am lost.

I climb upstairs to my bedroom, stand tiptoe on the desk chair, and raise choice onto the highest shelf. Squeezed among the books, trolls, and trinkets. One day I'll huff and puff and blow the lid off this can of spinach. Choice will leap off the shelf and sink into my arms.

1989

ANONYMOUS

A Rape

A twenty-year-old [college name] student was allegedly raped early this morning in [city] after a man who had crawled into the back seat of her car surprised her and ordered her to drive to a side street. County police said the victim was returning to her residence at 1:42 A.M. when the rapist confronted her. The man, wielding a gun, directed her to drive to [name of road], where the rape occurred. Following the attack, the victim ran to a [name of road] residence where she called the police. [City] police are investigating the rape, county police said this morning.

This newspaper account of a rape was printed in a college town daily on April 18, 1980, and the rape victim referred to in the account is me. It is still not easy to claim that experience as my own. How do you say it: I was raped? The rape victim was me? The story about rape refers to me? The rape was of my person? I am having a hard time with this simple acknowledgment. All I see is this abstract grammatical construction, like a sentence diagram, that goes: subject—rapist; verb—rape; object—me. *Rape* is just a word like any other word. If you say it ten times fast it will start to sound silly.

For five years I didn't talk to many people about my rape. I denied that it had had any effect at all. Now, though, I want to understand what happened to me and what it means that rape is a threat to every woman. If I'm to talk to someone about my experience of rape, it's important that I give the details, so that my experience isn't confused with any preconceived ideas. In order to understand what rape means, more people need to say what rape is.

I left Rhonda's just past midnight, David and Trish in the front seat of the car with me. Trish's car was parked on campus, so I dropped her and David there.

Said to Trish, "See you when we get home." Was told to drive carefully. Started home.

Was pulling over to the right of Clay Boulevard, to make a right turn onto Tyler Avenue. Heard noises in the back seat. Before I could react, I heard a voice.

"Just keep driving. I have a gun. You don't want me to use it, do you?"

I reacted—muffled scream. Turned around—man crouched in the back.

"Turn right here," he said.

I turned. I looked at the car door.

He locked the car door.

"Do what I say and you won't get hurt," he said. "I want simplicity. I won't hurt you if you do what I say. Feel that, that's a gun." He pushed the gun into the base of my skull.

"I thought your friends were gonna see me," he said. I looked in the rearview mirror—where's Trish's car? No cars behind me. He pushed the rearview mirror up.

"Turn left here," he said. This was at the 7-Eleven. "Don't do anything stupid," he said. "Just do what I say. I just want simplicity. Light me a cigarette."

I lit the cigarette and moved my pocketbook to the left, between the car door and me. "Just tell me what to do, I'll do anything you say, sir." He was surprised and pleased at the "sir."

"Keep driving," he said. "Were you all smoking reefer in there?"

"No. We were just drinking beer."

"Ugh." He grunted a lot.

I hesitated where I usually turn for home.

"You don't want me to use this gun, do you?" he said.

"No, sir," I said. "Stay right?" My voice was cracking.

"Are you afraid?" he said.

"Yes." We passed Jim Wheel's tavern.

"Just do what I say and I won't hurt you. I just want simplicity."

"Simplicity . . . what's that?" I asked. "I can't understand your words. I don't know what you're saying." He said something unintelligible.

By this point the car was weaving. I couldn't really drive. "I can't see very well," I said. "I'll do whatever you say but you're going to have to tell me. I want to do whatever you say."

"Shut up. I want simplicity."

"Where are you taking me?"

"There are trucks parked up ahead, on your left. Pull across the lot, beside the last truck."

What's going to happen now? Is he meeting someone? Am I going to die right here?

"What do you want?" I asked. "What are you going to do to me?"

"I'm gonna get some pussy," he said. "Do you understand that?" Then I understood that the whole time I had been hearing "simplicity," he had been saying "some pussy."

I was relieved—rape echoing in my mind felt better than murder. At the same time, I felt like my insides were dropping out.

"Take your clothes off," he said.

What was actually happening to me hit me in the face: I was about to be *raped*.

"I have a gun," he said. "You don't want me to hurt you, do you? Give me the keys."

I took my boots and socks off, then my sweater, then I unbuttoned my shirt and took my pants off. I was still hoping to find a moment when I could break away. I left my shirt and underwear on, thinking I could run away.

"Lie down and turn your head to the side."

"Which side? Like this?" My voice cracked—almost sobbing—then went into a high-pitched whine.

He climbed over the seat. Pants down around his hips. Work shoes. No underwear. Blue work pants. Dark blue jacket, zipped up. Couldn't see his face—couldn't turn my head that far. He eased himself on top of me, was straddling my body, on his knees. No weight on me. Saw my underwear.

"Are you gonna take your panties off, or do you want me to rip 'em off?" he said.

Remember thinking that line could be right out of a trashy novel. I pulled my underwear off.

He put the weight of his hips on me—not very heavy. His penis was very hard, pushed against me. Couldn't find my vagina. I couldn't see how he was going to enter me—bone dry.

"Spread your legs more. Do what I say," he said.

There was some fumbling. He was getting frustrated and angry. I was more scared.

"Here, do you want me to help you?" I said.

"Yeah, you do it," he said. Like it was his idea.

I managed to put his penis inside of me. Moved in and out—not all the way—up and down. Must have had leverage from the way he was positioned. He wasn't very far inside of me and didn't hurt me much.

He had an orgasm but was still hard. While he collapsed for a few seconds all kinds of possibilities went through my head—ways to get away.

He pulled completely out of me and we talked for a couple of minutes.

"What's your name?" he asked.

I told him my first name.

"What's your last name?"

I told him my last name.

"You gonna tell the police," he said.

"No I won't," I said. I started crying. "I just want to go home."

"I'm not going to hurt you," he said. "Are you still afraid?"

"Yes. I just want to go home. Will you let me go home?"

"No," he said. "I want to cream again. After this time."

I started crying again. "Don't hurt me!" I screamed. The whole time I was afraid he had a knife.

He entered me. This time it hurt more—he was deeper inside of me and he groaned a lot. I tried to look at his face.

"Keep your head turned, girl. You don't want me to slap you around, do you? I'll slap you around."

"I didn't mean to look, I'm sorry," I said.

He finally came to an orgasm for the second time.

"How old are you?" he asked.

"Seventeen," I said. I don't know why I lied, except that I was trying to give him the best answer, psychologically.

"No you're not."

"Yes I am. Will you let me go home now?"

"What grade you in?"

"Twelfth."

"Ugh," he said. "You gonna tell the police."

"No, I won't tell anyone. Just let me go home." I started crying.

Some of this conversation wasn't exactly in this order; some of it occurred while he was fucking me.

"You got a boyfriend?" he asked.

"No. I had one once."

"Was he white?"

"Yes. But this doesn't feel any different," I said.

"You ever done this before?" he asked.

"No. Yes." I was confused as to which answer would be better. "I just don't know what to do."

"Just do what I say. Feels good, huh? Never had a black cock before, huh?"

"No. But this feels the same. Can I go home now?"

"I just wanna cream one more time."

"You promised you'd let me go home," I said.

"I will. I wanna cream one more time first. I want you to cream too."

I tried to look at him, but I got caught.

"Turn your head, girl," he screamed.

"Please don't hurt me. Please let me go home."

"One more—you cream too," he said.

"I did the first time. You just didn't see," I said.

"I didn't see," he said. "One more time. Then you can go home."

"I don't believe you. Do you promise?"

"Yeah, I promise," he said.

"I still don't believe you. Promise?" I asked again.

"Yeah. Shut up."

This time he hurt me a lot and I felt rage—very hard to control. I thought about how to get away. Had my hand on the door handle but didn't know if the door was locked. Tried to reach the lock. Couldn't.

I moaned loudly.

"Yeah, you like it too, bitch," he said. "Let me see you. I want to see if you're fat."

"If I'm *what*?" I asked.

No answer. He stroked my chest and looked at me. I watched him do this. He struggled for a long time trying to reach an orgasm. Finally I pretended to have an orgasm and tried to push him away. He wasn't finished. I moaned some more. I don't know if he came or not. I assume so.

He collapsed onto me—all his weight.

"Let me go home now. I'll drive you anywhere you want to go. We better put on our clothes so nobody knows," I said. "I'll drive."

"Yeah, you drive," he said. "I can't drive anything 'cept my thing and that I can drive real well. I don't even have a license."

"I need my keys," I said.

"I'm going to go in the back seat again," he said. "Don't do anything stupid. I'm getting my gun."

He fumbled in his jacket pocket and handed me the keys.

"Light me another cigarette," he said.

I turned the key. Dear God, please start, I thought.

"How do I get out of here?" I asked.

I turned my headlights on.

"Go around these trucks," he said.

"It's muddy."

"You better hadn't get stuck. Uh, oh. You're gonna have to back up," he said.

I turned around but didn't look at him.

"I can't see," I said.

"Wait a minute," he said. He turned around and wiped the window with his left hand. I stared out and backed around.

"Turn right," he said. This put us on the road.

"Just tell me where you want to go. I'll take you anywhere."

He laughed.

He wanted me to turn into a little road on the left, but I missed it. Told me to turn around at the store. I got the door lock up while I was turning.

"Where are we going?" I asked.

"Just keep driving. Shut up," he said.

"There are trucks parked on your left. Turn there."

"Isn't that where we already were before?" I asked.

"Shut up!" he screamed. "Pull down beside the last truck."

"What are you gonna do to me?" I asked.

"I'm gonna—"

I jumped out of the car. I screamed, "You motherfucking bastard," and ran.

He yelled something but I couldn't make it out. Halfway to the nearest house, I heard the car crash. The people at the house let me in. Called the police. Called Trish.

She didn't answer at first because she was out searching for me. When I finally reached her, and heard her voice, I started sobbing. "I've just been raped," I said. It seemed overwhelming to me that I had talked to Trish such a short while before, maybe an hour earlier, and that the world had been a different place.

At the hospital later that night, the nurses made me sit in a wheelchair. Trish, trying to make me feel less like an invalid, started playing around, and pushed me pretty fast down the hall. I remember feeling completely out of control and panicked, even though it was my best friend pushing the chair and I knew she would never hurt me.

During the two days following the rape I lost ten pounds. Later, my weight dropped much further. I felt like I'd never be able to eat enough to regain my strength.

I still sleep with a light on. I will not watch anything resembling a horror film. I methodically check to make sure no one is in my apartment when I return home. I check back seats of cars often—even when I know no one is there but feel like there might be someone anyway. I wonder if the fear will ever go away.

There are other, more damaging effects of the rape. I am capable of incredible passivity and subject to feelings of powerlessness. I distrust people, especially men. I have not been involved in an intimate sexual relationship since the rape. I have not even had sexual intercourse since then. I don't have much to say about these reactions. It is all frustrating and embarrassing and sad. I am actively working through these things, but I am nowhere near where I want to be. I can't just will myself there. Healing is different from that. Wholeness is different from being hardened.

1986

BARBARA MOR

Amazing Rage

In this post-everything-real decade (postpolitics, postfeminism, postconsciousness: I see a row of fence posts along the road graffitied with careerist suits and mousse) there is a correspondingly decadent compunction to Look Good. Spiritually, physically, culturally: pose pretty. Even our goddesses. New Age spiritual guides, even we spiritual feminists, urge ourselves to image "positively": smiling, wise, benevolent, graciously nonconfrontational Ladies. Those who succor, shelter, soothe. Goddesses of therapy rather than bitches of politics; goddesses of personal well-being rather than witches of global change. Because we are all, as the whole doomed world is, alone, scared, in pain, stressed-out, terminally obstructed, overdosed, and confused. Naturally it follows we seek the Mother of Peace and Quiet, not an Amazonian Battle-Ax hounding us Out To Fight Again. In the midst of patriarchy's metallic noise and violent self-pollution, we consume tapes of our mother's last, lost waterfalls, forest winds, sweet silence. For our Goddess, we'd prefer the lovely and aerobic nurturer, Ms. Holistic Healing Sunshine—not that same old Bitch wrapped in stinking fragments of bloody moon.

But the primal power is Hers. In my mirror, cracked by time and strange choice, the face I most favor is the *Morrigan*. She is "le Faye," the fate of Ireland, my people's Black Goddess. In pre-Indo-European symbology, "black" is the color of female power. (In those myths, as well as in African and Asian myths, the color of death was white.) The power of Earth, of Night, of the womb: a stern power, often, but wholly real. "Blackness," to the Irish, is the mood of necessity, be it grim, glorious, or otherwise. It is the eventual doom of all things, the inevitable flowering of each thing, as we follow our natures utterly to the end: endless transformation on the wheel of change. The Gaelic "black mood" is akin to the Spanish *duende*, the black voice, black sound present in all true song. The Irish love this grave darkness of the Morrigan, her fatal necessity, because it has been with us so much, and for so long. It is our pagan face, indeed, our oldest face. Imagine a moon Goddess when almost all the lunations are dark ones. One learns to see, to believe in, the mothering dark. The black, uterine Cave of the Mind.

A triple Goddess, the Morrigan has three names: *Ana*, *Badb*, and *Macha*. Ana, "plenty," is the Mother, both good and awful. She gives abundance and blight, lush weather and foulness, laughter and loud screams. Her body is the land, all the happy and suffering creatures on it her children. We know this Mother well: she is everyone's Mother. Badb is more specific, terrible. She is met at river fords, crouched and smeared with gore, washing the weapons and armor of those about to die in battle. With a downturn of her hand, she can flood a land with blood; a finger-lift, the river goes dry, for easy crossing. Badb means "boiling," like a cauldron; also "crow." An *badb catha* is "the battle crow." Brains and belly stewing and bubbling always with blood heat, with the circling cries of black birds: life and death, cooking female energy, the natural magic. In Ireland and Gaelic Scotland still, the word badb is used to target "an unpleasant woman," a hag, a troublemaker. So you think you're badb, huh? A glorious name!

Macha is "the raven," Badb's big sister, goddess of prophetic warfare. This means she is a mind-zapper, rather than a physical participant in battles. With psychic energy alone, mental mojo, she can influence a fight, destroy an enemy, or win a war. She was invoked in ancient Irish battles by an imitation of a raven's croaking, on war horns. The sound alone, supposedly, could traumatize men's minds. Terror of her invisible always presence.

Morrigan means "Great Queen," but you can see: this is not anyone's idea of a legal, regal lady. The Irish chose wildness as their metaphor, particularly vis-à-vis the linear Anglo conquerors. They also chose female power over female beauty. In all descriptions, the Morrigan is a pugnacious sight.

A *big-mouthed black swift sooty woman, lame and squinting with her left eye. She wore a threadbare dingy cloak. Dark as the back of a stag beetle was every joint of her, from the top of her head to the ground.*

Her long gray hair falls back over her shoulder. A big, bony shoulder. Cruel and kind mother, warrior, virgin, hag, goddess of sex and fertility, the one who makes the land fruitful or barren, mother of seasons, the one who protects the flocks and seeds: the Morrigan shares all these classic attributes of Great Goddesses everywhere.

But she has this Gaelic twist. Smoky, lame, and cockeyed. Barefoot and filthy-fingered. A supernatural hagbag, a screeching *cailleach*, like her Welsh twin, *Cerridwen*. Solitary, she roams mountains with wild deer herds, haunts alleys of hard cities. A face often distraught, pissed, poor, swollen with anger or the planetary passion of ultimatums about to be explosively uttered. Mantic words spewed out like crazy crows against the world's official wind. She is called "big-mouthed." She is called "ugly and utterly abnormal." She is called mad. Mean. Nasty. Out of style. She is. So be it!

You see my bias. I love this Hag. One good leg, one eye, one tooth: the Stubborn One. Fist in the chest that clenches, opens, clenches again as the world's relentless pulse goes through it. Politics is not pretty. Earth today is not altogether serene. Nor is the Morrigan. Feisty; but she is frustrated. For this reason: she *is* the Earth. She cannot sell out, exploit herself. Take dishonest shortcuts to survival. Source of all wealth, power, work, real value, she cannot *therefore* turn herself into quick cash, properties, paper assets, profitable junk, or bombs. She is not a necrophiliac dealer, a stockbroker, a land developer, a sharky hustler of trends and markets. She cannot pimp her own flesh: her home, her body. Nor her children: animals, trees, humanity. Nor her imaginative power: her dreams. She pays herself lousy wages, indeed.

She can only boil in her belly, turning from day to night through all weathers, while the rage for poetry and justice flies out of her, continuously, circling and cawing in a mood of black wings. And hope that we are Her Daughters: to see, and listen, and do the same.

When they say anger is not spiritual, they lie. When they say spirituality and politics don't mix, they lie again. Politics can be a dream of the body. And the body of Earth is definitely spiritual. And definitely has a right to rage. Her righteous rage. Earth can be made sick, beat up, enslaved, can die: she has a right to defend herself. She is not obligated to be nice, negotiable, nonargumentative, nonthreatening. She does not need to Look Good: she is Real. All the moods are Hers, as are all the weathers of this planet. This is a model for Female Politics, 1990s (recalling that brief but fine feminist holism of the 1960s): no justifiable separation between "being spiritual" and "being political." No choice between personal well-being and global change. One signifies/necessitates the other, and She will kick shit if necessary. Anything less is a lie.

I like the way the Morrigan fights. A war goddess, her weapon is the female mind. She was responsible for this ultimate power to decide, to will the fate of Her people; it was recognized by male warriors as mightier than any weapon or stratagem. Celtic women engaged in battle, and fought in the Morrigan's name. In her mode. Rushing among the enemy ranks, they swirled blazing bundles of wood. Cursing, chanting, screaming. Enchanted, rooted, right: they totally confused the mind of the opponent, draining his muscles of strength, his heart of courage. This is guerrilla theater! Guerrilla warfare. Is it not? To short-circuit all opposing certitudes; eclipse the Moon, the mind. The Hag whose thoughts are black wings can do it. The Badb had a special posture, the stance of magicians. Approached by any hostile entity, scheming to take Her world, She: stood on one leg, shut one eye, and chanted. And the world remained Hers. To this day. Try it.

1990

PART FOUR

Women's Bodies,
Women's Choices

In the 1920s we believed that children should be

wanted and planned for.

MARGARET MEAD

MARGARET MEAD

On Having a Baby

I was always glad that I was a girl. I cannot re-
member ever wanting to be a boy. It seems to me this was because of the
way I was treated by my parents. I was a wanted child, and when I was born
I was the kind of child my parents wanted. This sense of satisfying one's
parents probably has a great deal to do with one's capacity to accept oneself
as a kind of person. As a girl, I knew that someday I would have children.
My closest models, my mother and my grandmother, had both had children and also had used their minds and had careers in the public world. So
I had no doubt that, whatever career I might choose, I would have children, too.

All through my childhood I enjoyed taking care of younger children.
At family parties I would collect the smaller children and play games with
them or tell them stories, and I enjoyed holding a baby in my arms until it
fell asleep. I had dolls, but I never cared very much for them; I preferred
real babies. And I never cared very much for pets, cats or dogs, because
babies were more interesting. And there always were babies, our own or
other people's babies, to hold, watch over, play with, and observe. I remember Ruth Benedict commenting that the baby of one of her acquain-
tances was "horrid." This surprised me. I had known horrid children and
horrid adults, but in my mind babies, before they could walk and talk, were

exempt. It was only later, when I watched births in the field, that I learned how the newborn baby does somehow embody the personality it will have and, if it dies soon after birth, epitomizes the person it would have become. But when Ruth made that remark I had seen only one newborn baby, my sister Priscilla, who was beautiful from her birth.

When I became engaged to Luther, I felt that this pledged us to have a child, and as he planned to enter the ministry I built up a picture of a rectory—modeled on Charlotte M. Yonge's stories of English rectories—with six children. Charlotte M. Yonge also wrote stirring stories of high adventure. These provided me with themes for adventurous daydreams, but in the end it was her domestic tales, in which she pictured children in the world of their day and night nurseries, that caught my imagination. When I was seventeen I gave a big Shrove Tuesday party for my sisters and made pancakes for some fifteen children. Grandma said, "Well, if you can keep as steady as you are now, with one in your arms and one pulling at your skirt, you'll do all right." And I never doubted that one day there would be one in my arms and one pulling at my skirt.

In the 1920s, we believed that children should be wanted and planned for. We were all very conscious of the new possibilities of birth control and safer childbirth, which meant that one could have a child even late in life. Luther and I wanted to finish our graduate work before we had a child, and then my field trip and Luther's traveling fellowship in Europe meant another postponement. But I was so sure that we would have children that Edward Sapir's advice that I would do better to stay at home and have a child than to go off to Samoa to study adolescent girls seemed peculiar to me. After all, men were not told to give up field work to have children! And I felt, rather than knew, that postponement—even postponement for a whole lifetime—need do no harm. A nun who loves children, but who devotes her life to the care of many of God's children, comes out unharmed, even though she may sometimes be wistful.

And then, in 1926, when I was told that I could never have children, I took this as a kind of omen about my future life. I had married Luther with the hope of rearing a houseful of children in a country parish. But now he was giving up the ministry and I was told that I could not have a child. I believed he would make a wonderful father, but this was no longer a possibility—for us.

On the other hand, I did not think that Reo, who wanted to marry me, would make an ideal father. He was too demanding and jealous of my attention; he begrudged even the attention I gave to a piece of mending. I had always felt that my father demanded too much of my mother and took her away from us to satisfy his own immediate and capricious requests to do something or find something for him. I did not want a marriage that repeated this pattern. But without children, the future looked quite different, and I decided to choose a life of shared field work and intellectual endeavor. I do not remember being terribly disappointed. There had always been the alternative of another kind of life. But Ruth was not pleased. Even though neither she nor anyone else questioned the doctor's verdict, she felt that I was somehow making an ascetic choice, a choice against the fullness of life.

So I married Reo. And, having made a commitment to work, I wrote to Professor Boas that he could send us anywhere he would send a man, since I would no longer need any special protection. I had accepted the need to give potentially childbearing women greater protection in the field than men. I still accept it, for the illness or death of a woman in the field makes for far more trouble for everyone—the people one is working with and the officials who have to deal with the situation. But this stricture no longer applied to me.

However, when we went to Mundugumor, I saw for the first time what the active refusal of children could do to a society. I had known many childless couples—some who did not want children and others, like the kings and queens in fairy tales, who had everything they wanted except a child. Mother had often spoken about the "selfishness" of childless couples who "preferred to go to Europe every summer," and she would say, self-righteously, "*Our* extravagances are our children." But as an anthropologist I learn best when I see what happens when a whole society embodies some particular trait—and among the Mundugumor both men and women actively disliked children. They are the only primitive people I have ever known who did not give an infant the breast when it cried. Instead, the child was hoisted up on the mother's shoulder. Sleeping babies were hung in rough-textured baskets in a dark place against the wall, and when a baby cried, someone would scratch gratingly on the outside of the basket.

The Mundugumor presented a harsh contrast to the Arapesh, whose whole meager and hardworking lives were devoted to growing their children. They had a strange kind of fascination for Reo, but I simply felt repelled. Added to this, we lived under constant tension. The Mundugumor had so recently been brought under control that it was not safe to let more than two or three people up into our house at a time, lest a head so easily taken might prove too tempting. In the village I walked about them quite freely, but I always kept the initiative. Probably this reinforced my distaste. But it was the Mundugumor attitude toward children that was decisive. I felt strongly that a culture that rejected children was a bad culture. And so I began to hope—not very logically, but with a kind of emotional congruence—that perhaps after all I could have a child, perhaps I could manage it.

I pointed out to Reo that one child would not interfere very much with our work. One child could always be put to bed in a bureau drawer. It was having two children that really changed life. Reo in no sense had made having no children a condition of our marriage, but I myself felt that our marriage had been a pact that committed us to field work as a way of life— and by this time we were very heavily committed to field work. And in spite of the difficulties, it was a more peaceful existence than our life in an academic setting, where Reo was almost unendurably harassed by his constant feelings of rivalry. A little later, while we were in Tchambuli, I had a miscarriage, but this did not weaken my renewed belief that somehow I was going to have a child.

Later, when Gregory and I were married and working in Bali, I continued to hope for a child, but once again I had several early miscarriages. Then, in 1938, when we went to the Sepik, it appeared that I might be having a premature menopause—again a doctor's theory. I was sad, but it was the kind of sadness that accompanies a hope that has been sustained. I wanted a child, but I did not feel, as Ruth had felt, that there was no possible compensation for not having a child. If I was now reaching a stage in my life in which it was certain that I could never have a child, I could face that, not with remorse or guilt, but only with regret.

Something very special sometimes happens to women when they know that they will not have a child—or any more children. It can happen to women who have never married, when they reach the menopause. It can happen to widows with children who feel that no new person can ever take the place of a loved husband. It can happen to young wives who discover that they never can bear a child. Suddenly, their whole creativity is released—they paint or write as never before or they throw themselves into academic work with enthusiasm, where before they had only half a mind to spare for it. I think that if I had had six children, I would have had energy to spare for other things, especially when the children were older, but they would have come first. And six children who come first take up most of one's time and energy, and, if they are deeply wanted, in a very satisfying way.

I remember the flash of insight I had in 1940 as I sat talking to a small delegation that had come to ask me to address a women's congress. I had my baby on my lap, and as we talked I recalled my psychology professor's explanation of why women are less productive than men. He had referred to a letter written by Harriet Beecher Stowe in which she said that she had in mind to write a novel about slavery, but the baby cried so much. It suddenly occurred to me that it would have been much more plausible if she had said "but the baby smiles so much." It is not that women have less impulse than men to be creative and productive. But through the ages having children, for women who wanted children, has been so satisfying that it has taken some special circumstance—spinsterhood, barrenness, or widowhood—to let women give their whole minds to other work.

When we returned to Bali for a brief stay in 1939, it appeared that I was, after all, pregnant. And so I was carried up and down the muddy, steep mile from the main road to Bajoeng Gede. The villagers had rigged up a kind of sedan from one of our old bamboo chairs. But the bamboo had dried out, and in the middle of the trip the chair suddenly collapsed on itself and held me as in a vise. That night, in the guesthouse in which we were staying in Kintamani, I had a rather bad miscarriage and the Dutch doctor was summoned. In those days Dutch doctors—indeed all the Dutch—strongly believed in having children. Every hotel room in the Indies had at least one crib, sometimes more. Instead of advising me not to try again for a while, the Dutch doctor said, "You want a child, yes?" and continued with homely advice.

By the time we reached Chicago, on our way back to New York, I thought I was pregnant again. One of the complications in the field is the difficulty of knowing whether you are, or are not, pregnant. But now it was possible to find out and to take precautions. However, we were visiting friends at the University of Chicago and had little time to ourselves; and so, instead of consulting a physician, I asked the secretary of the Anthropology Department to arrange for a test. The result was negative. I was heartbroken. Hope deferred was quite a different thing from resignation to what could not be changed.

Nevertheless, the first few weeks in New York were inexplicably peculiar. Without any good explanation for my mood, I was fretful, irritable, and cantankerous. I even had a sudden attack—the only one I ever had—of morning sickness. But I knew I was not pregnant. Finally, because I felt so strange, we went to a doctor, who said that either I was very pregnant or else I had a tumor and would have to be operated on immediately. The danger of a little knowledge! No one had warned me not to touch alcohol before taking a pregnancy test—and in Chicago, on the night before, we had gone to a big, gay party given by the Ogburns.

From the moment it was certain that I was pregnant, I took extreme precautions. I took a leave of absence from the Museum and gave up riding on streetcars, trains, and buses. I was given vitamin E as an aid to nidification, and I kept the baby.

We had planned to stay in the United States only briefly and then to go to England. There we intended to live in Cambridge, where Gregory held a fellowship in Trinity College. Now it appeared that I might have to have the baby in America and cope with all the tiresome regulations of hospitals and doctors that made breast-feeding difficult and prevented a mother from keeping the baby in the room with her.

But perhaps there was a way around the problem. I decided to start with the coming baby and work backward. I looked for a pediatrician first, and talked with Ben Spock, a young pediatrician who had been psychoanalyzed and who was recommended to me by my child development friends. I explained to Ben that I wanted him to be present at the birth, so that he could take over the baby's care immediately, that I wanted to have a film made of the baby's birth, so that afterward it could be referred to with some degree of accuracy; that I wanted a wet nurse if my milk was slow in coming in, and that I wanted permission to adjust the feeding schedule to the baby instead of the clock.

Ben replied genially—for after all he was dealing with someone more or less of his own age with a reputation in his field—that he would come to the delivery and that I could feed the baby as often as I pleased. He also knew of a good obstetrician, Claude Heaton, who had some odd ideas and might be willing to listen to me.

It turned out that Dr. Heaton was deeply interested in American Indian medicine and that he was delighted to consider my ideas—including the fact that I wanted no anesthesia unless it was absolutely necessary. He happily entered into plans to persuade the nursing sisters at the French Hospital to cooperate with my wish to breast-feed the baby in response to the baby's own needs. As part of his efforts in this direction he showed them one of our New Guinea films depicting a scene just after childbirth.

While all these arrangements were being made, we still hoped that it might be possible for me to travel to England before the baby was born. In August I was once more allowed to travel. As a first trial, we made the long, slow train journey to New Hampshire to visit Larry and Mary Frank, who were to provide a second home for all of us in the years to come. While we still were at Cloverly, the Franks' summer home, after several days' fascinating discussion with J. H. Woodger, the philosopher-biologist, the stunning news came of the Soviet-German neutrality pact. Then, when we were back in New York, the German armies invaded Poland.

It was clear that unless the British government could find some use for Gregory in the United States, he would have to leave for England immediately. He went to see the British consul, who told him, "If you were forty-nine and had a bad heart, I'd say stay. As it is, I'd advise you to go back." Four days later, when Geoffrey Gorer came to New York from a vacation in Yucatán, the orders had changed and he was advised to remain in America. Gregory, however, had to sail. He cabled his mother the date on which the ship was expected to arrive and added, "Inform National Register." He assumed that he would at once be used as a social scientist. Actually, although highly trained scientists were reserved from active military service, it was some time before the British were ready to put their intellectuals to work at specialized tasks.

And so it came about that at thirty-eight, after many years of experience as a student of child development and of childbirth in remote villages—watching children born on a steep wet hillside, in the "evil place" reserved for pigs and defecation, or while old women threw stones at the inquisitive children who came to stare at the parturient woman—I was to share in the wartime experience of young wives all around the world. My husband had gone away to take his wartime place, and there was no way of knowing whether I would ever see him again. We had a little money, a recent bequest from Gregory's aunt Margaret, so I would not have to work until after the baby was born. But that was all. Initially, we had thought that I might join Gregory in England, but my mother-in-law wrote that they were sending away busloads of pregnant women. Obviously it was better to stay in America than to become a burden in Britain as the country girded itself for war.

As a temporary measure, my friend Marie Eichelberger organized her ground-floor apartment so that I could live with her for the three months before the baby was expected. She even brought in a large armchair, strong enough for Gregory to sit in, if he should be able to return to New York. She carefully fed me low-calorie vegetables and rationed me on high-calorie foods. I also was given calcium and a little thyroid. This was about all that was known about feeding a pregnant woman.

At that time physicians were obsessed with the idea that pregnant women should not gain weight—in almost total disregard for the well-being of their unborn babies. Today, extravagant disregard for the safety of the baby has taken another form, as pregnant women, determined not to give in to coddling, engage in hazardous sports, work full time, take no precautions to have a responsible person nearby in the last weeks of pregnancy, and cheerfully risk having their babies born in taxis or police cars or at the office. Mothers even risk being alone when the new baby is born with all the difficulty of having to cope with the frightened older children. And wholly inexperienced young fathers aspire to act as midwives. These extreme rejections of our contemporary social regime are contrapuntal to "natural childbirth"—the elaborate and beneficent preparation for child bearing invented and elaborated by men to indoctrinate women (the phrase is a masculine one) with the idea that childbirth is natural!

I was rosily healthy and happy and had on my cheeks the rare "mask of pregnancy." I did not experience the extreme dimming of mental activity that affects some women—I suspect particularly women who very much enjoy carrying a child. During the whole summer Gregory and I had worked very hard cataloguing our Balinese films and 25,000 stills. The stills were on long rolls of film that Gregory would hold up to the light, while I followed my notes, to identify the scenes and the actors. Periodically we invited colleagues to come to see the films and help us to develop hypotheses from these first comparative films of human behavior. I also did some writing and in the autumn I taught at Vassar in the Child Development Department. While I lectured, Mary Fisher (Mary Fisher Langmuir Essex) sat on the steps of the little podium to be sure I would not fall off.

During these months I had all the familiar apprehensions about what the baby would be like. There was some deafness in my family, and there had been a child who suffered from Mongolism and a child with some severe form of cerebral palsy. There also were members of my family whom I did not find attractive or endearing, and I knew that my child might take after them. Distinguished forebears were no guarantee of normality. But what I dreaded most, I think, was dullness. However, I could do something about anxieties of this kind by disciplining myself not to expect the child to be any special kind of person—of my own devising. I felt deeply—as I still feel—that this is the most important point about bringing into the world a child that will have its own unique and clear identity.

So I schooled myself not to hope for a boy or a girl, but to keep an open mind. I schooled myself to have no image of what the child would look like and no expectations about the gifts he or she might, or might not, have. This was congenial to me, for I had already learned to watch carefully the power that my imagination could have over the thoughts and dreams of other people. People would come to me with some vague stirring of ambition, some vague glimpse of a possible future, and unless I was careful, I would find myself imagining a whole future and the course of action necessary to grasp it. As students or friends talked about what they wanted to be or do, a panorama would unfold before my eyes in which I could see how some special combination of talent and experience might make possible a unique contribution to the world. It was better, I had learned, to listen and occasionally suggest some alternatives or some of the complications of the course chosen by the other person. In the same way, I determined not to limit the child that was to be born—not to hope for it to be beautiful or intellectually gifted or temperamentally happy.

There was another problem, too, of which I was quite aware. I had been a "baby carriage peeker," as Dr. David Levy described the child with an absorbing interest in babies, and he identified this as one of the traits that predisposed one to become an overprotective mother. When I told him, in a telephone conversation, that I was expecting a baby, he asked, in that marvelous therapeutic voice which he could project even over the telephone, "Are you going to be an overprotective mother?" I answered, "I'm going to try not to be." But I realized that whatever predisposition in this direction I might have must have been reinforced by hope that was so often disappointed, and I knew that I would have to work hard not to overprotect my child, but to ensure my child's freedom to find its own way of taking hold of life and becoming a person.

I did not, of course, have to contend with the kinds of ambivalence that bedevil the newly married, who are afraid of sharing their so recently established intimacy with a newcomer. Nor did I worry about what having a child might do to my career. I already had a reputation on which I could rest for several years, and our Balinese and Iatmul field trip had provided materials on which I could work for the rest of my life. Before the war disrupted plans to live in England, I had intended to stay at home in Cambridge in order to look after the baby and work up our field notes. I had never cared about having any particular professional status; in the Cambridge of those days, in any case, feminine aspirations were meaningless. Men dined in hall several times a week and left their wives at home. I expected to have the baby to care for, and there was plenty of work to do.

The day before the baby was born, while I was working on Balinese films with Colin McPhee, a cable came from Gregory telling me that he had applied for a permit to come to America. There seemed to be nothing to be gained by staying in England. In fact, he had finally been rebuked for not getting on with the analysis of his field materials, the purpose for which he had been given the fellowship at Trinity.

The following night my father came over from Philadelphia and took me out to dinner. Soon after he brought me home, the water broke. It is astonishing how seldom things of this kind, which are apparently innerly determined, happen in the wrong place and at the wrong time. Six weeks earlier, I had spoken at Barnard's seventy-fifth anniversary celebration. When my former professor, Miss Howard, telephoned to ask whether I would do this, I had said, "But I'm expecting a baby at about that time." Her response came crisply, "Well, you won't have it at the dinner, will you?" And as I was getting ready to go to the hospital, Dr. Beatrice Hinkle telephoned to ask me about accepting an award and did not see any reason why the imminent birth of the baby should interfere with my speaking to her.

At the hospital I was made to time my own pains with an ordinary watch, and I remember my annoyance at not having a stopwatch. They were convinced that as a primipara I could not be so ready for birth and I was given medication to slow things down. In the end, the baby's birth had to be slowed down for another ten minutes while Myrtle McGraw, who was making the film of the birth, sent for a flashbulb that had been left in her car. All night I felt as if I were getting an attack of malaria, but I did not know—one of those things one does not know—whether the sensation of having a baby might not feel like malaria. And I was fascinated to discover that far from being "ten times worse than the worst pain you have ever had" (as our childless woman doctor had told us in college) or "worse than the worst cramps you ever had, but at least you get something out of it" (as my mother had said), the pains of childbirth were altogether different from the enveloping effects of other kinds of pain. These were pains one could follow with one's mind; they were like a fine electric needle outlining one's pelvis.

Today, preparation for natural childbirth gives women a chance to learn and to think about the task of labor, instead of simply fearing how they will endure the pains. In fact, the male invention of natural childbirth has had a magnificent emancipating effect on women, who for generations had been muffled in male myths instead of learning about a carefully observed actuality. I have never heard primitive women describe the pains of childbirth. But in societies in which men were forbidden to see birth, I have seen men writhing on the floor, acting out their conception of what birth pangs were like. In one such society, the wife herself had squatted quietly on a steep hillside in the dark and had cut the cord herself, following the instructions not of a trained midwife but of the woman who had most recently borne a child.

Mary Catherine Bateson was born on December 8, 1939, and looked very much herself.

But I did have malaria, and the day after the baby's birth my fever shot up. Now my original choice of an obstetrician, as someone who would support what I wanted for the baby, paid off in the mysterious way that a correct choice so often determines that the outcome will be felicitous. For Dr. Heaton, who was open-minded beyond most men of his day, believed me when I said that this was an ordinary attack of tertian malaria, with familiar timing. He said reasonably, "She's had it, and none of us knows anything about it." And he found an ancient book in which quinine was prescribed as a postpartum drug and let me have the thirty grains a day I was accustomed to taking. Someone else might well have diagnosed the malaria as puerperal fever. I would then have been banished from the birth pavilion and my baby would have been put into a nursery to learn the lazy habits of bottle-fed babies and perhaps would never have learned to feed from the breast.

For with all the positive forces at one's disposal—I had enough money, I had knowledge, I had reputation and prestige, I even had a film of a newborn baby in New Guinea to show to the nurses—there are limits to what one can do within a culture. The pressures of an economy building up for wartime were already felt in the hospital. Nurses were in short supply. Keeping one's baby in the same hospital room was forbidden by state law. Four-hour feeding intervals were enjoined for babies weighing more than seven pounds, and my baby was several ounces over that.

The best that could be done—the closest approximation to rooming-in and self-demand feeding, as these practices later came to be called—was to give me the baby to be fed every three hours, as if she weighed less than seven pounds, and to allow me to feed her at night. According to hospital practice, then and now, a baby should go home from the hospital ready to sleep the night through—already, at a few days old, resigned to a world whose imposed rhythms are strange and uncongenial. Although Dr. Heaton's wooing of the nurses' interest had been successful, they were too busy to manage any further alterations of the customary routine. The night I arrived the nursing sister in charge had said to me, "I understand we are to let you do just what you want." An astonishing statement, but however willing she was, there were limits beyond which she could not move.

Before Gregory left for England, we had discussed the question of the baby's name. We had already decided that if the baby were a boy, we would make our home in England, because the English did a better job of bringing up a boy; but if it were a girl, we would live in the United States, where girls are better off. But in any event, the child's surname would be Bateson, and so we considered Bateson names. We decided that we would name a girl Mary, after the most distinguished of Gregory's paternal aunts, a pioneer historian, who had died young, much loved and deeply regretted. Naming a child after someone who has died young is in some sense, I think, a promise that an interrupted pattern will, after all, be completed.

But when I suggested that a boy should be named William, Gregory dissented. "Too hard on librarians," he commented. His geneticist father was William Bateson and his theologian grandfather, Master of St. John's College, had been William H. Bateson. Evidently Gregory already expected that the child would one day write books. And in this case, another William would simply add confusion.

After a time I found that I did not really feel at home with the name Mary. I wanted to name our child Katherine after my lost little sister, whom I had named. I proposed that we spell the name Catherine, to match her Bateson grandmother's initials, C.B. I had written about this to Gregory, and he had agreed. We had also discussed circumcision, which Gregory disapproved of, but the question was left unresolved. When the cable was sent, "Mary Catherine Bateson, born December 8th," Gregory started to cable, in a return message, "Don't circumcise," and then, remembering he had a daughter, cabled instead, "Don't christen."

Three days after her birth, a package arrived in the mail addressed to Miss Mary Catherine Bateson. Reading this, I started the process of learning to treat my daughter as a separate person with an identity completely her own.

In my family I was treated as a person, never as a child who could not understand. My grandmother shared her worries about my parents with me as she combed my hair. My mother took me with her when she did field work among recently arrived immigrants. My father taught me to look him in the eye when I recited a poem to an audience. To them I was an individual. It might be necessary to keep me—as a child—from reading too much or sitting up too late. But it was never suggested that because I was a child I could not understand the world around me and respond to it responsibly and meaningfully.

Now there was Catherine, a new person.

1972

CAROLYN COMAN

Trying (and Trying and Trying) to Get Pregnant

I hear that Ann is trying to get pregnant. It's typical woman-news in our small New England community. I hold in my memory somewhere news of vaginal infections that will not be cured, suspected depressions, impossible husbands—all news of women I do not know well. I sometimes wonder what they know of me. All I know of Ann is that she is beautiful and trying to get pregnant.

"Trying to"—the phrase sounds odd to me in conjunction with pregnancy. I imagine a different kind of making love—a chore, a duty, homework. It does not sound easy, but mostly it sounds foreign to me, who unless otherwise confronted presumes fertility, presumes pregnancy waiting to happen, and "tries *not* to." Fertility for me and those around me has always been the given.

A few months later, I join a women's group and find myself sitting across from Ann. I look at her, study her. Brown curls frame her face in a natural, scattered perfection. She has a model's body, but full, round breasts. She is quiet and attentive. I am vaguely surprised that she is having trouble getting pregnant, as if women struggling with infertility would "look" a certain way. What did I think—a telltale spot on the face, a missing feature?

Ann works as a counselor at Family Planning. I hear she's wonderful at her job, especially with teenagers. Ironic, I think, that she must spend all her days talking to women who, for the most part, are "trying not to." She is informed about all the methods, all the statistics; she knows the body and its cycles.

I invite Ann and her husband to dinner with my family. Ann and Jack meet our daughter, Lily, with interest, play with her, give her their attention. Lily, with a child's nearly infallible detector for true liking, adores them.

Somewhere along the beginnings of our friendship, Ann mentions to me that she and Jack are trying to conceive, have been for a year. It is casually mentioned, over boiling noodles in the kitchen, or in the car. I unload the small bulk of my clichés on the subject, hasten to tell her that it all seems to be a matter of luck, just worrying about it can throw off your cycle. I tell her to just relax, she'll be pregnant as soon as she forgets about it. I underplay her concern with her "biological time clock"—I, two years her junior at twenty-eight, and a mother of one. She is concerned but not worried.

Months tick by. We see each other more and more. I begin to feel comfortable asking her about it—it?—her wanting and not getting a pregnancy. In the beginning I didn't ask, out of some curtsy to good manners, I suppose, shyness perhaps, awkwardness, the same inhibiting factors that keep people from acknowledging handicaps to a handicapped person. But it's what we *want* to talk about; our friendship deepens with it. There is a growing fear in Ann, not far behind the facts and statistics and biological theories that she understands so well. She tells me of marathons of love-making on the "right" days, and droughts of abstinence in between. She fears her longing for a child could consume her and so she keeps it in constant check.

I meet her father that summer: her parents are visiting from the Midwest. We are introduced at a party where her father, joke-telling, laughing, entertaining, parties hardest of all. He is taken with my two-year-old daughter, and she with him. He offers again and again to buy her. "Looks like she may be the only way I'll ever get a grandchild. And she has Irish blood in her too! I'll raise my offer!" Ann and Jack smile and joke along. Everything in me stops running when he says these things. I want to put my hand over his mouth. I am beginning to understand the stakes here.

At our women's group the following week, Ann mentions her father's yearning for a grandchild. I cannot help but blurt out my own frustration—"How can you stand hearing that, doesn't that hurt you?" She takes a breath, raises her hand to her face, and starts crying. Everyone in the group is stunned. Hands reach out to her; there is a murmur of sympathy. I am overwhelmed with her sadness. I want to get up and walk across the room and put my arms around her, but I do not. I do not for reasons having more to do with the extent of my caring than the limits of it. "Well," she says, dropping her hand from her face, tears still running down, "I guess I need to cry about that." Everyone lets out a laugh. Laughing and crying—most women I know combine them; I do, and my husband marvels at what seems a natural communion to me.

Ann laughs and cries as the other women, freed by her brave initiation of the subject, ask her where it all stands. "Have you seen a doctor yet?" one asks. She says yes. "He told me that we didn't have sex enough. Actually what he said was that the infrequency of sex was grounds for divorce. People my age who aren't even trying to get pregnant have sex on the average of five or six times a week." Everyone groans. "Yes," offers someone, "and the women are multi-orgasmic every time." We all laugh, even as I feel a rage rising up in me. "What did you say to him?" someone asks. "Nothing," she says. "I was lying flat on my back, naked underneath a paper sheet, and he was telling me that I was not even an average woman. I started to cry." I see her on that table, tears spilling sideways from her eyes. "And he got all grumpy and said, 'Now look what I've made you do,' and I was a good, sympathetic woman and told him that it wasn't his fault." We all shake our heads, juggling the ironies. "So that was my last visit. He said he wouldn't go through with more tests until the frequency of intercourse improved."

Ann's body keeps track of her time now. I have work days and weekends and job deadlines. She does too, but mostly she has cycles, and fertile times, and though the time passes slowly, it accumulates quickly, month after bloody month, because with the arrival of each period, there is the thought that the next month brings another chance—like getting to repeat a test endlessly. So her decisions and thoughts and feelings roll forward through time that is thick and liquid and slow, and she begrudges the slowness. She finds another doctor and makes arrangements for tests. Even as she does, she wishes her vagina would just produce a ticker tape every month and tell her Yes or No. Enough with the changing texture of her mucus, endless trips to the bathroom to peer down into her future. I tell her of the deals I used to make "if I would only get my period this one time"; and she tells me of the deals she makes "if there will be no blood . . ."

The new doctor is much better—sensitive, informative, gentle, not pushy. Ann sees him often for a series of tests. Jack's sperm are counted and are plentiful. His is the first and easiest test. There are postcoital sperm counts to test the thickness of Ann's mucus. Ann goes to the hospital for a scraping of the lining of her uterus. It hurts her a lot. I see her that night, and she is wearing a white cotton shirt with bright tulips appliquéd on the back—a present from Jack that is full of yearning for spring. The results trickle in, some right away, some in days or weeks. They are ambiguous. It might be the thickness of the mucus; it might be the the lack of a certain hormone to nourish a fertilized egg in the uterus; it might be the timing of the lovemaking. She is often taking samples of her body so that microscopes can magnify her and tell her when she is fertile. The doctor always says, "If you can," when he advises frequent though staggered intercourse during her fertile period.

Intercourse. That's the term, not lovemaking. Babymaking, perhaps. I see that the same process can take completely different forms. Ann tells me that lovemaking turns into taking—she takes the sperm and mission accomplished. She counts the days and schedules her desire. Her husband feels used, and is. They stop altogether.

I watch as she goes from concern to worry. I watch and realize that she is ultimately alone in it all. Surrounded by husband and friends, but ultimately alone with it: the desire and the not getting is hers—she owns it. Forging a merger of the emotional and the practical, she juggles decisions about fertility drugs with prayers for a miracle. I can only watch and listen and tell her again and again that she works hard at it, that she is honest and brave. The language of it all is hard—the terminology of the testing, the medical procedures. But the language of the heart is every bit as hard. I avoid using any word that encourages a sense of failure or guilt, but those are the senses that crop up in her over and over. Trying to become pregnant, and not, becomes a lesson in reduction for Ann—self-reduction— which I see as a beautiful, painful humanness.

Ann lets me in on an experience bigger than my own, and it is humbling. Knowing what I know, I hear the innocent comments of friends and neighbors and recognize them for the bludgeons they are. Again and again she is made the victim of others' jealousy or misunderstanding of her situation. "You're so lucky," she is assured, "you can actually sit down and read a book when you feel like it." Jack and Ann's activities, their travels, are safely dismissed by onlookers—"Well, it's not as if they have kids to consider . . ." It is assumed that since they do not have children, they do not want children, and it is that presumption which seems to step on toes. So why doesn't she tell everyone, set them all straight? Why should she have to? She tells so much as it is. I need not tell outside observers and professionals how often my husband and I make love, the times and dates, chart my cycles for them. My deepest desires are my own.

Over two years now, into the attempts at pregnancy, Ann refers to herself as infertile. She says it without fanfare or dramatics; the term is worked into the middle of a sentence, used appropriately, hooked up with the simple subject and predicate: I am. How many times do I avoid naming because of how final and true a name can make things sound? The power of words: old, dying, cancer, lonely, lost. I blanch at the label Ann has given herself, learn finally from her to embrace it for its usefulness.

Forward motion: for several months Ann takes a drug to increase the level of a certain hormone. Of all the fertility drugs available it is the one that seems the safest, most understood. To know and understand her choices and decide to take a drug are all efforts of mind and heart, and take time. There are more tests to measure the levels of hormones and quantities of sperm within the fertile mucus, but after several months there is still no pregnancy, and Ann decides to stop taking the drug, and to stop insisting on timed intercourse, and to let go for a while. To open a clenched fist, a clenched jaw. Acts of determined relaxation, as hard won as the other.

Ann makes contact with the adoption agency most respected, and most likely to have a child available at some point. My own mother became pregnant when the adoption papers were already being processed, after the gynecologist had told my parents that they could never have children. And I also know of a woman who became pregnant weeks after her adopted son was brought home. I hear a lot of stories like that. So must Ann. Sometimes I tell her stories I know, and sometimes I don't, but I tell them differently now from the way I spoke a year ago. We speak to each other with more understanding and acceptance of chance and no guarantees. There are no deals to be made, no charms, no spells to cast, even if Ann still wants the doctor to pull out a baby from his desk drawer at the end of their meetings.

She battles her desire to give birth to her own child, to have her body produce, to sing her fertility. "Primitive bullshit," she tells me. "It's crap, but it still hurts." I learn again that healthy attitudes are forged, hammer to metal; they do not just appear on cue in a society and culture where definitions of womankind are ancient, mythical, loaded.

At the adoption agency, there are facts and dates and histories to be supplied. It is just the beginning of another process, more tests to come to ensure competency, the meeting of requirements, measuring up. All that before the waiting can even begin. Some processes that are very different can seem very much the same. The slowness of it all—the need for letters and proof, and the nod from the parish priest claiming them as one of the fold blesses and stings too. The need for time is essential now, to change course, renew, prepare, but the thing that Ann wants the most seems always to take a long time, more waiting for decisions that she does not get to make but must ultimately accept.

I watch Ann within all the waiting, with time enough to doubt even wanting a child. I hear her tallying up the wealth of her life with Jack, without a child, which is plentiful. Infertility is one aspect of Ann's life, not everything. This is not tragedy. She wonders if it might not be better to learn to live contentedly in the world she has now. She tries out every idea and plan for size, like hats, to test them for beauty, comfort, warmth, price. She returns to wanting a child, but there is a constant taking stock of plans, career, marriage, sex, that is exhausting.

Summer comes, and the pace and activity of life are stepped up, and for a while take over. We do not talk of pregnancy or fertility or infertility much. The adoption application is in limbo somewhere, and the drugs and the working at pregnancy are on hold. Ann is trying to make decisions about career, about returning to school. She would like one definite answer.

"Good thing I didn't marry Prince Charles," she tells me as we hear yet another news item about the new Prince William. What she says hangs in midair between us for a moment and then falls into a deep, still pool. "That's not funny," I say. "I know it isn't," she answers, "and I know you know." But there's truth there too: sometimes not getting what you want when you want it feels like a bad joke. She tells me she is going to have lunch with a woman she met who has been unable to become pregnant, and who has had one ovary removed. They are going to talk about their infertility. Ann has been on her way to this meeting for more than two years now, building an understanding, acceptance, and empathy large enough to share with others. I bet they have a glass of wine with lunch and toast each other.

1983

ANNE TAYLOR FLEMING

Sperm in a Jar

On a beautiful spring day in 1988 I am driving
down the Santa Monica freeway with a jar of my sixty-year-old husband's
sperm in my purse, en route to the Institute for Reproductive Research at
the Hospital of the Good Samaritan in downtown Los Angeles. He is at
home sleeping after having yielded up this specimen, and I am gingerly
maneuvering through the heavy morning traffic with my stash, careful not
to swerve or speed lest I upset my cargo or get stopped by a cop.

This is what we have come to, after sixteen years of marriage: this clin-
ical breeding. Oh, my, how did I get here? I ask myself as I park the car,
surrender the sperm to the lab technician, and take my place in the waiting
room. What quirk of fate, of timing, of biology, has brought me to this
clinic, presided over by Dr. Richard Marrs, one of the new crop of infertility experts who do the procreative bidding of those of us who cannot do
it on our own? A soft-spoken forty-year-old Texan with a specialty in reproductive endocrinology, Dr. Marrs spouts abbreviations for all the out-of-
body pregnancy procedures—I. V. F. (in-vitro fertilization), GIFT (gamete
intra-Fallopian transfer), ZIFT (zygote intra-Fallopian transfer), IUI
(intra-uterine insemination), ITI (intertubal insemination)—with opti-
mism and assurance. His waiting room is full of anxious women from all
over the country, from all over the world.

I am one of them, this sisterhood of the infertile. At thirty-eight, I have entered the high-tech world of postsexual procreation. As I look around at the other women—some in blue jeans, like me, some in suits en route to work, just stopping by to get a shot of sperm before heading out to do battle in corporate America—I smile a small, repressed smile at them and for them. We have sailed together into a strange, surreal country, the Country of the Disembodied Procreators, mutually dedicated to practicing biological warfare against our very own bodies in the hope of reversing time, cheating fate, and getting our hands on an embryo, a baby, a life.

We're hard-core, those of us here. Last-ditchers. And there's a kind of stubborn, exhilarating pride radiating from us. No wimps, we. Toting our small white paper bags of hypodermic needles and hundreds of dollars' worth of fertility drugs, we shoot up once or twice daily with the expertise of junkies, our hips tight and swollen like cheeks with wads of tobacco in them. We are fearless, Amazonian in our baby hunger, bereft. The small waiting room vibrates with our hope.

"Anne."

I go into an examining room, strip from the waist down and take my place in the stirrups. The doctor appears. Boyish and solicitous, his hair beginning to gray like that of many of his patients, he is perfectly cast for his role as procreative assistant to a bunch of desperate women. Gently he inserts the dildo-like scanner and, voilà, my ovaries appear as if by magic on the grainy screen next to me. The doctor and I count together: One, two, three, on the left side; one, two, on the right.

"You have the ovaries of a twenty-five-year-old," he says, reaching for the syringe of my husband's sperm, now washed and sorted and counted. And with one deft whoosh through a thin catheter inserted up through my vagina and cervix, the sperm are sent spinning into my uterus.

I feel nothing, no pain; but strangely enough, tears hover. There is something in the matter-of-fact gentleness with which the doctor folds my legs back up off the stirrups that affects me, a reminder of touch and flesh, normal procreation instead of this cold, solo breeding. I hold the tears until the doctor leaves. In my supine position, which I must maintain for at least fifteen minutes, I imagine the sperm settling in, looking around after their frantic, accelerated journey. I implore my eggs to make their move, to come down my Fallopian tubes into the sperm's frenzied midst, there to be pursued and penetrated.

I drift into a reverie, remembering being pursued and won and indeed penetrated myself as a young college girl in Northern California in the late 1960s. I remember the wonderfully sticky smells that hung over those years, an erotic brew of sweat and incense and marijuana. I remember the aromatic afternoons in bed in my small dorm room, the sun filtering in through the redwoods, the light filigreed across our skin and the spines of my books—Rousseau and Thoreau and Marx and Marcuse. From a record player down the hall Janis Joplin wailed about freedom. A cocoon of passion and politics, of pine trees and patchouli oil. Armed with my contraceptives and my fledgling feminism, I was on the cusp of a fabulous journey. My sisters and I were. We were the golden girls of the brave new world, ready, willing and able to lay our contraceptively endowed bodies across the chasm between the feminine mystique and the world the feminists envisioned. Strong, smart, educated, we were the beneficiaries of unique historical timing, when the doors were opening, the old male-female roles were falling and the world was ours to conquer: the world of men, of lawyers and doctors, astronauts and poets. I wanted in that world. I wanted to matter. I wanted to be somebody. I wanted to send dazzling words out into that world.

Babies didn't cross my mind back then. And not for a long, long time after. I took contraception for granted: birth-control pills briefly in my late teens, then a diaphragm. It became not only a fixed part of my body but also a fixed part of my mind—entrenched, reflexive, the ticket to my female freedom. Not for me an unexpected pregnancy, the fate of women throughout the millennia.

In the early 1970s, when my husband, Karl, whispered above me about wanting to have a baby, I shrank from his ardor. I couldn't imagine it, didn't even feel the connection between lovemaking and baby making, so methodically had I put contraception—and ambition—between my womb and pregnancy. I had been adamant, powerful in my rebuff of the sperm ejaculated into my body, the sperm I am now importuning to do its fertilizing dance.

After all those years of sex without procreation, here I lie, engaged in this procreation without sex. It is a stunning reversal, a cosmic joke. It contains my history, that arc—from all that sex to no sex—a lifetime of trying to be somebody, my whole own woman in the latter half of twentieth-century America, a lifetime of holding motherhood at bay. The nurse gently knocks and I am released. On the freeway heading home, I am already beginning the fourteen-day countdown to the pregnancy test—am I, am I not; am I, am I not—a moment-by-moment monitoring, an imaginary ear to the womb intent on picking up any uterine sign of life.

In my hope and in my angst, I am tempted to roll down the window and shout: "Hey, hey, Gloria! Germaine! Kate! Tell us: How does it feel to have ended up without babies, children, flesh of your flesh? Did you mean to thumb your noses at motherhood, or is that what we heard or intuited for our own needs? Simone, Simone de Beauvoir and Virgina Woolf, can you wade in here too, please, share any regrets, my barren heroines from the great beyond? Tell me: Was your art worth the empty womb—predicated on it, in fact—no children to divert attention, to splinter the focus? Can you tell me, any of you: Am I going to get over this?"

The clouds do not part; no feminist goddess peers down with a benediction on my emptiness. I am on my own here, an agnostic midlife feminist sending up silent prayers to the fertility gods on high. (I also send up apologies to the mothers of yore, the station-wagon moms with their postpartum pounds who felt denigrated in the liberationist heyday by the young, lean, ambitious women like me so intent on making our way.) In my most aggrieved moments I think of infertility as comeuppance for having so fervently and so long delayed motherhood. The data are irrefutable: Fertility declines with age.

How could something as primal as this longing to procreate have been so long repressed, so long buried? Not only am I infertile but, worse, a cliché, a humbled renegade haunting the national imagination, held up as some sort of dupe of feminism, rather a double dupe of the sexual revolution and the women's revolution.

I will persevere in this pregnancy quest. I know that about myself. And as I turn into the driveway I breathe a pride-filled sigh. I can manage this. If it doesn't work this time, I will try again next month and the next. I will be optimistic, as dogged in my pursuit of motherhood as in everything else: Our Lady of the Stirrups, shooting up and running up and down the smoggy L.A. freeways with jars of sperm if need be.

Dr. Marrs and I are having our procreative postmortem. It has been only a matter of months, but it seems a thousand years ago that I was here. After countless inseminations and surgical procedures,

I still do not have a baby. He says the only thing left to offer women like me is—and I almost want to cover my ears because I know full well what's coming—those damn donor eggs. That's the panacea now for us older women who aren't getting pregnant even with high-tech intervention. Am I willing to buy eggs from another woman to make embryos with my husband's sperm and carry them as my own—if I can carry them? This is a daunting new edge to dance on somehow.

He says the odds for donor eggs on an I.V.F. or GIFT procedure go as high as a 25 to 33 percent success rate per cycle, no matter the recipient's age. Big, fat, juicy odds from where I'm sitting. So, are eggs and sperm totally analogous finally, equally purchasable? Is this the logical reduction of liberation, this absolute biological equality?

It strikes me as conceptual hanky-panky—my husband's sperm and another woman's egg. I imagine a stranger floating in my amniotic fluid. What do I tell this child, and when? Ninety percent of the couples who buy eggs do so anonymously, I am told—most clinics won't do otherwise— the same way couples have been buying sperm for so many years. They simply pretend to all concerned that the baby is 100 percent genetically theirs.

Can I do that, be matched up with a woman whose physical characteristics approximate mine and just carry the conceit on to the grave? No. I would have to know that down the road my child could see and meet his or her biological mother. I get dizzy with the moral and emotional ramifications of this. But I am not ready to shut the door, especially since doctors can work their magic even on postmenopausal women. Still, do I really want to be a fifty-year-old first-time mother?

Isn't that finally beyond the limit, procreating in the final trimester of life? Do I want it so bad—to have someone, anyone, doing somersaults in my gut? I can't answer. In fact, there is one other alternative that will allow me my own embryo—not a pregnancy but an embryo. Gestational surrogacy. Rent-a-womb.

A friend of proven fertility has offered to try to carry my embryos for me. It is one of those offers that transcends love. Why not? I can make them, that we know; and she can certainly carry them, or at least has carried her own. But in an offhand moment she says ebulliently, "I'll breast feed them too for a few days, just to get them started," and something in me tenses despite the overweening generosity of her offer.

My babies? You will breast feed my babies? And in that instant I have a sharp inkling of how fine the lines are in all this talk of scrambled eggs and borrowed wombs.

In the meantime, I mourn. Karl doesn't really. We have survived. As the father of four grown sons, he feels no stubborn need for our baby, as I do, as the younger husbands of my friends do. His detachment is faintly annoying but mostly restful.

For me now, it's over, and I set about, as is my writer's wont, trying to reckon with all the mixed messages and complicated choices faced by women over the last decades, looking for clues always to my delayed and unconsummated motherhood. True, those bedeviling baby-making possibilities remain, and I toss them around in the days and weeks and months after I have officially declared my independence from Dr. Marrs and his seductive magic. But I don't begrudge anyone else's choices. Going through this, with all the disapproval from various quarters—friend and foe, feminist and counterfeminist—I am aware of how lonely some decisions can be.

1994

FELICITA GARCIA

I Just Came Out Pregnant

In the following oral history, taped in 1980, Felicita Garcia, a twenty-year-old Puerto Rican who grew up in New York City, talks about what it meant in her life to become pregnant at sixteen. Her narrative brings into question a number of prevailing assumptions about the problems of teen-age pregnancy and promiscuity.

When Felicita became pregnant, she was forced to leave school, and she went to live with the man she calls "my daughter's father." For four years, she stayed home with her daughter Zindy, but she never gave up her zeal to "be somebody." When Zindy learned to talk, Felicita left her daughter's father, in part because he wouldn't allow her to go back to school, and moved back in with her mother, a forty-seven-year-old woman who still has young children at home. For the next few years, Felicita continued to work and she also tried to save money for school. She attended Drake Business School and is currently enrolled at the College of Staten Island, where she is studying social work. She doesn't know how she will pay for four years of college, since welfare "told me that it is against the law for me to go to school for four years," but she plans to do it "somehow or other." Despite the uncertain conditions of her life, Felicita has an extraordinary buoyancy and warmth. She tells the teenage girls she meets now, "If you're not a virgin, take pills and think about your future," but, she says, in her own life she found the strength to struggle for a future at least in part because she had her daughter. "I want a future for myself," she says, "to show her that she could do it too."

As Felicita spoke, her daughter—a gravely beautiful child in a red smock dress, her hair tied neatly to the sides with red yarn—tended a brindled puppy in a cardboard box. Sharon Thompson conducted the interview. It is one of a series she is gathering on teenage romance and sexuality.

I was only sixteen when I came out pregnant. I had to leave school and everything. The school didn't want me. They wanted to send me away, and it was like, "No, I don't want to go away. I don't want to lose my family. This is all I am."

I went through changes with her father. He hurt me a lot. I was fifteen when I met him and I was a virgin. He'll be twenty-six now. He's five years older than me. He claimed I wasn't a virgin and maybe that kid is not his. He hurt me, I guess, because I was his first virgin and I was young. I was his only girlfriend that was a virgin. They were always womens that he had. He was just scared. He told my girlfriend he was just scared I was going to leave him. He said I was so pretty and there were a lot of guys that would look at me. That's why he was the way he was to me—because he was afraid he was going to lose me. I told him it was wrong of him because if he would have trusted me and given me a little space to breathe, then I would have been with him. It would have been different and gotten me what I wanted. But I like my freedom.

I hadn't expected to come out pregnant. I was so naive. I didn't figure I would come out pregnant in a couple of months, and when I found out, I broke down. "Oh my God, my mother's going to kill me." That's what I kept saying. "My mother's going to kill me." Father was the one who was the strict one in the house. Father always said, "If your mother wouldn't have broke up, this wouldn't have happened to none of you. You know, it wouldn't have been like that." 'Cause we were straight A's in school. We all had 95's always in school, and we were straight because of my father. We knew how strict he was, and we were always goody-goody in school. We were with my father until my brother was about two years old. I was about twelve or thirteen. I cried because I was so close to my father. I was daddy's little girl, and my father spoiled me in his own way, and I was so hurt because I didn't have my father, and I didn't want to live down here in Manhattan. We used to live in Brooklyn in the projects, and there were nights down here I couldn't sleep because I would hear the mice, and there were roaches crawling onto the walls, and I wasn't used to all that. It blew my mind because down here I found everything strange. So strange. I was used to living with mainly black people. There were a few Puerto Rican but the majority were black people. When I came down here, it freaked me out because there was so much dope out on the street, all the shooting out here. I couldn't understand.

Before I moved here, all I knew about sex was where the baby came from—in the stomach. I was very naive when I first moved down here, and then I started learning about sex. My girlfriend? Her brother had little porno films and I was watching and it was like, "Oh my God!" You know, you'd be watching. You'd always find somebody touching somebody out in the street or somewhere. Somebody would take off their clothes. You always would catch somebody doing something. It was like, "Oh my God, look what they doing!" In the hall, behind the stairs, on the roof, you'd catch somebody going to bed with each other. Anywhere. They're going to bed with anybody anywhere. It was like, "Oh my God, I didn't know they do that."

You had to be fast to live out here. To catch up on life out here, and that's how it is. That's how come so many girls come out pregnant, 'cause they're so grown. You grow up fast over here. When I was fourteen, I thought I was a woman. I came over here when I was thirteen. When I hit fourteen, I thought I was about eighteen years old. I was going out dancing and partying, coming home at three and four o'clock in the morning. Sometimes I'd come home at ten o'clock in the morning. My mother would slap me down, but there were places that let you in. I had a fake ID. I went in. I partied all night. I came home like nothing.

But you had to be grown to live out here. You had to catch up on everything. The guys just wanted to get something out of you and that's it. I didn't let nobody touch me until I met my daughter's father, and my girlfriend said, "It's all right. Nothing will happen." I said, "I don't want to come out pregnant." She said, "It doesn't matter if you come out pregnant. You'll have your baby. It'll be all right." Everything was the positive side. She never told me, "Well, you're going to go through changes and get stuck up." Everything was the positive side.

In my mother's house, I had so much freedom. I used to have guy friends, and they used to come to my room, and it was all right. But then my mother was living with this man in my house, and it blew all our minds. She was living with somebody else, and he was fresh. I guess that's what made me want to leave out of my house more. Because I told my mother, "Before he abuses me, I'd rather let somebody else do it, a man that I would really want for him to do it." She didn't say nothing back. It blew her mind. She didn't know what to do. I was always going out. I would just tell her, "Mommy, I'll be back in a couple hours," and disappear. He was following me, too. I didn't know it, but there were times that he would follow me, and his daughter told me that he tried to abuse her. I was scared, and I didn't know what to do. Then my father found out, and he wanted to take my mother to court, and I told him, "Don't do that to her." He said, "I'm going to take her to court and put her away." I said, "No, no, please. Leave her alone. Don't bother her." Because wherever my mother went, we went behind her. She always took us everywhere. She never left us behind with nobody at all. So it was always, "Mommy, mommy, mommy, mommy," everything.

Then when I first had sex, I felt dirty. I felt real dirty. I said, "Oh my God, my mother's going to know that I'm dirty and that I let him touch me." I didn't talk to him for a while. I had sex at his mother's house the first time. It was in his mother's house.

I was four months when I told my sister I come out pregnant. I didn't tell nobody till four months. To this day, I never told my mother I was pregnant. She knew. The mothers know, I guess.

I was scared. I didn't know what was going to happen. Where was I going to live? I had my own room in my mother's house and my mother gave me everything I wanted. I didn't know what was going to happen with the baby's father. Are we going to last? What about the baby? I thought ahead to her future. How was it going to be for her? I said, "When I have my baby, I want the best for my baby. No matter how I am going to do it, I am going to give her the best."

My sister said, "Well, think about it. It's hard. It's really hard to have a baby." I would tell her, "I know," but it was like, I don't know it yet because I haven't gone through it. But I was telling her, "I know." So I said, "Don't worry, don't worry. Her father is going to get us an apartment." And I would tell her, "Don't tell me what to do. You have your own life, so live your own life." We weren't close. We were never close until we came out pregnant and our bellies were real big. Now we are like best of friends. I'm close with my mother now, too. Very close. And there are times when I tell her I'm sorry.

When I was about six months pregnant, I moved out of my mother's house, and I went to live with my daughter's father. I used to wash his clothes in the washing machine around two blocks away, and I had to carry a big basket full of clothes down the stairs with my belly. I had nobody to help me. Or I was always kneeling and washing his clothes by hand. I was doing like oldtime rough work, and I couldn't believe it. My mother used to tell me, "Felicita, if you want, stay with me. You don't have to go to that." And I told her, "No, mommy. That's my baby's father. I have to do it." I was always cooking and cleaning and mopping, and I used to get pains in my stomach because I was constantly moving dressers and everything. I was moving the clothes up and down from off the floor.

I went to the hospital one day for my appointment, and the doctor told me he'd leave me in because I was carrying my baby so low, and I was swollen. I used to eat a lot, and I was gaining a lot of weight. I went up to 179 pounds from 100, and the doctor told me my ankles were swollen, I had toxemia, and he told me he was going to leave me in. I said, "I'm not supposed to give birth yet. I've still got two more weeks." He said, "No, we've got to leave you in." They took me downstairs. They said, "We're going to check you in, Felicita." I called up my mommy. I said, "Mommy, mommy, they're going to leave me in the hospital." My daughter's father came and he brought my pajamas and clothes, and then they took me down, and they induced labor. I was having convulsions when I was in labor, and my blood pressure went up, and I had fever, too.

When I was in labor, I kept telling my mother to forgive me for everything I've done to her. That's what I kept telling her. "Mommy, mommy, I'm sorry. I'm sorry for all the pain I gave you." I said, "Now I know what it is for you to have a child." She started crying and crying, and I told her, "I'm sorry, mommy. I'm sorry. I didn't mean for it to end this way." I told her I was sorry because I hurt her. I yelled at her. All the things that a kid does when they yell at their mother and talk back and because I just came out pregnant and never told her and I hurt her a lot because I was the baby of the girls. Because it was just me and my sister were the only girls, and I got four brothers. When I was pregnant, she'd ask me what was wrong and

I'd tell her, "Nothing, mommy, nothing nothing." There was nothing wrong. And I just told her, "Mommy, forgive me. I didn't mean for it to end this way." She had wanted me to finish school. She would tell me, "Felicita, do you want the baby? You could keep it. It's up to you. If you want to have an abortion, it's up to you." She said, "You're not a little girl anymore. It's up to you. Just remember it's a big responsibility," and I told her, "Mommy, this is my first child. If I'm woman enough to do something like this, then I'm woman enough to keep this child. If other girls want to give up their babies, that's them. But I feel that if I'm woman enough to make a mistake like this, then this is my responsibility to keep this child."

As the baby came out, that's when they put me to sleep. I didn't get to see her. I didn't see her for two days because my fever was up and my blood pressure was up high. Everybody saw my baby except me. And then I had her. I just remember her head was smashed a little on one side, and I said, "Oh my God, my baby's going to come out with a busted head," and I thought it was all the struggling I did. That I hurt her. But the lady said, "It'll grow back to normal," and that's what happened. In a couple of days, her head went round. She was real hairy. All over her face, she had hair. I got scared. I said, "Wow, I got a hairy baby."

After a while, I couldn't believe that she was mine. I was tripped on it. I took off all her clothes. I said, "This is mine. Really mine." I cried nights with her because I couldn't sleep. I wouldn't take naps during the day while she was asleep. I was always cleaning. You know, washing her clothes. Taking care of the house. Cooking for my mother. I stayed for a while with my mother. Not too long. About a week. Then I moved out. Then I was doing everything on my own. Then I was living with her father. Then I had to deal with him. We lived together for almost four years and then I decided to leave him.

He always wanted me to be a housewife, and I wanted to be some-body. I wanted to go to school, to do something. He wouldn't let me go to school or do something. He stopped me from school and everything. He always had me home. Home, home, home, home. I would go out with my daughter to my girlfriend's house in Brooklyn and that's it. Home. He would go out, go to the movies with his friends and everything. He only took me to the movies twice in three years and that's it. I never got to go anywhere. After we broke up, I went crazy. I went dancing. I went to places I hadn't been—to museums that I haven't been to since I was young, and I got to see New York. And it's been fun. I've been enjoying every minute of it. I've been dressing up better. I've lost weight. I make myself look good. Before, I didn't care what I looked like. I was getting fat, and he was helping me get fat. He was no help. He didn't care if I blew up like an elephant.

About a year after we were living together, he hit me. He slapped me when we were arguing, and I went to hit him back, and he slapped me, and I said, "I can't hit him because he's going to beat me." Then I ran away from home for a week. He said, "I'm sorry. I'll never do it again." I said, "No, I don't want to live with you anymore, because if I keep living with you, you're going to keep hitting me. No," I said, "I'm not a ragdoll for you to be hitting on me." He said, "Okay." He apologized. He said, "I won't hit you anymore." I said, "Okay." I went back to him and three years later I left him. He gave me two black eyes after we left each other and everything because I answered him back, you know. He started to talk to me dirty. He never talked to me dirty and I told him, "I am not no cheap little tramp for you to talk to me like that. You know." But he hit me and I just went in back of him and he just whacked me one, you know. And I said, "No, I don't need to deal with that. I don't need it. I don't need no mens to touch me." I said, "The next man that touched me, I'll pick up a stick or something. I am going to crack his head to show him that I'm no little piece of doll that he should beat me. Or his child." I used to tell my daughter's father, "I'm not your child. I might be young, but I am not your child for you to scold me and demand me to do something. If I want to do it, I'll do it of my own will—not because you say so or because you're the boss." I tell him, "I could be my own boss. It's not always what you say."

Finally, I decided, I'll wait until my baby goes to the bathroom and when she stops her bottle and her Pampers, I'll wait till she's three, and she's learned how to talk well, and then I'll leave him and go to work, and I'll leave her with my mother to babysit. Because I'll know then if something happens, she talks to me. She tells me everything. Because I said in case mama is not around, and I need to leave her with a babysitter, if anything happened, my daughter could tell me. So I said, "I'd rather wait until she is big enough before I go to work." I wanted to go to school, but I needed money, so I said I'd have to get a job.

I want the best for my little girl. I want to give her everything. I don't take money from him for myself. I tell him, "You want to see your daughter? You buy her things, because I don't want you to say that I used up her money. So you buy her what she needs and that'll be good enough for me."

In the beginning, he threatened to cut my face when I left him. It took almost a year for him to leave me alone. He was always pushing and pulling me and telling me and trying to put me down. I went into a depression. I was getting sick, and I almost had a nervous breakdown. I was afraid to leave my house. He was always threatening me. Finally I told him how sick I was getting, and, well, then he stopped. He said, "Okay. I'm sorry. I didn't mean to get you like that, but I couldn't believe that you left me." I said, "But I told you I was leaving a month before." And then he understood.

Now everything is his daughter, and he always says, "Take care of yourself." He's always asking if I need anything. I tell him, "No, I don't need nothing." I never asked him for anything, not even when we lived together. I always supported myself because I didn't want to ask him for anything. If I would ask him for anything, he would tell me, "For what?" I would tell him, "What do you do with your money?" He would tell me, "It's none of your business." So I said, "Okay. You keep your money. I'll take care of myself. I don't need you. Put it that way: I don't need you or any other man."

I like it better this way.

I don't want no more kids because I don't want to have a child from another father and go through the changes that my daughter has a stepfather. That father will treat my daughter a little different than the second child I have, and I don't want her to go through that because I seen what my sister went through with my father. My father raised her since she was two but my father was always hard on her, and I said, "But that's not her father, for him to be hitting her." I say now, "I don't want no man to touch my child." I guess I'm selfish with her. I say, "If I want, I'll remarry when she's big and on her own." I don't want no more children unless me and her father decide, well, okay, we'll have another one. But I wouldn't want to have competition with two kids. It could be different. Maybe he'll treat my daughter good, but I don't want to take a chance with that. I don't want nobody to hurt my child. I've been hurt too much in my life. My sister's been hurt and I guess the pain that she's hurt I feel, and I don't want my daughter to go through that. I'm so afraid for somebody to push or hit her. You know, I have this boyfriend, and he hit her one time, and I practically jumped him. He hit her on the hand, and I told him, "If you ever touch my child again, I will kill you. Don't touch my child." Nobody touches my child but my mother while she's with her. That's it. Nobody. Not even her father hits her.

This organization I work for, it works with youth, and there are a lot of young girls come around here. I tell them, "If you're not a virgin, take pills and think about the future. Go to school." I tell them, "Look where I'm at now. Without a diploma, it's hard to find a job. I've got a lot of experience because I volunteered and everything. But you can't volunteer for the rest of your life. You have to get somewhere in this world." I tell them, "Keep going to school and if you're a virgin, don't make the mistake." I tell them, it's a big responsibility to have a child. I say, "You know what you do? Babysit somebody's child and you'll know what it is to have that child all day with you." They don't know what it is. "Babysit," I tell them. "You babysit a small baby, a couple months old? Ask if you can stay with that baby for overnight. Stay in their house and let the baby sit in your room, and you'll see how it feels to be a mother in one night." I say, "Think about your life, your future." I say, "Be free and enjoy life as much as you could and don't get no man that can't give you anything." I say, "Because none of these mens out here ain't going to give you anything." I say, "Suppose you get a boyfriend that gets $125 a week, and the rent is $200. How do you expect to support each other with $125 a week? You can't do nothing," I tell them. "You can't." I say, "I could barely make it, me and my child, and I live with my mother, and you're going to go living with somebody else?" They say, "It's true, what you're saying." I say, "I'm not saying that don't have a child. Don't get a boyfriend. But look for your happiness first. What you want in life. What you want to be in life. And try to be somebody, and not just fall back. Keep going up ahead." I remind them all the time. I ask them everyday, "Did you go to school?" They tell me, "Yes." I say, "Good. How did you do in school?" And they tell me like, "I did okay." If they're not in school, I ask them why. I tell them, "I don't want to find out that you're out of school, because I'm going to squeal on you. I'm going to call up the school and say you played hooky. I'm only playing, but it's for your own good. It's not for me," I tell them. "It's for you." I say, "Be somebody. That's all. Just be somebody." And I say, "Once you're somebody, you don't have to worry about nothing else. As long as you got a good-paying job, then if you feel like you want to have a child, then you have a child. But go to school and enjoy yourselves. That's all. Don't get hooked up. Enjoy life." I tell them, "Don't let no man beat you. Don't let no man hit on you." I tell them, "He'll make you stay home and be a housewife."

I still mean to make something of myself. I want to be like a social worker or a counselor. I always like to work with young people or kids. Since I was little, I was always babysitting. Now I see the kids I babysat for and they are taller than I am, and I say, "I used to babysit him! I used to change his Pampers!" And that's still what I want to be.

I like my life now. I do what I want. I don't need to do anything for nobody but for my child. I try my best for her. I want a future for myself to show her that she could do it too. I don't want her to have the teenage life I had. I want her to see the world. I want her to go places. I want her to go out and enjoy herself and not to get caught up as young as I did for nobody. I want for her to be free. I don't want her to go through changes. I went through changes my whole teenage life. I can't say I enjoyed my teenage life. Now is when I'm enjoying myself.

1983

MARY GORDON

A Moral Choice

I am having lunch with six women. What is unusual is that four of them are in their seventies, two of them widowed, the other two living with husbands beside whom they've lived for decades. All of them have had children. Had they been men, they would have published books and hung their paintings on the walls of important galleries. But they are women of a certain generation, and their lives were shaped around their families and personal relations. They are women you go to for help and support. We begin talking about the latest legislative act that makes abortion more difficult for poor women to obtain. An extraordinary thing happens. Each of them talks about the illegal abortions she had during her young womanhood. Not one of them was spared the experience. Any of them could have died on the table of whatever person (not a doctor in any case) she was forced to approach, in secrecy and in terror, to end a pregnancy that she felt would blight her life.

I mention this incident for two reasons: first as a reminder that all kinds of women have always had abortions; second because it is essential that we remember that an abortion is performed on a living woman who has a life in which a terminated pregnancy is only a small part. Morally speaking, the decision to have an abortion doesn't take place in a vacuum. It is connected to other choices that a woman makes in the course of an adult life.

Anti-choice propagandists paint pictures of women who choose to have abortions as types of moral callousness, selfishness, or irresponsibility. The woman choosing to abort is the dressed-for-success yuppie who gets rid of her baby so that she won't miss her Caribbean vacation or her chance for promotion. Or she is the feckless, promiscuous ghetto teenager who couldn't bring herself to just say no to sex. A third, purportedly kinder, gentler picture has recently begun to be drawn. The woman in the abortion clinic is there because she is misinformed about the nature of the world. She is having an abortion because society does not provide for mothers and their children, and she mistakenly thinks that another mouth to feed will be the ruin of her family, not understanding that the temporary truth of family unhappiness doesn't stack up beside the eternal verity that abortion is murder. Or she is the dupe of her husband or boyfriend, who talks her into having an abortion because a child will be a drag on his life-style. None of these pictures created by the anti-choice movement assumes that the decision to have an abortion is made responsibly, in the context of a morally lived life, by a free and responsible moral agent.

THE ONTOLOGY OF THE FETUS

How would a woman who habitually makes choices in moral terms come to the decision to have an abortion? The moral discussion of abortion centers on the issue of whether or not abortion is an act of murder. At first glance it would seem that the answer should follow directly upon two questions: Is the fetus human? and Is it alive? It would be absurd to deny that a fetus is alive or that it is human. What would our other options be—to say that it is inanimate or belongs to another species? But we habitually use the terms "human" and "live" to refer to parts of our body—"human hair," for example, or "live red-blood cells"—and we are clear in our understanding that the nature of these objects does not rank equally with an entire personal existence. It then seems important to consider whether the fetus, this alive human thing, is a *person*, to whom the term "murder" could sensibly be applied. How would anyone come to a decision about something so impalpable as personhood? Philosophers have struggled with the issue of personhood, but in language that is so abstract that it is unhelpful to ordinary people making decisions in the course of their lives. It might be more productive to begin thinking about the status of the fetus by examining the language and customs that surround it. This approach will encourage us to focus on the choosing, acting woman, rather than the act of abortion—as if the act were performed by abstract forces without bodies, histories, attachments.

This focus on the acting woman is useful because a pregnant woman has an identifiable, consistent ontology, and a fetus takes on different ontological identities over time. But common sense, experience, and linguistic usage point clearly to the fact that we habitually consider, for example, a seven-week-old fetus to be different from a seven-month-old one. We can tell this by the way we respond to the involuntary loss of one as against the other. We have different language for the experience of the involuntary expulsion of the fetus from the womb depending upon the point of gestation at which the experience occurs. If it occurs early in the pregnancy, we call it a miscarriage; if late, we call it a stillbirth.

We would have an extreme reaction to the reversal of those terms. If a woman referred to a miscarriage at seven weeks as a stillbirth, we would be alarmed. It would shock our sense of propriety; it would make us uneasy; we would find it disturbing, misplaced—as we do when a bag lady sits down in a restaurant and starts shouting, or an octogenarian arrives at our door in a sailor suit. In short, we would suspect that the speaker was mad. Similarly, if a doctor or a nurse referred to the loss of a seven-month-old fetus as a miscarriage, we would be shocked by that person's insensitivity: could she or he not understand that a fetus that age is not what it was months before?

Our ritual and religious practices underscore the fact that we make distinctions among fetuses. If a woman took the bloody matter—indistinguishable from a heavy period—of an early miscarriage and insisted upon putting it in a tiny coffin and marking its grave, we would have serious concerns about her mental health. By the same token, we would feel squeamish about flushing a seven-month-old fetus down the toilet—something we would quite normally do with an early miscarriage. There are no prayers for the matter of a miscarriage, nor do we feel there should be. Even a Catholic priest would not baptize the issue of an early miscarriage.

The difficulties stem, of course, from the odd situation of a fetus's ontology: a complicated, differentiated, and nuanced response is required when we are dealing with an entity that changes over time. Yet we are in the habit of making distinctions like this. At one point we know that a child is no longer a child but an adult. That this question is vexed and problematic is clear from our difficulty in determining who is a juvenile offender and who is an adult criminal and at what age sexual intercourse ceases to be known as statutory rape. So at what point, if any, do we on the pro-choice side say that the developing fetus is a person, with rights equal to its mother's?

The anti-choice people have one advantage over us; their monolithic position gives them unity on this question. For myself, I am made uneasy by third-trimester abortions, which take place when the fetus could live outside the mother's body, but I also know that these are extremely rare and often performed on very young girls who have had difficulty comprehending the realities of pregnancy. It seems to me that the question of late abortions should be decided case by case, and that fixation on this issue is a deflection from what is most important: keeping early abortions, which are in the majority by far, safe and legal. I am also politically realistic enough to suspect that bills restricting late abortions are not good-faith attempts to make distinctions about the nature of fetal life. They are, rather, the cynical embodiments of the hope among anti-choice partisans that technology will be on their side and that medical science's ability to create situations in which younger fetuses are viable outside their mothers' bodies will increase dramatically in the next few years. Ironically, medical science will probably make the issue of abortion a minor one in the near future. The RU-486 pill, which can induce abortion early on, exists, and whether or not it is legally available (it is not on the market here, because of pressure from anti-choice groups), women will begin to obtain it. If abortion can occur through chemical rather than physical means, in the privacy of one's home, most people not directly involved will lose interest in it. As abortion is transformed from a public into a private issue, it will cease to be perceived as political; it will be called personal instead.

AN EQUIVOCAL GOOD

But because abortion will always deal with what it is to create and sustain life, it will always be a moral issue. And whether we like it or not, our moral thinking about abortion is rooted in the shifting soil of perception. In an age in which much of our perception is manipulated by media that specialize in the sound bite and the photo op, the anti-choice partisans have a twofold advantage over us on the pro-choice side. The pro-choice moral position is more complex, and the experience we defend is physically repellent to contemplate. None of us in the pro-choice movement would suggest that abortion is not a regrettable occurrence. Anti-choice proponents can offer pastel photographs of babies in buntings, their eyes peaceful in the camera's gaze. In answer, we can't offer the material of an early abortion, bloody, amorphous in a paper cup, to prove that what has just been removed from the woman's body is not a child, not in the same category of being as the adorable bundle in an adoptive mother's arms. It is not a pleasure to look at the physical evidence of abortion, and most of us don't get the opportunity to do so.

The theologian Daniel Maguire, uncomfortable with the fact that most theological arguments about the nature of abortion are made by men who have never been anywhere near an actual abortion, decided to visit a clinic and observe abortions being performed. He didn't find the experience easy, but he knew that before he could in good conscience make a moral judgment on abortion, he needed to experience through his senses what an aborted fetus is like: he needed to look at and touch the controversial entity. He held in his hand the bloody fetal stuff; the eight-week-old fetus fit in the palm of his hand, and it certainly bore no resemblance to either of his two children when he had held them moments after their birth. He knew at that point what women who have experienced early abortions and miscarriages know: that some event occurred, possibly even a dramatic one, but it was not the death of a child.

Because issues of pregnancy and birth are both physical and metaphorical, we must constantly step back and forth between ways of perceiving the world. When we speak of gestation, we are often talking in terms of potential, about events and objects to which we attach our hopes, fears, dreams, and ideals. A mother can speak to the fetus in her uterus and name it; she and her mate may decorate a nursery according to their vision of the good life; they may choose for an embryo a college, a profession, a dwelling. But those of us who are trying to think morally about pregnancy and birth must remember that these feelings are our own projections onto what is in reality an inappropriate object. However charmed we may be by an expectant father's buying a little football for something inside his wife's belly, we shouldn't make public policy based on such actions, nor should we force others to live their lives conforming to our fantasies.

As a society, we are making decisions that pit the complicated future of a complex adult against the fate of a mass of cells lacking cortical development. The moral pressure should be on distinguishing the true from the false, the real suffering of living persons from our individual and often idiosyncratic dreams and fears. We must make decisions on abortion based on an understanding of how people really do live. We must be able to say that poverty is worse than not being poor, that having dignified and meaningful work is better than working in conditions of degradation, that raising a child one loves and has desired is better than raising a child in resentment and rage, that it is better for a twelve-year-old not to endure the trauma of having a child when she is herself a child.

When we put these ideas against the ideas of "child" or "baby," we seem to be making a horrifying choice of life-style over life. But in fact we are telling the truth of what it means to bear a child, and what the experience of abortion really is. This is extremely difficult, for the object of the discussion is hidden, changing, potential. We make our decisions on the basis of approximate and inadequate language, often on the basis of fantasies and fears. It will always be crucial to try to separate genuine moral concern from phobia, punitiveness, superstition, anxiety, a desperate search for certainty in an uncertain world.

One of the certainties that is removed if we accept the consequences of the pro-choice position is the belief that the birth of a child is an unequivocal good. In real life we act knowing that the birth of a child is not always a good thing: people are sometimes depressed, angry, rejecting, at the birth of a child. But this is a difficult truth to tell; we don't like to say it, and one of the fears preyed on by anti-choice proponents is that if we cannot look at the birth of a child as an unequivocal good, then there is nothing to look toward. The desire for security of the imagination, for typological fixity, particularly in the area of "the good," is an understandable desire. It must seem to some anti-choice people that we on the pro-choice side are not only murdering innocent children but also murdering hope. Those of us who have experienced the birth of a desired child and felt the joy of that moment can be tempted into believing that it was the physical experience of the birth itself that was the joy. But it is crucial to remember that the birth of a child itself is a neutral occurrence emotionally: the charge it takes on is invested in it by the people experiencing or observing it.

THE FEAR OF
SEXUAL AUTONOMY

These uncertainties can lead to another set of fears, not only about abortion but about its implications. Many anti-choice people fear that to support abortion is to cast one's lot with the cold and technological rather than with the warm and natural, to head down the slippery slope toward a brave new world where handicapped children are left on mountains to starve and the old are put out in the snow. But if we look at the history of abortion, we don't see the embodiment of what the anti-choice proponents fear. On the contrary, excepting the grotesque counterexample of the People's Republic of China (which practices forced abortion), there seems to be a real link between repressive anti-abortion stances and repressive governments. Abortion was banned in Fascist Italy and Nazi Germany; it is illegal in South Africa and in Chile. It is paid for by the governments of Denmark, England, and the Netherlands, which have national health and welfare systems that foster the health and well-being of mothers, children, the old, and the handicapped.

Advocates of outlawing abortion often refer to women seeking abortion as self-indulgent and materialistic. In fact these accusations mask a discomfort with female sexuality, sexual pleasure, and sexual autonomy. It is possible for a woman to have a sexual life unriddled by fear only if she can be confident that she need not pay for a failure of technology or judgment (and who among us has never once been swept away in the heat of a sexual moment?) by taking upon herself the crushing burden of unchosen motherhood.

It is no accident, therefore, that the increased appeal of measures to restrict maternal conduct during pregnancy—and a new focus on the physical autonomy of the pregnant woman—have come into public discourse at precisely the time when women are achieving unprecedented levels of economic and political autonomy. What has surprised me is that some of this new anti-autonomy talk comes to us from the left. An example of this new discourse is an article by Christopher Hitchens that appeared in *The Nation* last April, in which the author asserts his discomfort with abortion. Hitchens's tone is impeccably British: arch, light, we're men of the left.

> Anyone who has ever seen a sonogram or has spent even an hour with a textbook on embryology knows that the emotions are not the deciding factor. In order to terminate a pregnancy, you have to still a heartbeat, switch off a developing brain, and whatever the method, break some bones and rupture some organs. As to whether this involves pain on the "Silent Scream" scale, I have no idea. The "right to life" leadership, again, has cheapened everything it touches.

"It is a pity," Hitchens goes on to say, "that . . . the majority of feminists and their allies have stuck to the dead ground of 'Me Decade' possessive individualism, an ideology that has more in common than it admits with the prehistoric right, which it claims to oppose but has in fact encouraged." Hitchens proposes, as an alternative, a program of social reform that would make contraception free and support a national adoption service. In his opinion, it would seem, women have abortions for only two reasons: because they are selfish or because they are poor. If the state will take care of the economic problems and the bureaucratic messiness around adoption, it remains only for the possessive individualists to get their act together and walk with their babies into the communal utopia of the future. Hitchens would allow victims of rape or incest to have free abortions, on the grounds that since they didn't choose to have sex, the women should not be forced to have the babies. This would seem to put the issue of volition in a wrong and telling place. To Hitchens's mind, it would appear, if a woman chooses to have sex, she can't choose whether or not to have a baby. The implications of this are clear. If a woman is consciously and volitionally sexual, she should be prepared to take her medicine. And what medicine must the consciously sexual male take? Does Hitchens really believe, or want us to believe, that every male who has unintentionally impregnated a woman will be involved in the lifelong responsibility for the upbringing of the engendered child? Can he honestly say that he has observed this behavior—or, indeed, would want to see it observed—in the world in which he lives?

REAL CHOICES

It is essential for a moral decision about abortion to be made in an atmosphere of open, critical thinking. We on the pro-choice side must accept that there are indeed anti-choice activists who take their position in good faith. I believe, however, that they are people for whom childbirth is an emotionally overladen topic, people who are susceptible to unclear thinking because of their unrealistic hopes and fears. It is important for us in the pro-choice movement to be open in discussing those areas involving abortion which are nebulous and unclear. But we must not forget that there are some things that we know to be undeniably true. There are some undeniable bad consequences of a woman's being forced to bear a child against her will. First is the trauma of going through a pregnancy and giving birth to a child who is not desired, a trauma more long-lasting than that experienced by some (only some) women who experience an early abortion. The grief of giving up a child at its birth—and at nine months it is a child whom one has felt move inside one's body—is underestimated both by anti-choice partisans and by those for whom access to adoptable children is important. This grief should not be forced on any woman—or, indeed, encouraged by public policy.

We must be realistic about the impact on society of millions of unwanted children in an overpopulated world. Most of the time, human beings have sex not because they want to make babies. Yet throughout history sex has resulted in unwanted pregnancies. And women have always aborted. One thing that is not hidden, mysterious, or debatable is that making abortion illegal will result in the deaths of women, as it has always done. Is our historical memory so short that none of us remember aunts, sisters, friends, or mothers who were killed or rendered sterile by septic abortions? Does no one in the anti-choice movement remember stories or actual experiences of midnight drives to filthy rooms from which aborted women were sent out, bleeding, to their fate? Can anyone genuinely say that it would be a moral good for us as a society to return to those conditions?

Thinking about abortion, then, forces us to take moral positions as adults who understand the complexities of the world and the realities of human suffering, to make decisions based on how people actually live and choose, and not on our fears, prejudices, and anxieties about sex and society, life and death.

1990

Consequences

In 1958, I had an illegal abortion. I was nineteen, a senior in college, an English major. Marriage was not an option: the boyfriend was my age but he was a sophomore majoring in basketball. When I met him after practice and told him I was pregnant, the panic in his eyes infuriated me. I assured him I didn't want to get married. The panic remained. The poor guy was terrified for my sake but he didn't know what to say or do. He started to cry, then caught himself and punched the cinderblock wall of the gym, breaking his hand and getting himself benched for the season.

I didn't know what to do, either. In all honesty, I wasn't even sure how I'd gotten into this fix. Many women of my generation believed you could get pregnant from a toilet seat but were never quite clear about how you got pregnant from a man. Our sexual gospel was full of axioms like "you can't get pregnant if you do it standing up" and "no one gets pregnant the first time." I needed two missed periods to believe that it had happened to me.

Finally I told my roommate. She was as innocent as I was of such matters, but she persuaded me to confide in our dorm counselor, a kindly woman who coached girls' field hockey. The coach hugged me as I sobbed, but didn't lecture me; she let me vent my misery, answered my questions, and made sure I understood my options and their repercussions. In biology texts, I'd seen that at this stage a pregnancy is a mass of cells, not a "child." I told her I had decided to have an abortion, an early, immediate abortion.

She was nonjudgmental, but given the criminal penalties at the time was afraid to get involved in my search for a doctor. She convinced me to have a pregnancy test, at least, to confirm my suspicions. The test came back positive. For about forty-eight hours, I thought about killing myself.

For those who didn't live through the '50s, it's hard to believe the suffocating terror of sexual shame and the coercive power of social propriety. In those years, etiquette demanded that women not wear white before Memorial Day or after Labor Day, so you can imagine the moral absolutes. For a well-bred middle-class girl, pregnancy "out of wedlock" was the ultimate disgrace, and in the Jewish community in which I grew up, it was a *shonda*, a scandal discussed in contemptuous whispers behind closed doors.

The category "single mothers" did not exist then. A woman could be a married mother, a widow with children, or a "divorcée" with children, but unless her body was legitimized by marriage, the fruit of her womb was "illegitimate," and she herself forfeited the right to travel in polite company or win a respectable husband in the future. As a result, young pregnant women were quickly pressed into "shotgun" marriages or else, under a canopy of lies—"she's caring for a sick aunt in Cleveland"—were spirited away to "homes for unwed mothers" where they disappeared from view, like lepers, until the pregnancy ran its course. Until they gave birth among strangers and left their babies to be adopted by strangers.

I could not tolerate that idea. It seemed wrong to make pregnancy the punishment for my sexual activity (especially when, for the same activity, the young man would get off with some angst and a broken hand). And it seemed crazy to consider adoption a "solution." I would not carry a child for a full nine months, feel it move inside my body, endure morning sickness, swollen legs, and the pain of labor only to have my baby taken away from me. I could never live in a world where a child of mine was being raised by someone else.

I wanted to be a mother, someday. I wanted to create a new life and give it the same loving, well-fed childhood my mother gave me. But I would not be an accidental mother, an ashamed mother, an impoverished mother, a hostile mother, or what today is termed a "birth mother"—one who brings a child into the world but cannot share its life.

Even in 1958, I did not confuse my capacity to breed with my capability to mother. One day, I thought, I will be a terrific parent, but at nineteen I was still raising myself out of adolescence, four years after my own mother died. She was my model of sensitivity, understanding, and patience. Because of her, I had great respect for what it takes to be a good parent. I wanted to be worthy of the job. I would not be a mother before I could be an adult.

With single parenthood and adoption out of the question, abortion was my choice, the *only* choice for me. But where could I turn for money and help?

My father, a lawyer, subscribed to traditional gender roles except when it came to me and money. Earning his own living at an early age had been the making of him, he said, and he insisted it would be character-building for me, even though I was a girl. He paid for college, but I had to earn my spending money, which I did by taking summer jobs, tutoring athletes, and working for the Hillel rabbi on campus. For all my bootstrap efforts, $12 was what I had left in the bank after I paid for the pregnancy test. I had to ask my father for help; there was no one else.

He was the sort of man who could talk about French conjugations or the First Amendment but not about problems or emotions. Paralyzed with fear, I finally breathed out the words: "Daddy, I'm pregnant, and I can't afford an abortion." His expression never changed; there was no moralizing, no scolding, but also no comfort. Nurturing wasn't his style. He went straight for the practical issues: who, when, and how much. He said he would take care of the arrangements and lend me the money.

Although I had been warned about kitchen-table hacks, my father found a real doctor who did abortions on the side. Late one night, I hurried into a darkened medical office, accompanied by my father and his new wife. I hated having her along, but he insisted we might need a woman in case there were complications.

There were no complications.

These memories came flooding back last December, when a friend stunned me with the news that she'd just heard from the child she gave up for adoption thirty-two years ago. I know this woman's twenty-eight-year-old son, but I never knew about the secret daughter, the one who got born because a bogus abortionist took an unsuspecting young woman's money and left her pregnant. Now the baby she last saw in the delivery room was coming for Christmas with *her* baby.

"I'm excited to be a grandmother," my friend told me, "but I feel such regret, loss, and guilt about my daughter that it overpowers all my other feelings."

I hope my friend's reunion story ends well. All I know is what it aroused in me. Relief. Waves of God-grateful relief. Had I not been able to terminate that pregnancy in 1958, I might now have a thirty-two-year-old daughter (or son) looking for *me*, and surely I would be a very different me for having carried the misery that burdened my friend all these years.

It's never simple. That's why public policy on abortion and adoption must be filtered through the experiences of women like us. When adoption is heralded as the answer to unwanted pregnancy, the targets of concern are infertile parents, not the woman, her feelings, her body, and her future— or the future feelings of the child she must give away.

I was grateful I never had to leave a child of mine with strangers or unwittingly pass a legacy of rejection to an infant at birth. If such a child existed today, no matter how happy our reunion, I would forever mourn the thirty-two lost years.

The fact that I was able to choose abortion made possible the life that was and is. Above all, the child-who-wasn't made possible the three wanted children who are my family today.

1991

JANE SHAPIRO

Standard Operating Procedure

After Amy was born, I took the Pill for five years straight, and I stopped, for no real reason, when I was thirty. Then I bled incredibly, long swells of black blood full of clots, and I figured that was what happened when you went off. Walking up the stairs, I crouched to breathe; I quarreled with Eddie because I wanted him to cook me two kinds of liver, full of iron, at once, and it was a craving that made me weep. When I couldn't walk easily on level ground, I dropped the kids at the library with the babysitter and drove over to the medical group office to have Dr. Flynn look at me. Dr. Flynn held my cold hands and looked at my fingernails, gone to white and then gray, then looked at my eyeballs, which he compared to the white albumen of an old hard-boiled egg, and was concerned.

"I've been bleeding," I said.

Dr. Flynn said, "I'm sending you down the hall, my good lady. Sit here a minute."

Down the hall was young Dr. Blandish, my gynecologist by default. (There is a long waiting list for the one female gynecologist, a cool and reserved person with a breathtakingly professional style.) I sucked breath that wouldn't come, and I was getting scared. Just before he checked me into the hospital, Dr. Blandish began to address me as Tiger.

"Tiger," Dr. Blandish said, "if you were fifty years old with a hemoglobin this low, you'd be dead."

Before Dr. Blandish could do a D&C, he said he had to transfuse me and hoped it wouldn't, uh, you know. Hoped it wouldn't bleed right out the other end, I suppose he meant. Two lively young nurses came giggling into my room to find the big vein in my arm and hook me up to plastic bags of blood which they keep in the refrigerator so that it drips into your body slowly, drop by freezing drop. The nurses shoved each other, and a bag of blood thumped onto the floor so the nurses had to giggle and get down on hands and knees together to feel under the bed. Two days later, after the D&C was over, Dr. Blandish came and said that now, Tiger, everything was fine, and we'd just see what happened.

Every month for the next four I bled the rivers of blood, and every month Dr. Blandish did what he could to stop it. Each month he tried something different. After Dr. Blandish examines you, as he turns away to strip off the rubber glove, that translucent membrane that separates his hand from the vagina of the patient, he puts his head to the side and on his usually controlled, actually impassive face is an unmistakable look: disgust. Knowing this, I figured Dr. Blandish would be doing his all to get the blood stopped.

We had planned another D&C for July, but as it approached I began to know I didn't want to return to that hospital and Dr. Blandish, and then after a while Dr. Blandish called and said: "Look, Tiger, we looked at the cells. It's hard to explain. They're in what you call a, uh, pre-malignant condition. Not even that. *Pre*-premalignant. It's nothing to sweat, believe me. I wouldn't con you."

"It's hard to believe you," I said.

"Believe me, Tiger, let's just get you in here, friend, and do the next one. Let's quit stalling."

"I can't help stalling."

"Look," Blandish said. "You may have heard stories about this hospital that aren't true. And this is nothing to worry about. *Pre*-premalignant. But we ought to take a peek, because we may have to just, uh, go in and take out the uterus."

"Thank you," I said. "I'll talk to you later."

Talking later was fine with him, because Dr. Blandish had said that thing about removing the uterus in a sort of toneless blurt, and during the hasty sign-off he seemed to imply that he hadn't actually said it, or at least if he had he was very sorry.

On Saturday night I was bleeding again. Eddie and I fought and made up. At Lila's party I would get up and start across toward the bathroom on my way to change my sodden purple diaper, and Arthur Resnick would grab me, his eager arm shooting out like The Hook, and I was a fading vaudevillian, too weak to protest. I even danced with wild-eyed Charles Burns, a great hopper and leaper, a wiry fellow so bursting with politeness and cheer that he freezes your mind in its tracks, and when I began to feel big clots burping out into the napkin under my African skirt and when I began to see them in my mind, I still kept following the leaps of Charles Burns, although genteelly—my restrained jogs nothing like his ferocious gestures—and I never said, for the longest time, "Excuse me, I have to go to the bathroom."

I was terrified. The blood was still streaming out of my body. So Eddie wrapped me in sheets and I lay on the couch while he made phone calls, and in that way we finally got to New York and a big hospital where there is a famous wonderful team of doctors who specialize in these things, headed by Dr. Alexander Baron.

No young women with big bellies sit in Dr. Baron's waiting room, lined up for a monthly check; the room is full of men: husbands and friends, holding their jackets on their laps, waiting for women who might have cancer. Nobody comes alone.

Dr. Baron is a big man, very grand, and his young subordinates call him Baron Al when he isn't listening. Occasionally, Baron Al looks at the patient with a sincere concerned look, crinkling up his eyes.

"After you discontinued the Pill," said Dr. Baron, "did you notice any change in sexual desire?"

"Yes," I said. "An increase."

"Aha," Dr. Baron said, and made a note. "Many girls say that."

I said to myself, "I'm thirty now; my age is on that paper he's got there. I'm not a famous surgeon, or a surgeon at all, but on the other hand I'm no longer a girl. On the other hand again, my useful third hand, don't be touchy, keep the facts in mind: you are pre-premalignant, and that is his field."

When Dr. Baron examines you, he hurts you. He shoves the speculum in; he shoves his fingers in fast and prods around hard, roughing you up.

"That hurts," I said.

"You have two children, Jane?"

"You're hurting me."

"A boy and a girl?"

Afterward, he does a curious thing: he leans down toward you where you're lying on the table, and he holds out his hand exactly like a man in the movies who has just won a fight. He stands that way, looking at you and waiting so that you'll take his hand and shake it and forgive him. Now he did that. I shook the hand. Then he put one cordovan shoe up on a stool and got the sincere look back on his face as he spoke in a low tone. He said that many girls believed that taking the Pill caused cancer, which was not by any means necessarily the case.

I told the children I would be back on Friday, and I checked into Dr. Baron's huge hospital. When I was wearing my nightgown and sitting up in my electric bed, Dr. Baron's Fellow came to take down my data. He was a young dark man, short and handsome, Turkish, shaved to pink and dressed for the evening. He was Dr. Göknil, whose name means "the feeling of the petal of the rose." He waived the pelvic examination, since I inhabited a private room. He murmured and smiled gently. I was of course a nice housewife? A writer, I said, causing him to lower his eyes and grin at his papers. I hated him.

"A little minor surgery tomorrow. Minor, minor. Put your mind at ease, utterly, Janie," he said.

After the D&C, Dr. Baron stopped into my room for a few seconds with his residents and helpers. I saw him in my sleep; he was a gigantic mother duck, plump with bread crusts, trailing her white ducklings after her on a string. I looked gorgeous, he said. Perhaps Mr. S. would step out here a minute? Everything fine. Sincere eyes, a three-second hold, now he's gone and I turn my head, hazy, to see the tail of the last duckling flutter out the door.

Eddie stepped to the lounge for a minute, and Dr. Baron told him that surprisingly enough our girl Jane had endometrial cancer, and they would have to remove her uterus and ovaries, and would he according to his own notions of appropriateness please let her know? It was a rare thing at this age, but there it was.

On Tuesday they will do the hysterectomy. Dr. Baron is gone for the weekend, and the resident says I have to stay so that I don't start bleeding again. I feel heartbroken, a forgotten child myself, phoning the children to say: "I'm so sorry. I can't come home for a while."

At night, images of death visit and comfort me. I think about Viet Nam—we all do, all the time. Many men are back in our lives, who were boys when they were sent, and now they're among us, busy all day and struggling all night not to remember.

What about special kinds of murderers, who come in dreams? Men who stab people or break open their brittle bodies, those little piñatas, with lengths of pipe.

Everyone else is in danger, not me. My children will be killed in the squealing crash of a car, with the glass flying in bits and their small bodies tossed against the walls. They will fall from trees and crush their legs and arms; they'll pick up the cleaver and sever their fingers so that their hands will end in red round squid-eyes streaming blood; they'll swallow lye. My husband's plane will fall soundlessly into the sea trailing a string of gray smoke, and he will die with a look of astonishment on his face.

"Why did I have to spend the weekend here?" I ask on Monday.

"It's easier, Janie," Dr. Göknil says. He smiles so that I will be calm and think positively. "Oh, Janie, darling, it was easier for you, wasn't it? You don't have to check out, check in again—"

Dr. Baron stops in. "Why did I spend the weekend?" I ask.

"We didn't want your head getting muddled."

What?

"Sometimes a girl gets into a tight situation like this, her head can tend to get muddled."

I hear screaming in my head now. I could have gone home. I had promised my children I would come.

"It's all for the best," Dr. Baron says. "I have to go. Dr. Göknil will take good care here?"

Zeki Göknil brings me stories.

The woman upstairs who yelled and threw her cigarettes on the floor.

A cr-razy girl! She shouted, she threw the Baron right out of her room! Out! Get out! she yelled at him. We had to call the psychiatrist to talk to her. Absolutely crazy.

"Oh, they are so crazy some of them, yet do you know? They all love me. It's very difficult. I want to help them, I listen to their troubles, sit on the bed, perhaps hold the hand, you know. And then what happens, they call up: I want Zeki. Only Zeki.

"They ask for me, and, Janie, what can I say? This one calls up today, send Zeki to me. So I get a few minutes, I go to her room, she is weeping, what does she want? Talk to me, she says, I'm lonely."

He grins. Rolls his eyes. Aah. Women.

One of Zeki's colleagues on Baron's team is a woman fifteen years older than Zeki, and his superior. "Ah, Ellie," Zeki says. "Yes, Eleanor. That girl. Always, Zeki, do this for me, will you? Stop in and speak to the patient, will you? Zeki, I go home early today, you don't mind? Hah, but she is a lazy, lazy girl, that Ellie."

After the hysterectomy, after the blinding pain dropped off, my nurse said that now I had better watch my pies and cakes if I didn't want to be a fatty like so many of them. Dr. Baron came and stood around in my room smoking a cigar and looking trapped, and I asked him what the nurse meant, and he said that the old wives thought this operation would make women get fat, but it's probably that the women just feel better and *heh-heh*. Just, as a result, eat more. And that I shouldn't worry, I'll still be gorgeous.

At this point it condenses. I escaped with my life, and two weeks later Dr. Baron called me at home to say the lab found tumor cells in the cervix and I'd better come back and talk about it, and in September I was back for more surgery.

This time I was filled with a racing terror. I had tests, those ingenious slow assaults. I lay on the X-ray tables, a fat fish at the market with pink and silver scales, thinking about nothing. I lay on my back holding my feet still second by second for six hours while a young doctor made cuts on the tops of my feet and probed in the slits, trying to find some tiny canals to thread with dye. When that doctor called me Janie, I called him Larry, although I didn't know his name, and that made his helpers laugh out of discomfort and boredom, and wounded him so that for the next three hours he whined and addressed me as "Dear." A doctor came and punctured my body under the collarbone, popped in a tube, and the nurses in white were swimming above me with their caps growing into wide wings. I had the operation, all the lymphatics removed from the pelvis. I was wheeled in my rolling chair, walked down the hall an inch at a step, and my fear and pain hung ahead of me in the air.

The times have run together in my mind, and now it seems that years have passed and I was floating, far away and drifting. Eddie sat in my room, and at night he went to restaurants and stayed among the people until he had escaped my world. Dr. Baron almost never stopped in; I thought he didn't like talking with surgical patients, cancer patients, women, or composites. Zeki said No, that Baron Al was just preoccupied with his divorce proceedings.

Time to unveil the "wound"—Zeki's word. Zeki and a resident peel back the bandages, Zeki peers at my stomach, clasps his hands, stands back to sigh. "Janie! It's absolutely beautiful."

"Is it?"

"Oh, it's pretty hard to make that kind of stitches, but they sure make a nice incision, says the resident, admiring his own needlework.

"Beautiful, Janie," Zeki says, staring reality down. "Perfect! Just a tiny bikini line."

Then every morning for three weeks Zeki came to my room to examine the beautiful wound, and he would smile and speak gently, and he always said something about the world I had forgotten, outside. What we'll all do when this is over. Every afternoon he rushed in laughing, whispering, pulling Eddie aside for a sexual allusion too frank for my delicate pink ears. Two lively men together, talking mantalk, and the woman quietly reclining, subdued, looking beautiful though wounded: Zeki was directing a pantomime of his vision of normal life. He talked as if he were obsessed with sex, the pursuit of women; he thought he ought to be. He postured and danced, although I couldn't share his view of the world, for now I shared his real obsession, his terror of death.

In the end, to my astonishment, I was wheeled down the ramp and out onto the sidewalk, and I left the hospital and came home after all. Several months later, walking down a street, I saw that I was alive.

1975

PART FIVE

What the Lover Knows

Essays on Nature

The secret of seeing, then, is the pearl of great price.

ANNIE DILLARD

ANNIE DILLARD

Sight into Insight

WHAT YOU SEE
IS WHAT YOU GET

When I was six or seven years old, growing up in Pittsburgh, I used to take a precious penny of my own and hide it for someone else to find. It was a curious compulsion; sadly, I've never been seized by it since. For some reason I always "hid" the penny along the same stretch of sidewalk up the street. I'd cradle it at the roots of a maple, say, or in a hole left by a chipped-off piece of sidewalk. Then I'd take a piece of chalk and, starting at either end of the block, draw huge arrows leading up to the penny from both directions. After I learned to write I labeled the arrows "SURPRISE AHEAD" or "MONEY THIS WAY." I was greatly excited, during all this arrow-drawing, at the thought of the first lucky passerby who would receive in this way, regardless of merit, a free gift from the universe. But I never lurked about. I'd go straight home and not give the matter another thought, until, some months later, I would be gripped by the impulse to hide another penny.

There are lots of things to see, unwrapped gifts and free surprises. The world is fairly studded and strewn with pennies cast broadside from a generous hand. But—and this is the point—who gets excited by a mere penny?

If you follow one arrow, if you crouch motionless on a bank to watch a tremulous ripple thrill on the water, and are rewarded by the sight of a muskrat kit paddling from its den, will you count that sight a chip of copper only, and go your rueful way? It is very dire poverty indeed for a man to be so malnourished and fatigued that he won't stoop to pick up a penny. But if you cultivate a healthy poverty and simplicity, so that finding a penny will make your day, then, since the world is in fact planted in pennies, you have with your poverty bought a lifetime of days. What you see is what you get.

Unfortunately, nature is very much a now-you-see-it, now-you-don't affair. A fish flashes, then dissolves in the water before my eyes like so much salt. Deer apparently ascend bodily into heaven; the brightest oriole fades into leaves. These disappearances stun me into stillness and concentration; they say of nature that it conceals with a grand nonchalance, and they say of vision that it is a deliberate gift, the revelation of a dancer who for my eyes only flings away her seven veils.

For nature does reveal as well as conceal: now-you-don't-see-it, now-you-do. For a week this September migrating red-winged blackbirds were feeding heavily down by Tinker Creek at the back of the house. One day I went out to investigate the racket; I walked up to a tree, an Osage orange, and a hundred birds flew away. They simply materialized out of the tree. I saw a tree, then a whisk of color, then a tree again. I walked closer and another hundred blackbirds took flight. Not a branch, not a twig budged: the birds were apparently weightless as well as invisible. Or, it was as if the leaves of the Osage orange had been freed from a spell in the form of red-winged blackbirds; they flew from the tree, caught my eye in the sky, and vanished. When I looked again at the tree, the leaves had reassembled as if nothing had happened. Finally I walked directly to the trunk of the tree and a final hundred, the real diehards, appeared, spread, and vanished. How could so many hide in the tree without my seeing them? The Osage orange, unruffled, looked just as it had looked from the house, when three hundred red-winged blackbirds cried from its crown. I looked upstream where they flew, and they were gone. Searching. I couldn't spot one. I wandered upstream to force them to play their hand, but they'd crossed the creek and scattered. One show to a customer. These appearances catch at my throat; they are the free gifts, the bright coppers at the roots of trees.

It's all a matter of keeping my eyes open. Nature is like one of those line drawings that are puzzles for children: Can you find hidden in the tree a duck, a house, a boy, a bucket, a giraffe, and a boot? Specialists can find the most incredibly hidden things. A book I read when I was young recommended an easy way to find caterpillars: you simply find some fresh caterpillar droppings, look up, and there's your caterpillar. More recently an author advised me to set my mind at ease about those piles of cut stems on the ground in grassy fields. Field mice make them; they cut the grass down by degrees to reach the seeds at the head. It seems that when the grass is tightly packed, as in a field of ripe grain, the blade won't topple at a single cut through the stem; instead, the cut stem simply drops vertically, held in the crush of grain. The mouse severs the bottom again and again, the stem keeps dropping an inch at a time, and finally the head is low enough for the mouse to reach the seeds. Meanwhile the mouse is positively littering the field with its little piles of cut stems into which, presumably, the author is constantly stumbling.

If I can't see these minutiae, I still try to keep my eyes open. I'm always on the lookout for ant lion traps in sandy soil, monarch pupae near milkweed, skipper larvae in locust leaves. These things are utterly common, and I've not seen one. I bang on hollow trees near water, but so far no flying squirrels have appeared. In flat country I watch every sunset in hopes of seeing the green ray. The green ray is a seldom-seen streak of light that rises from the sun like a spurting fountain at the moment of sunset; it throbs into the sky for two seconds and disappears. One more reason to keep my eyes open. A photography professor at the University of Florida just happened to see a bird die in midflight; it jerked, died, dropped, and smashed on the ground.

I squint at the wind because I read Stewart Edward White: "I have always maintained that if you looked closely enough you could *see* the wind—the dim, hardly-made-out, fine débris fleeing high in the air." White was an excellent observer, and devoted an entire chapter of *The Mountains* to the subject of seeing deer: "As soon as you can forget the naturally obvious and construct an artificial obvious, then you too will see deer."

But the artificial obvious is hard to see. My eyes account for less than 1 percent of the weight of my head; I'm bony and dense; I see what I expect. I just don't know what the lover knows; I can't see the artificial obvious that those in the know construct. The herpetologist asks the native, "Are there snakes in that ravine?" "No, sir." And the herpetologist comes home with, yessir, three bags full. Are there butterflies on that mountain? Are the bluets in bloom? Are there arrowheads here, or fossil ferns in the shale?

Peeping through my keyhole I see within the range of only about 30 percent of the light that comes from the sun; the rest is infrared and some little ultraviolet, perfectly apparent to many animals, but invisible to me. A nightmare network of ganglia, charged and firing without my knowledge, cuts and splices what I do see, editing it for my brain. Donald E. Carr points out that the sense impressions of one-celled animals are *not* edited for the brain: "This is philosophically interesting in a rather mournful way, since it means that only the simplest animals perceive the universe as it is."

A fog that won't burn away drifts and flows across my field of vision. When you see fog move against a backdrop of deep pines, you don't see the fog itself, but streaks of clearness floating across the air in dark shreds. So I see only tatters of clearness through a pervading obscurity. I can't distinguish the fog from the overcast sky; I can't be sure if the light is direct or reflected. Everywhere darkness and the presence of the unseen appalls. We estimate now that only one atom dances alone in every cubic meter of intergalactic space. I blink and squint. What planet or power yanks Halley's Comet out of orbit? We haven't seen it yet; it's a question of distance, density, and the pallor of reflected light. We rock, cradled in the swaddling band of darkness. Even the simple darkness of night whispers suggestions to the mind. This summer, in August, I stayed at the creek too late.

STRANGERS TO DARKNESS

Where Tinker Creek flows under the sycamore log bridge to the tear-shaped island, it is slow and shallow, fringed thinly in cattail marsh. At this spot an astonishing bloom of life supports vast breeding populations of insects, fish, reptiles, birds, and mammals. On windless summer evenings I stalk along the creek bank or straddle the sycamore log in absolute stillness, watching for muskrats. The night I stayed too late I was hunched on the log staring spellbound at spreading, reflected stains of lilac on the water. A cloud in the sky suddenly lighted as if turned on by a switch; its reflection just as suddenly materialized on the water upstream, flat and floating, so that I couldn't see the creek bottom, or life in the water under the cloud. Downstream, away from the cloud on the water, water turtles smooth as beans were gliding down with the current in a series of easy, weightless push-offs, as men bound on the moon. I didn't know whether to trace the progress of one turtle I was sure of, risking sticking my face in one of the bridge's spider webs made invisible by the gathering dark, or take a chance on seeing the carp, or scan the mudbank in hope of seeing a muskrat, or follow the last of the swallows who caught at my heart and trailed it after them like streamers as they appeared from directly below, under the log, flying upstream with their tails forked, so fast.

But shadows spread and deepened and stayed. After thousands of years we're still strangers to darkness, fearful aliens in an enemy camp with our arms crossed over our chests. I stirred. A land turtle on the bank, startled, hissed the air from its lungs and withdrew to its shell. An uneasy pink here, an unfathomable blue there, gave great suggestion of lurking beings. Things were going on. I couldn't see whether that rustle I heard was a distant rattlesnake, slit-eyed, or a nearby sparrow kicking in the dry flood debris slung at the foot of a willow. Tremendous action roiled the water everywhere I looked, big action, inexplicable. A tremor welled up beside a gaping muskrat burrow in the bank and I caught my breath, but no muskrat appeared. The ripples continued to fan upstream with a steady, powerful thrust. Night was knitting an eyeless mask over my face, and I still sat transfixed. A distant airplane, a delta wing out of nightmare, made a gliding shadow on the creek's bottom that looked like a stingray cruising upstream. At once a black fin slit the pink cloud on the water, shearing it in two. The two halves merged together and seemed to dissolve before my eyes. Darkness pooled in the cleft of the creek and rose, as water collects in a well. Untamed, dreaming lights flickered over the sky. I saw hints of hulking underwater shadows, two pale splashes out of the water, and round ripples rolling close together from a blackened center.

At last I stared upstream where only the deepest violet remained of the cloud, a cloud so high its underbelly still glowed, its feeble color reflected from a hidden sky lighted in turn by a sun halfway to China. And out of that violet, a sudden enormous black body arced over the water. Head and tail, if there was a head and tail, were both submerged in cloud. I saw only one ebony fling, a headlong dive to darkness; then the waters closed, and the lights went out.

I walked home in a shivering daze, up hill and down. Later I lay open-mouthed in bed, my arms flung wide at my sides to steady the whirling darkness. At this latitude I'm spinning 836 miles an hour round the earth's axis; I feel my sweeping fall as a breakneck arc like the dive of dolphins, and the hollow rushing of wind raises the hairs on my neck and the side of my face. In orbit around the sun I'm moving 64,800 miles an hour. The solar system as a whole, like a merry-go-round unhinged, spins, bobs, and blinks at the speed of 43,200 miles an hour along a course set east of Hercules. Someone has piped, and we are dancing a tarantella until the sweat pours. I open my eyes and I see dark, muscled forms curl out of water, with flapping gills and flattened eyes. I close my eyes and I see stars, deep stars giving way to deeper stars, deeper stars bowing to deepest stars at the crown of an infinite cone.

"Still," wrote Van Gogh in a letter, "a great deal of light falls on everything." If we are blinded by darkness, we are also blinded by light. Sometimes here in Virginia at sunset low clouds on the southern or northern horizon are completely invisible in the lighted sky. I only know one is there because I can see its reflection in still water. The first time I discovered this mystery I looked from cloud to nocloud in bewilderment, checking my bearings over and over, thinking maybe the ark of the covenant was just passing by south of Dead Man Mountain. Only much later did I learn the explanation: polarized light from the sky is very much weakened by reflection, but the light in clouds isn't polarized. So invisible clouds pass among visible clouds, till all slide over the mountains; so a greater light extinguishes a lesser as though it didn't exist.

In the great meteor shower of August, the Perseid, I wail all day for the shooting stars I miss. They're out there showering down, committing hara-kiri in a flame of fatal attraction, and hissing perhaps at last into the ocean. But at dawn what looks like a blue dome clamps down over me like a lid on a pot. The stars and planets could smash and I'd never know. Only a piece of ashen moon occasionally climbs up or down the inside of the dome, and our local star without surcease explodes on our heads. We have really only that one light, one source for all power, and yet we must turn away from it by universal decree. Nobody here on the planet seems aware of this strange, powerful taboo, that we all walk about carefully averting our faces, this way and that, lest our eyes be blasted forever.

Darkness appalls and light dazzles; the scrap of visible light that doesn't hurt my eyes hurts my brain. What I see sets me swaying. Size and distance and the sudden swelling of meanings confuse me, bowl me over. I straddle the sycamore log bridge over Tinker Creek in the summer. I look at the lighted creek bottom: snail tracks tunnel the mud in quavering curves. A crayfish jerks, but by the time I absorb what has happened, he's gone in a billowing smoke screen of silt. I look at the water: minnows and shiners. If I'm thinking minnows, a carp will fill my brain till I scream. I look at the water's surface: skaters, bubbles, and leaves sliding down. Suddenly, my own face, reflected, startles me witless. Those snails have been tracking my face! Finally, with a shuddering wrench of the will, I see clouds, cirrus clouds. I'm dizzy, I fall in.

This looking business is risky. Once I stood on a humped rock on nearby Purgatory Mountain, watching through binoculars the great autumn hawk migration below, until I discovered that I was in danger of joining the hawks on a vertical migration of my own. I was used to binoculars, but not, apparently, to balancing on humped rocks while looking through them. I reeled. Everything advanced and receded by turns; the world was full of unexplained foreshortenings and depths. A distant huge object, a hawk the size of an elephant, turned out to be the browned bough of a nearby loblolly pine. I followed a sharp-shinned hawk against a featureless sky, rotating my head unawares as it flew, and when I lowered the glass a glimpse of my own looming shoulder sent me staggering. What prevents the men on Palomar from falling, voiceless and blinded, from their tiny, vaulted chairs?

I reel in confusion; I don't understand what I see. With the naked eye I can see two million light-years to the Andromeda galaxy. Often I slop some creek water in a jar, and when I get home I dump it in a white china bowl. After the silt settles I return and see tracings of minute snails on the bottom, a planarian or two winding round the rim of water, roundworms shimmying frantically, and finally, when my eyes have adjusted to these dimensions, amoebae. At first the amoebae look like *muscae volitantes*, those curled moving spots you seem to see in your eyes when you stare at a distant wall. Then I see the amoebae as drops of water congealed, bluish, translucent, like chips of sky in the bowl. At length I choose one individual and give myself over to its idea of an evening. I see it dribble a grainy foot before it on its wet, unfathomable way. Do its unedited sense impressions include the fierce focus of my eyes? Shall I take it outside and show it Andromeda, and blow its little endoplasm? I stir the water with a finger, in case it's running out of oxygen. Maybe I should get a tropical aquarium with motorized bubblers and lights, and keep this one for a pet. Yes, it would tell its fissioned descendants, the universe is two feet by five, and if you listen closely you can hear the buzzing music of the spheres.

Oh, it's mysterious, lamplit evenings here in the galaxy, one after the other. It's one of those nights when I wander from window to window, looking for a sign. But I can't see. Terror and a beauty insoluble are a riband of blue woven into the fringes of garments of things both great and small. No culture explains, no bivouac offers real haven or rest. But it could be that we are not seeing something. Galileo thought comets were an optical illusion. This is fertile ground: since we are certain that they're not, we can look at what our scientists have been saying with fresh hope. What if there are *really* gleaming, castellated cities hung upside-down over the desert sand? What limpid lakes and cool date palms have our caravans always passed untried? Until, one by one, by the blindest of leaps, we light on the road to these places, we must stumble in darkness and hunger. I turn from the window. I'm blind as a bat, sensing only from every direction the echo of my own thin cries.

LEARNING TO SEE

I chanced on a wonderful book called *Space and Sight*, by Marius Von Senden. When Western surgeons discovered how to perform safe cataract operations, they ranged across Europe and America operating on dozens of men and women of all ages who had been blinded by cataracts since birth. Von Senden collected accounts of such cases; the histories are fascinating. Many doctors had tested their patients' sense perceptions and ideas of space both before and after the operations. The vast majority of patients, of both sexes and all ages, had, in Von Senden's opinion, no idea of space whatsoever. Form, distance, and size were so many meaningless syllables. A patient "had no idea of depth, confusing it with roundness." Before the operation a doctor would give a blind patient a cube and a sphere; the patient would tongue it or feel it with his hands, and name it correctly. After the operation the doctor would show the same objects to the patient without letting him touch them; now he had no clue whatsoever to what he was seeing. One patient called lemonade "square" because it pricked on his tongue as a square shape pricked on the touch of his hands. Of another postoperative patient the doctor writes, "I have found in her no notion of size, for example, not even within the narrow limits which she might have encompassed with the aid of touch. Thus when I asked her to show me how big her mother was, she did not stretch out her hands, but set her two index fingers a few inches apart."

For the newly sighted, vision is pure sensation unencumbered by meaning. When a newly sighted girl saw photographs and paintings, she asked, "'Why do they put those dark marks all over them?' 'Those aren't dark marks,' her mother explained, 'those are shadows. That is one of the ways the eye knows that things have shape. If it were not for shadows, many things would look flat.' 'Well, that's how things do look,' Joan answered. 'Everything looks flat with dark patches.'"

In general the newly sighted see the world as a dazzle of "color-patches." They are pleased by the sensation of color, and learn quickly to name the colors, but the rest of seeing is tormentingly difficult. Soon after his operation a patient "generally bumps into one of these color-patches and observes them to be substantial, since they resist him as tactual objects do. In walking about it also strikes him—or can if he pays attention—that he is continually passing in between the colors he sees, that he can go past a visual object, that a part of it then steadily disappears from view; and that in spite of this, however he twists and turns—whether entering the room from the door, for example, or returning back to it—he always has a visual space in front of him. Thus he gradually comes to realize that there is also a space behind him, which he does not see."

The mental effort involved in these reasonings proves overwhelming for many patients. It oppresses them to realize, if they ever do at all, the tremendous size of the world, which they had previously conceived of as something touchingly manageable. It oppresses them to realize that they have been visible to people all along, perhaps unattractively so, without their knowledge or consent. A disheartening number of them refuse to use their new vision, continuing to go over objects with their tongues, and lapsing into apathy and despair.

On the other hand, many newly sighted people speak well of the world, and teach us how dull our own vision is. To one patient, a human hand, unrecognized, is "something bright and then holes." Shown a bunch of grapes, a boy calls out, "It is dark, blue and shiny. . . . It isn't smooth, it has bumps and hollows." A little girl visits a garden. "She is greatly astonished, and can scarcely be persuaded to answer, stands speechless in front of the tree, which she only names on taking hold of it, and then as 'the tree with the lights in it.'" Another patient, a twenty-two-year-old girl, was dazzled by the world's brightness and kept her eyes shut for two weeks. When at the end of that time she opened her eyes again, she did not recognize any objects, but "the more she now directed her gaze upon everything about her, the more it could be seen how an expression of gratification and astonishment overspread her features; she repeatedly exclaimed: 'Oh God! How beautiful!'"

I saw color-patches for weeks after I read this wonderful book. It was summer; the peaches were ripe in the valley orchards. When I woke in the morning, color-patches wrapped round my eyes, intricately, leaving not one unfilled spot. All day long I walked among shifting color-patches that parted before me like the Red Sea and closed again in silence, transfigured, wherever I looked back. Some patches swelled and loomed, while others vanished utterly, and dark marks flitted at random over the whole dazzling sweep. But I couldn't sustain the illusion of flatness. I've been around for too long. Form is condemned to an eternal danse macabre with meaning: I couldn't unpeach the peaches. Nor can I remember ever having seen without understanding; the color-patches of infancy are lost. My brain then must have been smooth as any balloon. I'm told I reached for the moon; many babies do. But the color-patches of infancy swelled as meaning filled them; they arrayed themselves in solemn ranks down distance which unrolled and stretched before me like a plain. The moon rocketed away. I live now in a world of shadows that shape and distance color, a world where space makes a kind of terrible sense. What Gnosticism is this, and what physics? The fluttering patch I saw in my nursery window—silver and green and shape-shifting blue—is gone; a row of Lombardy poplars takes its place, mute, across the distant lawn. That humming oblong creature pale as light that stole along the walls of my room at night, stretching exhilaratingly around the corners, is gone, too, gone the night I ate of the bittersweet fruit, put two and two together and puckered forever my brain. Martin Buber tells this tale: "Rabbi Mendel once boasted to his teacher Rabbi Elimelekh that evenings he saw the angel who rolls away the light before the darkness, and mornings the angel who rolls away the darkness before the light. 'Yes,' said Rabbi Elimelekh, 'in my youth I saw that too. Later on you don't see these things anymore.'"

Why didn't someone hand those newly sighted people paints and brushes from the start, when they still didn't know what anything was? Then maybe we all could see color-patches too, the world unraveled from reason, Eden before Adam gave names. The scales would drop from my eyes; I'd see trees like men walking; I'd run down the road against all orders, hallooing and leaping.

SILVER FLASHES

Seeing is of course very much a matter of verbalization. Unless I call my attention to what passes before my eyes, I simply won't see it. If Tinker Mountain erupted, I'd be likely to notice. But if I want to notice the lesser cataclysms of valley life, I have to maintain in my head a running description of the present. It's not that I'm observant; it's just that I talk too much. Otherwise, especially in a strange place, I'll never know what's happening. Like a blind man at the ball game, I need a radio.

When I see this way I analyze and pry. I hurl over logs and roll away stones; I study the bank a square foot at a time, probing and tilting my head. Some days when a mist covers the mountains, when the muskrats won't show and the microscope's mirror shatters, I want to climb up the blank blue dome as a man would storm the inside of a circus tent, wildly, dangling, and with a steel knife claw a rent in the top, peep, and, if I must, fall.

But there is another kind of seeing that involves a letting go. When I see this way I sway transfixed and emptied. The difference between the two ways of seeing is the difference between walking with and without a camera. When I walk with a camera I walk from shot to shot, reading the light on a calibrated meter. When I walk without a camera, my own shutter opens, and the moment's light prints on my own silver gut. When I see this second way I am above all an unscrupulous observer.

It was sunny one evening last summer at Tinker Creek; the sun was low in the sky, upstream. I was sitting on the sycamore log bridge with the sunset at my back, watching the shiners the size of minnows who were feeding over the muddy sand in skittery schools. Again and again, one fish, then another, turned for a split second across the current and flash! the sun shot out from its silver side. I couldn't watch for it. It was always just happening somewhere else, and it drew my vision just as it disappeared: flash! like a sudden dazzle of the thinnest blade, a sparking over a dun and olive ground at chance intervals from every direction. Then I noticed white specks, some sort of pale petals, small, floating from under my feet on the creek's surface, very slow and steady. So I blurred my eyes and gazed toward the brim of my hat and saw a new world. I saw the pale white circles roll up, roll up, like the world's turning, mute and perfect, and I saw the linear flashes, gleaming silver, like stars being born at random down a rolling scroll of time. Something broke and something opened. I filled up like a new wineskin. I breathed an air like light; I saw a light like water. I was the lip of a fountain the creek filled forever; I was ether, the leaf in the zephyr; I was flesh-flake, feather, bone.

When I see this way I see truly. As Thoreau says, I return to my senses. I am the man who watches the baseball game in silence in an empty stadium. I see the game purely; I'm abstracted and dazed. When it's all over and the white-suited players lope off the green field to their shadowed dugouts, I leap to my feet, I cheer and cheer.

But I can't go out and try to see this way. I'll fail, I'll go mad. All I can do is try to gag the commentator, to hush the noise of useless interior babble that keeps me from seeing just as surely as a newspaper dangled before my eyes. The effort is really a discipline requiring a lifetime of dedicated struggle; it marks the literature of saints and monks of every order east and west, under every rule and no rule, discalced and shod. The world's spiritual geniuses seem to discover universally that the mind's muddy river, this ceaseless flow of trivia and trash, cannot be dammed, and that trying to dam it is a waste of effort that might lead to madness. Instead you must allow the muddy river to flow unheeded in the dim channels of consciousness; you raise your sights; you look along it, mildly, acknowledging its presence without interest and gazing beyond it into the realm of the real where subjects and objects act and rest purely, without utterance. "Launch into the deep," says Jacques Ellul, "and you shall see."

The secret of seeing, then, is the pearl of great price. If I thought he could teach me to find it and keep it forever I would stagger barefoot across a hundred deserts after any lunatic at all. But although the pearl may be found, it may not be sought. The literature of illumination reveals this above all: although it comes to those who wait for it, it is always, even to the most practiced and adept, a gift and a total surprise. I return from one walk knowing where the killdeer nests in the field by the creek and the hour the laurel blooms. I return from the same walk a day later scarcely knowing my own name. Litanies hum in my ears; my tongue flaps in my mouth, *Alim non*, alleluia! I cannot cause light; the most I can do is try to put myself in the path of its beam. It is possible, in deep space, to sail on solar wind. Light, be it particle or wave, has force: you rig a giant sail and go. The secret of seeing is to sail on solar wind. Hone and spread your spirit till you yourself are a sail, whetted, translucent, broadside to the merest puff.

When her doctor took her bandages off and led her into the garden, the girl who was no longer blind saw "the tree with the lights in it." It was for this tree I searched through the peach orchards of summer, in the forests of fall and down winter and spring for years. Then one day I was walking along Tinker Creek thinking of nothing at all and I saw the tree with the lights in it. I saw the backyard cedar where the mourning doves roost charged and transfigured, each cell buzzing with flame. I stood on the grass with the lights in it, grass that was wholly fire, utterly focused and utterly dreamed. It was less like seeing than like being for the first time seen, knocked breathless by a powerful glance. The flood of fire abated, but I'm still spending the power. Gradually the lights went out in the cedar, the colors died, the cells unflamed and disappeared. I was still ringing. I had been my whole life a bell, and never knew it until at that moment I was lifted and struck. I have since only very rarely seen the tree with the lights in it. The vision comes and goes, mostly goes, but I live for it, for the moment when the mountains open and a new light roars in spate through the crack, and the mountains slam.

1974

Walking

It began in dark and underground weather, a slow hunger moving toward light. It grew in a dry gully beside the road where I live, a place where entire hillsides are sometimes yellow, windblown tides of sunflower plants. But this one was different. It was alone, and larger than the countless others who had established their lives further up the hill. This one was a traveler, a settler, and like a dream beginning in conflict, it grew where the land had been disturbed.

I saw it first in early summer. It was a green and sleeping bud, raising itself toward the sun. Ants worked around the unopened bloom, gathering aphids and sap. A few days later, it was a tender young flower, soft and new, with a pale green center and a troop of silver gray insects climbing up and down the stalk.

Over the summer this sunflower grew into a plant of incredible beauty, turning its face daily toward the sun in the most subtle of ways, the black center of it dark and alive with a deep blue light, as if flint had sparked an elemental fire there, in community with rain, mineral, mountain air, and sand.

As summer changed from green to yellow there were new visitors daily: the lace-winged insects, the bees whose legs were fat with pollen, and grasshoppers with their clattering wings and desperate hunger. There were other lives I missed, lives too small or hidden to see. It was as if this plant with its host of lives was a society, one in which moment by moment, depending on light and moisture, there was great and diverse change.

There were changes in the next larger world around the plant as well. One day I rounded a bend in the road to find the disturbing sight of a dead horse, black and still against a hillside, eyes rolled back. Another day I was nearly lifted by a wind and sandstorm so fierce and hot that I had to wait for it to pass before I could return home. On this day the faded dry petals of the sunflower were swept across the land. That was when the birds arrived to carry the new seeds to another future.

In this one plant, in one summer season, a drama of need and survival took place. Hungers were filled. Insects coupled. There was escape, exhaustion, and death. Lives touched down a moment and were gone.

I was an outsider. I only watched. I never learned the sunflower's golden language or the tongues of its citizens. I had a small understanding, nothing more than a shallow observation of the flower, insects, and birds. But they knew what to do, how to live. An old voice from somewhere, gene or cell, told the plant how to evade the pull of gravity and find its way upward, how to open. It was instinct, intuition, necessity. A certain knowing directed the seedbearing birds on paths to ancestral homelands they had never seen. They believed it. They followed.

There are other summons and calls, some even more mysterious than those commandments to birds or those survival journeys of insects. In bamboo plants, for instance, with their thin green canopy of light and golden stalks that creak in the wind. Once a century, all of a certain kind of bamboo flower on the same day. Whether they are in Malaysia or in a greenhouse in Minnesota makes no difference, nor does the age or size of the plant. They flower. Some current of an inner language passes between them, through space and separation, in ways we cannot explain in our language. They are all, somehow, one plant, each with a share of communal knowledge.

John Hay, in *The Immortal Wilderness*, has written: "There are occasions when you can hear the mysterious language of the Earth, in water, or coming through the trees, emanating from the mosses, seeping through the undercurrents of the soil, but you have to be willing to wait and receive."

Sometimes I hear it talking. The light of the sunflower was one language, but there are others, more audible. Once, in the redwood forest, I heard a beat, something like a drum or heart coming from the ground and trees and wind. That underground current stirred a kind of knowing inside me, a kinship and longing, a dream barely remembered that disappeared back to the body.

Another time, there was the booming voice of an ocean storm thundering from far out at sea, telling about what lived in the distance, about the rough water that would arrive, wave after wave revealing the disturbance at center.

Tonight I walk. I am watching the sky. I think of the people who came before me and how they knew the placement of stars in the sky, watched the moving sun long and hard enough to witness how a certain angle of light touched a stone only once a year. Without written records, they knew the gods of every night, the small, fine details of the world around them and of immensity above them.

Walking, I can almost hear the redwoods beating. And the oceans are above me here, rolling clouds, heavy and dark, considering snow. On the dry, red road, I pass the place of the sunflower, that dark and secret location where creation took place. I wonder if it will return this summer, if it will multiply and move up to the other stand of flowers in a territorial struggle.

It's winter and there is smoke from the fires. The square, lighted windows of houses are fogging over. It is a world of elemental attention, of all things working together, listening to what speaks in the blood. Whichever road I follow, I walk in the land of many gods, and they love and eat one another.

Walking, I am listening to a deeper way. Suddenly all my ancestors are behind me. Be still, they say. Watch and listen. You are the result of the love of thousands.

1990

LINDA HOGAN

Waking Up the Rake

In the still dark mornings, my grandmother would rise up from her bed and put wood in the stove. When the fire began to burn, she would sit in front of its warmth and let down her hair. It had never been cut and it knotted down in two long braids. When I was fortunate enough to be there, in those red Oklahoma mornings, I would wake up with her, stand behind her chair, and pull the brush through the long strands of her hair. It cascaded down her back, down over the chair, and touched the floor.

We were the old and the new, bound together in front of the snapping fire, woven like a lifetime's tangled growth of hair. I saw my future in her body and face, and her past was alive in me. We were morning people, and in all of earth's mornings the new intertwines with the old. Even new, a day itself is ancient, old with earth's habit of turning over and over again.

Years later, I was sick, and I went to a traditional healer. The healer was dark and thin and radiant. The first night I was there, she also lit a fire. We sat before it, smelling the juniper smoke. She asked me to tell her everything, my life spoken in words, a case history of living, with its dreams and losses, the scars and wounds we all bear from being in the world. She smoked me with cedar smoke, wrapped a sheet around me, and put me to bed, gently, like a mother caring for her child.

The next morning she nudged me awake and took me outside to pray. We faced east where the sun was beginning its journey on our side of earth.

The following morning in red dawn, we went outside and prayed. The sun was a full orange eye rising up the air. The morning after that we did the same, and on Sunday we did likewise.

The next time I visited her it was a year later, and again we went through the same prayers, standing outside facing the early sun. On the last morning I was there, she left for her job in town. Before leaving, she said, "Our work is our altar."

Those words have remained with me.

Now I am a disciple of birds. The birds that I mean are eagles, owls, and hawks. I clean cages at the Birds of Prey Rehabilitation Foundation. It is the work I wanted to do, in order to spend time inside the gentle presence of the birds.

There is a Sufi saying that goes something like this: "Yes, worship God, go to church, sing praises, but first tie your camel to the post." This cleaning is the work of tying the camel to a post.

I pick up the carcasses and skin of rats, mice, and of rabbits. Some of them have been turned inside out by the sharp-beaked eaters, so that the leathery flesh becomes a delicately veined coat for the inner fur. It is a boneyard. I rake the smooth fragments of bones. Sometimes there is a leg or shank of deer to be picked up.

In this boneyard, the still-red vertebrae lie on the ground beside an open rib cage. The remains of a rabbit, a small intestinal casing, holds excrement like beads in a necklace. And there are the clean, oval pellets the birds spit out, filled with fur, bone fragments and now and then, a delicate sharp claw that looks as if it were woven inside. A feather, light and soft, floats down a current of air, and it is also picked up.

Over time, the narrow human perspective from which we view things expands. A deer carcass begins to look beautiful and rich in its torn redness, the muscle and bone exposed in the shape life took on for a while as it walked through meadows and drank at creeks.

And the bone fragments have their own stark beauty, the clean white jaw bones with ivory teeth small as the head of a pin still in them. I think of medieval physicians trying to learn about our private, hidden bodies by cutting open the stolen dead and finding the splendor inside, the grace of every red organ, and the smooth, gleaming bone.

This work is an apprenticeship, and the birds are the teachers. Sweet-eyed barn owls, such taskmasters, asking us to be still and slow and to move in time with their rhythms, not our own. The short-eared owls with their startling yellow eyes require the full presence of a human. The marsh hawks, behind their branches, watch our every move.

There is a silence needed here before a person enters the bordered world the birds inhabit, so we stop and compose ourselves before entering their doors, and we listen to the musical calls of the eagles, the sound of wings in air, the way their feet with sharp claws, many larger than our own hands, grab hold of a perch. Then we know we are ready to enter, and they are ready for us.

The most difficult task the birds demand is that we learn to be equal to them, to feel our way into an intelligence that is different from our own. A friend, awed at the thought of working with eagles, said, "Imagine knowing an eagle." I answered her honestly, "It isn't so much that we know the eagles. It's that they know us."

And they know that we are apart from them, that as humans we have somehow fallen from our animal grace, and because of that we maintain a distance from them, though it is not always a distance of heart. The places we inhabit, even sharing a common earth, must remain distinct and separate. It was our presence that brought most of them here in the first place, nearly all of them injured in a clash with the human world. They have been shot, or hit by cars, trapped in leg hold traps, poisoned, ensnared in wire fences. To ensure their survival, they must remember us as the enemies that we are. We are the embodiment of a paradox; we are the wounders and we are the healers.

There are human lessons to be learned here, in the work. Fritjof Capra wrote: "Doing work that has to be done over and over again helps us to recognize the natural cycles of growth and decay, of birth and death, and thus become aware of the dynamic order of the universe." And it is true, in whatever we do, the brushing of hair, the cleaning of cages, we begin to see the larger order of things. In this place, there is a constant coming to terms with both the sacred place life occupies, and with death. Like one of those early physicians who discovered the strange, inner secrets of our human bodies, I'm filled with awe at the very presence of life, not just the birds, but a horse contained in its living fur, a dog alive and running. What a marvel it is, the fine shape life takes in all of us. It is equally marvelous that life is quickly turned back to the earth-colored ants and the soft white maggots that are time's best and closest companions. To sit with the eagles and their flutelike songs, listening to the longer flute of wind sweep through the lush grasslands, is to begin to know the natural laws that exist apart from our own written ones.

One of those laws, that we carry deep inside us, is intuition. It is lodged in a place even the grave-robbing doctors could not discover. It's a blood-written code that directs us through life. The founder of this healing center, Sigrid Ueblacker, depends on this inner knowing. She watches, listens, and feels her way to an understanding of each eagle and owl. This vision, as I call it, directs her own daily work at healing the injured birds and returning them to the wild.

"Sweep the snow away," she tells me. "The Swainson's hawks should be in Argentina this time of year and should not have to stand in the snow."

I sweep.

And that is in the winter when the hands ache from the cold, and the water freezes solid and has to be broken out for the birds, fresh buckets carried over icy earth from the well. In summer, it's another story. After only a few hours the food begins to move again, as if resurrected to life. A rabbit shifts a bit. A mouse turns. You could say that they have been resurrected, only with a life other than the one that left them. The moving skin swarms with flies and their offspring, ants, and a few wasps, busy at their own daily labor.

Even aside from the expected rewards for this work, such as seeing an eagle healed and winging across the sky it fell from, there are others. An occasional snake, beautiful and sleek, finds its way into the cage one day, eats a mouse and is too fat to leave, so we watch its long muscular life stretched out in the tall grasses. Or, another summer day, taking branches to be burned with a pile of wood near the little creek, a large turtle with a dark and shining shell slips soundlessly into the water, its presence a reminder of all the lives beyond these that occupy us.

One green morning, an orphaned owl perches nervously above me while I clean. Its downy feathers are roughed out. It appears to be twice its size as it clacks its beak at me, warning me: stay back. Then, fearing me the way we want it to, it bolts off the perch and flies, landing by accident onto the wooden end of my rake, before it sees that a human is an extension of the tool, and it flies again to a safer place, while I return to raking.

The word "rake" means to gather or heap up, to smooth the broken ground. And that's what this work is, all of it, the smoothing over of broken ground, the healing of the severed trust we humans hold with earth. We gather it back together again with great care, take the broken pieces and fragments and return them to the sky. It is work at the borderland between species, at the boundary between injury and healing.

There is an art to raking, a very fine art, one with rhythm in it, and life. On the days I do it well, the rake wakes up. Wood that came from dark dense forests seems to return to life. The water that rose up through the rings of that wood, the minerals of earth mined upward by the burrowing tree roots, all come alive. My own fragile hand touches the wood, a hand full of my own life, including that which rose each morning early to watch the sun return from the other side of the planet. Over time, these hands will smooth the rake's wooden handle down to a sheen.

Raking. It is a labor round and complete, smooth and new as an egg, and the rounding seasons of the world revolving in time and space. All things, even our own heartbeats and sweat, are in it, part of it. And that work, that watching the turning over of life, becomes a road into what is essential. Work is the country of hands, and they want to live there in the dailiness of it, the repetition that is time's language of prayer, a common tongue. Everything is there, in that language, in the humblest of labor. The rake wakes up and the healing is in it. The shadows of leaves that once fell beneath the tree the handle came from are in that labor, and the rabbits that passed this way, on the altar of our work. And when the rake wakes up, all earth's gods are reborn and they dance and sing in the dusty air around us.

1988

The Bowl

There was a woman who left the city, left her husband, and her children, left everything behind to retrieve her soul. She came to the desert after seeing her gaunt face in the mirror, the pallor that comes when everything is going out and nothing is coming in. She had noticed for the first time the furrows under her eyes that had been eroded by tears. She did not know the woman in the mirror. She took off her apron, folded it neatly in the drawer, left a note for her family, and closed the door behind her. She knew that her life and the lives of those she loved depended on it.

The woman returned to the place of her childhood, where she last remembered her true nature. She returned to the intimacy of a small canyon that for years had loomed large in her imagination, and there she set up camp. The walls were as she had recalled them, tall and streaked from rim to floor. The rock appeared as draped fabric as she placed her hand flat against its face. The wall was cold; the sun had not yet reached the wash. She began wading the shallow stream that ran down the center of the canyon, and chose not to be encumbered by anything. She shed her clothing, took out her hairpins, and squeezed the last lemon she had over her body. Running her hands over her breasts and throat and behind her neck, the woman shivered at her own bravery. This is how it should be, she thought. She was free and frightened and beautiful.

For days, the woman wandered in and out of the slickrock maze. She drank from springs and ate the purple fruit of prickly pears. Her needs were met simply. Because she could not see herself, she was unaware of the changes—how her skin became taut and tan, the way in which her hair relaxed and curled itself. She even seemed to walk differently as her toes spread and gripped the sand.

All along the wash, clay balls had been thrown by a raging river. The woman picked one up, pulled off the pebbles until she had a mound of supple clay. She kneaded it as she walked, rubbed the clay between the palms of her hands, and watched it lengthen. She finally sat down on the moist sand and, with her fingers, continued moving up the string of clay. And then she began to coil it, around and around, pinching shut each rotation. She created a bowl.

The woman found other clay balls and put them inside the bowl. She had an idea of making dolls for her children, small clay figurines that she would let dry in the sun. Once again, she stopped walking and sat in the sand to work. She split each clay ball in two, which meant she had six small pieces to mold out of three balls she had found. One by one, tiny shapes took form. A girl with open arms above her head; three boys—one standing, one sitting, and one lying down (he was growing, she mused); and then a man and a woman facing each other. She had re-created her family. With the few scraps left over she made desert animals: a lizard, a small bird, and a miniature coyote sitting on his haunches. The woman smiled as she looked over her menagerie. She clapped her hands to remove the dried clay and half expected to see them dance. Instead, it began to rain.

Within minutes, the wash began to swell. The woman put the clay creatures into the bowl and sought higher ground up a side canyon, where she found shelter under a large overhang. She was prepared to watch if a flash flood came. And it did. The clear water turned muddy as it began to rise, carrying with it the force of wild horses running with a thunderstorm behind them. The small stream, now a river, rose higher still, gouging into the sandy banks, hurling rocks, roots, and trees downstream. The woman wondered about the animals as she heard stirrings in the grasses and surmised they must be seeking refuge in the side canyons as she was—watching as she was. She pulled her legs in and wrapped her arms around her shins, resting her cheekbones against her knees. She closed her eyes and concentrated on the sound of water bursting through the silence of the canyon.

The roar of the flood gradually softened until it was replaced by bird-song. Swifts and swallows plucked the water for insects as frogs announced their return. The woman raised her head. With the bowl in both hands, she tried to get up, but slipped down the hillside, scraping the backs of her thighs on rabbitbrush and sage. She finally reached the wash with the bowl and its contents intact. And then she found herself with another problem: she sank up to her knees in the wet, red clay, only to find that the more she tried to pull her foot free, the deeper she sank with the other. Finally, letting go of her struggle, she put the bowl and her family aside, and wallowed in it. She fell sideways and rolled onto her stomach, then over onto her back. She was covered in slimy, wet clay, and it was delicious. She stretched her hands above her head, flexed her calves, and pointed her toes. The woman laughed hysterically until she became aware of her own echo.

Her body contracted.

She must get control of herself, she thought; what would her husband think? What kind of example was she setting for her children? And then she remembered—she was alone. She sat up and stared at the coiled bowl full of clay people. The woman took out the figurines and planted them in the wash. She placed the animals around them.

"They're on their own," she said out loud. And she walked back to the spring where she had drunk, filled up her bowl with water, and bathed.

The next morning, when the woman awoke, she noticed that the cottonwood branches swaying above her head had sprouted leaves.

She could go home now.

1989

A Woman's Dance

She came to the desert to dance. The woman gathered a variety of plants: mullen, sage, chamisa, mint, Oregon grape, aster, equisetum, and yarrow. She carried them in the folds of her long, red skirt to a clearing. It was a meadow defined by juniper. She placed the plants in the center and returned to the trees. She took off her paisley bandana wrapped around her forehead and knelt on the red soil.

"Good death," she said, as her hands sifted the wood dust of a decaying tree. She opened her scarf and placed the henna wood chips on the silk square. After she had gathered enough for the task, she brought the four corners together, tied them, and walked back to the clearing. She was not alone. Flickers, robins, magpies, and jays accompanied her. The woman carefully untied one of the corners and let the wood dust sprinkle to the ground as she walked in a circle. Next, she retrieved the plants from the center and arranged them end to end on top of the wood dust to define her circle more clearly. She liked what she saw.

Movement surrounded her. The wind, clouds, grasses, and birds—all reminded her that nothing stands still. She held up the hem of her skirt in both hands and began walking briskly around the circle. Deep breaths took the aroma of mint and sage down to her toes. Her long, spirited stride broke into short leaps with extended arms as she entered the circle dancing, without guile, without notice, without any thought of herself. She danced from the joy of all she was a part.

Pronghorn Antelope entered the circle through her body. She danced Eagle, Raven, and Bear. The Four Seasons sent her swirling as she danced to ignite the Moon. She danced until gravity pulled her down, and then she rested, her eyes closed, with nothing moving but her heart and lungs, beating, breathing, against the hot, dry desert.

With her ear against the earth, the woman listened. A chant began to rise. Slowly, she raised her body like a lizard. An audience had gathered. Each individual sat cross-legged around the plant circle with a found instrument: rocks, bones, sticks, stumps, whistles, and voices. For hours, they played music, organic and whole, as she danced. Her hands, like serpents, encouraged primal sounds as she arched forward and back with the grasses. She was the wind that inspired change. They were a tribe creating a landscape where lines between the real and imagined were thinly drawn.

The light deepened, shadows lengthened, and the woman began to turn. Her turns widened with each rotation until she stopped, perfectly balanced. The woman stepped outside the circle and kissed the palms of her hands and placed them on the earth. The dance was over.

The audience rose, refreshed. Each picked up one of the plants that held the circle and took a handful of wood dust to scatter, leaving no clues in the clearing of ever having been there. They disappeared as mysteriously as they had arrived.

And the woman who came to the desert to dance simply ran her fingers through her long, black hair and smiled.

1989

URSULA K. LE GUIN

A Very Warm Mountain

An enormous region extending from north-central Washington to
northeastern California and including most of Oregon east of the
Cascades is covered by basalt lava flows. . . . The unending cliffs
of basalt along the Columbia River . . . seventy-four volcanoes in the
Portland area . . . A blanket of pumice that averages about fifty
feet thick . . .

ROADSIDE GEOLOGY OF OREGON,

ALT AND HYNDMAN, 1978

Everybody takes it personally. Some get mad.
Damn stupid mountain went and dumped all that dirty gritty glassy gray
ash that flies like flour and lies like cement all over their roofs, roads, and
rhododendrons. Now they have to clean it up. And the scientists are a real
big help, all they'll say is we don't know, we can't tell, she might dump
another load of ash on you just when you've got it all cleaned up. It's an
outrage.

Some take it ethically. She lay and watched her forests being cut and
her elk being hunted and her lakes being fished and fouled and her ecology
being tampered with and the smoky, snarling suburbs creeping closer to her
skirts, until she saw it was time to teach the White Man's Children a lesson.

And she did. In the process of the lesson, she blew her forests to match-sticks, fried her elk, boiled her fish, wrecked her ecosystem, and did very little damage to the cities: so that the lesson taught to the White Man's Children would seem, at best, equivocal.

But everybody takes it personally. We try to reduce it to human scale. To make a molehill out of the mountain.

Some got very anxious, especially during the dreary white weather that hung around the area after May 18 (the first great eruption, when she blew 1300 feet of her summit all over Washington, Idaho, and points east) and May 25 (the first considerable ashfall in the thickly populated Portland area west of the mountain). Farmers in Washington State who had the real fallout, six inches of ash smothering their crops, answered the reporters' questions with police stoicism; but in town a lot of people were cross and dull and jumpy. Some erratic behavior, some really weird driving. "Everybody on my bus coming to work these days talks to everybody else, they never used to." "Everybody on my bus coming to work sits there like a stone instead of talking to each other like they used to." Some welcomed the mild sense of urgency and emergency as bringing people together in mutual support. Some—the old, the ill—were terrified beyond reassurance. Psychologists reported that psychotics had promptly incorporated the volcano into their private systems; some thought they were controlling her, and some thought she was controlling them. Businessmen, whom we know from the Dow Jones Reports to be an almost ethereally timid and emotional breed, read the scare stories in Eastern newspapers and cancelled all their conventions here; Portland hotels are having a long cool summer. A Chinese Cultural Attaché, evidently preferring earthquakes, wouldn't come farther north than San Francisco. But many natives were irrationally exhilarated, secretly, heartlessly welcoming every steam-blast and earth-tremor: Go it, mountain!

Everybody read in the newspapers everywhere that the May 18 eruption was "five hundred times greater than the bomb dropped on Hiroshima." Some reflected that we have bombs much more than five hundred times more powerful than the 1945 bombs. But these are never mentioned in the comparisons. Perhaps it would upset people in Moscow, Idaho, or Missoula, Montana, who got a lot of volcanic ash dumped on them, and don't want to have to think, what if that stuff had been radioactive? It really isn't nice to talk about it, is it. I mean, what if something went off in New

Jersey, say, and *was* radioactive—Oh, stop it. That volcano's way out west there somewhere anyhow.

Everybody takes it personally.

I had to go into hospital for some surgery in April, while the mountain was in her early phase—she jumped and rumbled, like the Uncles in *A Child's Christmas in Wales*, but she hadn't done anything spectacular. I was hoping she wouldn't perform while I couldn't watch. She obliged and held off for a month. On May 18 I was home, lying around with the cats, with a ringside view: bedroom and study look straight north about forty-five miles to the mountain.

I kept the radio tuned to a good country western station and listened to the reports as they came in, and wrote down some of the things they said. For the first couple of hours there was a lot of confusion and contradiction, but no panic, then or later. Late in the morning a man who had been about twenty miles from the blast described it: "Pumice-balls and mud-balls began falling for about a quarter of an hour, then the stuff got smaller, and by nine it was completely and totally black dark. You couldn't see ten feet in front of you!" He spoke with energy and admiration. Falling mud-balls, what next? The main West Coach artery, I-5, was soon closed because of the mud and wreckage rushing down the Toutle River toward the highway bridges. Walla Walla, 160 miles east, reported in to say their street lights had come on automatically at about ten in the morning. The Spokane-Seattle highway, far to the north, was closed, said an official expressionless voice, "on account of darkness."

At one-thirty that afternoon, I wrote:

It has been warm with a white high haze all morning, since six A.M., when I saw the top of the mountain floating dark against yellow-rose sunrise sky above the haze.

That was, of course, the last time I saw or will ever see that peak.

Now we can see the mountain from the base to near the summit. The mountain itself is whitish in the haze. All morning there has been this long, cobalt-bluish drift to the east from where the summit would be. And about ten o'clock there began to be visible clots, like cottage cheese curds, above the summit. Now the eruption cloud is visible from the summit of the mountain till obscured by a cloud layer at about twice the height of the mountain, i.e., 25–30,000 feet. The eruption cloud is very solid-looking, like sculptured marble, a beautiful blue in the deep relief of baroque curls, sworls, curled-cloud-shapes—darkening towards the top—a wonderful color. One is aware of motion, but (being shaky, and looking through shaky binoculars) I don't actually see the carven-blue-sworl-shapes move. Like the shadow on a sundial. It is *enormous*. Forty-five miles away. It is so much bigger than the mountain itself. It is silent, from this distance. Enormous, silent. It looks not like anything earthy, from the earth, but it does not look like anything atmospheric, a natural cloud, either. The blue of it is stormcloud blue but the shapes are far more delicate, complex, and immense than stormcloud shapes, and it has this solid look; a weightiness, like the capital of some unimaginable column—which in a way indeed it is, the pillar of fire being underground.

At four in the afternoon a reporter said cautiously, "Earthquakes are being felt in the metropolitan area," to which I added, with feeling, "I'll say they are!" I had decided not to panic unless the cats did. Animals are supposed to know about earthquakes, aren't they? I don't know what our cats know; they lay asleep in various restful and decorative poses on the swaying floor and the jiggling bed, and paid no attention to anything except dinner time. I was not allowed to panic.

At four-thirty a meteorologist, explaining the height of that massive, storm-blue pillar of cloud, said charmingly, "You must understand that the mountain is very warm. Warm enough to lift the air over it to 75,000 feet."

And a reporter: "Heavy mud flow on Shoestring Glacier, with continuous lightning." I tried to imagine that scene. I went to the television, and there it was. The radio and television coverage, right through, was splendid. One forgets the joyful courage of reporters and cameramen when there is something worth reporting, a real Watergate, a real volcano.

On the 19th, I wrote down from the radio, "A helicopter picked the logger up while he was sitting on a log surrounded by a mud flow." This rescue was filmed and shown on television: the tiny figure crouching hopeless in the huge abomination of ash and mud. I don't know if this man was one of the loggers who later died in the Emanuel Hospital burn center, or if he survived. They were already beginning to talk about the "killer eruption," as if the mountain had murdered with intent. Taking it personally

. . . Of course she killed. Or did they kill themselves? Old Harry who wouldn't leave his lodge and his whiskey and his eighteen cats at Spirit Lake, and quite right too, at eighty-three; and the young cameraman and the young geologist, both up there on the north side on the job of their lives; and the loggers who went back to work because logging was their living; and the tourists who thought a volcano is like Channel Six, if you don't like the show you turn it off, and took their RVs and their kids up past the roadblocks and the reasonable warnings and the weary county sheriffs sick of arguing: they were all there to keep the appointment. Who made the appointment?

A firefighter pilot that day said to the radio interviewer, "We do what the mountain says. It's not ready for us to go in."

On the 21st I wrote:

Last night a long, strange, glowing twilight; but no ash has yet fallen west of the mountain. Today, fine, gray, mild, dense Oregon rain. Yesterday afternoon we could see her vaguely through the glasses. Looking appallingly lessened—short, flat—That is painful. She was so beautiful. She hurled her beauty in dust clear to the Atlantic shore, she made sunsets and sunrises of it, she gave it to the Western wind. I hope she erupts magma and begins to build herself again. But I guess she is still unbuilding. The Pres. of the U.S. came today to see her. I wonder if he thinks he is on her level. Of course he could destroy much more than she has destroyed if he took a mind to.

On June 4th I wrote:

Could see her through the glasses for the first time in two weeks or so. It's been dreary white weather with a couple of hours sun in the afternoons.—Not the new summit, yet; that's always in the roil of cloud/plume. But both her long lovely flanks. A good deal of new snow has fallen on her (while we had rain), and her SW face is white, black, and gray, much seamed, in unfamiliar patterns.

"As changeless as the hills—"

Part of the glory of it is being included in an event on the geologic scale. Being enlarged. "I shall lift up mine eyes unto the hills," yes: "whence cometh my help."

In all the Indian legends dug out by newspaper writers for the occasion, the mountain is female. Told in the Dick-and-Jane style considered appropriate for popular reportage of Indian myth, with all the syllables hyphenated, the stories seem even more naive and trivial than myths out of context generally do. But the theme of the mountain as woman—first ugly, then beautiful, but always a woman—is consistent. The mapmaking whites of course named the peak after a man, an Englishman who took his title, Baron St. Helens, from a town in the North Country: but the name is obstinately feminine. The Baron is forgotten, Helen remains. The whites who lived on and near the mountain called it The Lady. Called her The Lady. It seems impossible not to take her personally. In twenty years of living through a window from her I guess I have never really thought of her as "it."

She made weather, like all single peaks. She put on hats of cloud, and took them off again, and tried a different shape, and sent them all skimming off across the sky. She wore veils: around the neck, across the breast: white, silver, silver-gray, gray-blue. Her taste was impeccable. She knew the weathers that became her, and how to wear the snow.

Dr. William Hamilton of Portland State University wrote a lovely piece for the college paper about "volcano anxiety," suggesting that the silver cone of St. Helens had been in human eyes a breast, and saying:

> St. Helens' real damage to us is not . . . that we have witnessed a denial of the trustworthiness of God (such denials are our familiar friends). It is the perfection of the mother that has been spoiled, for part of her breast has been removed. Our metaphor has had a mastectomy.
>
> At some deep level, the eruption of Mt. St. Helens has become a new metaphor for the very opposite of stability—for that greatest of twentieth-century fears—cancer. Our uneasiness may well rest on more elusive levels than dirty windshields.

This comes far closer to home than anything else I've read about the "meaning" of the eruption, and yet for me it doesn't work. Maybe it would work better for men. The trouble is, I never saw St. Helens as a breast. Some mountains, yes: Twin Peaks in San Francisco, of course, and other round, sweet California hills—breasts, bellies, eggs, anything maternal, bounteous, yielding. But St. Helens in my eyes was never part of a woman; she is a woman. And not a mother but a sister.

These emotional perceptions and responses sound quite foolish when written out in rational prose, but the fact is that, to me, the eruption was all mixed up with the women's movement. It may be silly but there it is; along the same lines, do you know any woman who wasn't rooting for Genuine Risk to take the Triple Crown? Part of my satisfaction and exultation at each eruption was unmistakably feminist solidarity. You men think you're the only ones can make a really nasty mess? You think you got all the firepower, and God's on your side? You think you run things? Watch this, gents. Watch the Lady act like a woman.

For that's what she did. The well-behaved, quiet, pretty, serene, domestic creature peacably yielding herself to the uses of man all of sudden said NO. And she spat dirt and smoke and steam. She blackened half her face, in those first March days, like an angry brat. She fouled herself like a mad old harridan. She swore and belched and farted, threatened and shook and swelled, and then she spoke. They heard her voice two hundred miles away. Here I go, she said. I'm doing my thing now. Old Nobodaddy you better JUMP!

Her thing turns out to be more like childbirth than anything else, to my way of thinking. But not on our scale, not in our terms. Why should she speak in our terms or stoop to our scale? Why should she bear any birth that we can recognize? To us it is cataclysm and destruction and deformity. To her—well, for the language for it one must go to the scientists or to the poets. To the geologists. St. Helens is doing exactly what she "ought" to do—playing her part in the great pattern of events perceived by that noble discipline. Geology provides the only time-scale large enough to include the behavior of a volcano without deforming it. Geology, or poetry, which can see a mountain and a cloud as, after all, very similar phenomena. Shelley's cloud can speak for St. Helens:

> I silently laugh
> At my own cenotaph . . .
> And arise, and unbuild it again.

So many mornings waking I have seen her from the window before any other thing: dark against red daybreak, silvery in summer light, faint above river-valley fog. So many times I have watched her at evening, the faintest outline in mist, immense, remote, serene: the center, the central stone. A self across the air, a sister self, a stone. "The stone is at the center,"

I wrote in a poem about her years ago. But the poem is impertinent. All I can say is impertinent.

When I was writing the first draft of this essay in California, on July 23, she erupted again, sending her plume to 60,000 feet. Yesterday, August 7, as I was typing the words "the 'meaning' of the eruption," I checked out the study window and there it was, the towering blue cloud against the quiet northern sky—the fifth major eruption. How long may her labor be? A year, ten years, ten thousand? We cannot predict what she may or might or will do, now, or next, or for the rest of our lives, or ever. A threat: a terror: a fulfillment. This is what serenity is built on. This unmakes the metaphors. This is beyond us, and we must take it personally. This is the ground we walk on.

1980

CONTRIBUTORS

Marcia Aldrich has published essays in *The North American Review* and *Northwest Review*.

Maya Angelou is perhaps best known for her *I Know Why the Caged Bird Sings* (1970), the first work in her series of autobiographical books. Other volumes in the series include *Gather Together in My Name* (1974), *The Heart of a Woman* (1981), and *All God's Children Need Traveling Shoes* (1986). Her collections of poetry include *And Still I Rise* (1978) and *I Shall Not Be Moved* (1990). Her account of her marriage forms a chapter in *Singin' and Swingin' and Gettin' Merry Like Christmas* (1976).

Gwendolyn Brooks, one of the foremost American poets of the twentieth century, was born in Topeka, Kansas, and grew up in Chicago. She has taught poetry at numerous colleges and universities. Her honors include a Guggenheim Fellowship (1946), the Pulitzer Prize for Poetry in 1950 for her *Annie Allen* (1949), and being named Poet Laureate of Illinois in 1968. Brooks was the first African American woman to serve as Poetry Consultant to the Library of Congress (1985–86). Among her volumes of poetry are *A Street in Bronzeville* (1945), *Bronzeville Boys and Girls* (1956), *In the Mecca* (1968), and *Family Pictures* (1970). Brooks records her thoughts on living as an African American in America in *Aloneness (1971)*, *Report from Part One: An Autobiography* (1972), *Primer for Blacks* (1980), and *To Disembark* (1981).

Sandra Cisneros is a prose and poetry writer and teacher whose published works include *The House on Mango Street* (1988), a book of linked stories, and the poetry collections *My Wicked Wicked Ways* (1987) and *Loose Woman* (1994). She has twice received fellowships from the National Endowment for the Humanities, for poetry in 1982 and prose in 1988. Her recent work of fiction is *Woman Hollering Creek, and Other Stories* (1991).

Carolyn Coman has run a bookbinding business in Massachusetts. Her essay first appeared in *Ms.* magazine (May, 1983).

Linda Katherine Cutting, a concert pianist, has recently completed *In Sanctuary*, a novel.

Joan Didion grew up in Sacramento, California, and attended the University of California at Berkeley. She served as an associate feature editor at *Vogue* for seven years and has contributed to numerous periodicals, including the *Saturday Evening Post*, *New York Review of Books*, and *National Review*. Her essays appear in her collections *Slouching Towards Bethlehem* (1968), *The White Album* (1979), and *After Henry* (1992). Didion's novels include *Run River* (1963), *Play It as It Lays* (1970), which was nominated for the 1970 National Book Award, *A Book of Common Prayer* (1977), and *Democracy* (1984).

Annie Dillard was awarded the Pulitzer Prize in nonfiction in 1975 for *Pilgrim at Tinker Creek*. Her other books include *An American Childhood* (1987), *The Writing Life* (1989), and *Holy the Firm* (1977). Her work has appeared in the *Atlantic*, *Harper's*, the *New York Times Magazine*, the *Yale Review*, *American Heritage*, and many anthologies. She has received grants from the Guggenheim Foundation and the National Endowment for the Arts and many other prestigious awards. Her first novel, *The Living*, was published in 1992.

Kathy Dobie's essays have appeared in *Mother Jones* and *Vogue*.

Susan Faludi is the author of *Backlash: The Undeclared War Against American Women* (1991), a remarkable study of women, feminism, and history in the United States. A Pulitzer Prize-winning journalist, Faludi has contributed essays to numerous periodicals, including the *San Jose Mercury News* Sunday Magazine, *West*, *Ms.*, and the *Wall Street Journal*.

Anne Taylor Fleming has written essays for *Glamour*, *New York Times Magazine*, *Vogue*, and *Woman's Day*. Her most recent book is *Motherhood Deferred* (1994).

Betty Friedan's 1963 book, *The Feminine Mystique*, still stirs provocative debate today for its role in defining the early stages of the Women's Movement in the

United States. She remains an important commentator on feminism and the status of women. She has recently written *The Fountain of Age* (1993). Friedan is a visiting professor at the University of Southern California.

Felicita Garcia's essay first appeared in *Powers of Desire* (1983).

Mary Gordon was born in Far Rockaway, New York, and was educated at Barnard College and Syracuse University's Writing Program. Her first novel, *Final Payments* (1978), received wide critical acclaim and established her as a leading voice in contemporary American fiction. Her later works include her novels, *The Company of Women* (1980) and *Men and Angels* (1985), and two collections of fiction, *Temporary Shelter* (1975) and *The Rest of Life: Three Novellas* (1993). Gordon's stories have also appeared in numerous periodicals, including *Antæus*, the *Atlantic Monthly*, *Ms.*, *Mademoiselle*, and *Southern Review*.

Linda Hogan, a descendent of the Chickasaw Native Americans, was educated at the University of Colorado. Her 1985 collection of poetry, *Seeing Through the Sun*, received the American Book Award from the Before Columbus Foundation. She has also received awards from the Guggenheim Foundation and the National Endowment for the Arts. Hogan's other books include *Calling Myself Home* (1979), *I Love You* (1981), and *Mean Spirit* (1990). Hogan's writings appear in many anthologies of Native American writing, including *The Remembered Earth: Anthology of Contemporary Native American Literature* (1978), *Spiderwoman's Granddaughters* (1989), and *Earth Power Coming: Short Fiction in Native American Literature* (1983). Her recent collection of poetry, *Book of Medicines: Poems*, was published in 1993. She currently teaches for the University of Minnesota's American Studies Program in Idledale, Colorado, and in the Creative Writing Program at the University of Colorado.

bell hooks writes primarily on gender and race relations in the United States. Her three most recent books are *Talking Back: Thinking Feminist, Thinking Black* (1989), *Yearning: Race, Gender, and Cultural Politics* (1990), and *Breaking Bread: Insurgent Black Intellectual Life* (1991).

LeAnne Howe, a Choctaw Native American, has worked as a print journalist for the *Dallas Morning News* and *USA Today*. Her books include *Coyote Papers* (1985) and *A Stand Up Reader* (1987). Her play, *Big PowWow* (written with Roxy Gordon), was performed in Fort Worth, Texas.

Ursula K. Le Guin writes both poetry and prose, and in several modes or genres, including realistic fiction, science fiction, fantasy, young children's books, books for young adults, screenplays, essays, verbal texts for musicians, and voicetexts for performance or recording. She has won numerous awards, including five Hugos,

four Nebulas, the National Book Award, the Harold D. Vurcell Memorial Award
from the American Academy and Institute of Arts and Letters, and the Pushcart
Prize. Her Earthsea Trilogy includes the novels *A Wizard of Earthsea* (1968), *The
Tombs of Atuan* (1971), and *The Farthest Shore* (1972). Other books include *The
Dispossessed: An Ambiguous Utopia* (1974), which won the Nebula, Hugo, and
Jupiter awards, *The Beginning Place* (1980), *Always Coming Home* (1985), *Buffalo
Gals and Other Animal Presences* (1987), *Dancing at the Edge of the World:
Thoughts on Words, Women, Places* (1989), and *Searoad: The Chronicles of Klat-
sand* (1991).

Mary McCarthy, who died in 1989, was born in Seattle and orphaned during her
early childhood. After graduating from Vassar College in 1933, she was book reviewer for the *Nation* and *New Republic,* and later drama reviewer for *Partisan
Review.* McCarthy chronicled both her childhood and adult life in her many autobiographical writings, including *Memories of a Catholic Girlhood* (1957), *How
I Grew* (1987), and *Intellectual Memoirs: New York, 1936–1938* (1992). Recipient
of two Guggenheim Fellowships (1949 and 1959) and the National Medal for Literature in 1984, McCarthy contributed to many distinguished periodicals and au-
thored numerous volumes of essays, social commentary, and fiction. *Vietnam*
(1967) and *The Writing on the Wall, and Other Literary Essays* (1978) record her
thoughts on American politics and society. Short story collections include *Cast a
Cold Eye* (1952) and *The Hounds of Summer and Other Stories* (1981). Among
McCarthy's novels are *The Company She Keeps* (1942), *The Oasis* (1949), *The
Groves of Academe* (1952), *Winter Visitors* (1970), and *Birds of America* (1971).

Nancy Mairs writes on sex, physical disability, and the status of women as depicted
in literature and in contemporary society. Her book-length works include *Carnal
Acts* (1990), *Ordinary Time* (1993), *Plaintext* (1986), *Voice Lessons* (1994), and
Remembering the Bone House (1995).

Margaret Mead (1901–1978) was an anthropologist, essayist, autobiographer, and
a nonfiction writer. Her field-work experience in the South Pacific formed the basis of her widely read books: *Coming of Age in Samoa* (1928), *Growing Up in New
Guinea* (1930), and *Sex and Temperament in Three Primitive Societies* (1935). Her
numerous works of cultural criticism include *Aspects of the Present* (1980) and
Culture and Commitment: A Study of the Generation Gap (1970).

Nancy K. Miller's writing stems primarily from her scholarly work in French literature. She is editor of *The Poetics of Gender* (1986) and co-editor of *Displace-
ments: Women, Tradition, Literatures in French* (1991). She has also written *Subject to Change: Reading Feminist Writing* (1988) and the book from which her
essay here is taken, *Getting Personal: Feminist Occasions and Other Autobiographical Acts* (1991).

Barbara Mor is co-author of *The Great Cosmic Mother: Rediscovering the Religion of the Earth* (1987). Mor has also written a volume of poetry, *Winter Ditch and Other Poems* (1982).

Cherríe Moraga has co-edited *Cuentos: Stories by Latinas* (1983) and *This Bridge Called My Back* (1981), both published by Women of Color Press. Her recent work includes a collection of prose and poetry titled *The Last Generation*, published in 1993 by South End Press.

Toni Morrison is the 1993 recipient of the Nobel Prize for Literature for her 1987 novel *Beloved*. Her most recent novel, *Jazz* (1992), has also received critical acclaim. Morrison writes extensively on social and political issues as well. She has recently written *Race-ing Justice, En-gendering Power: Essays on Anita Hill, Clarence Thomas, and the Construction of Social Reality* (1992).

Shana Penn is a founding member and executive director of the Network of East-West Women (NEWW). At present, she is completing a book about the role of women in opposition movements in Central Europe, entitled *Talking Revolutions: Women, Communism, and Opposition in Poland, Hungary, and the Czech and Slovak Republics* (Ballantine Books). Ms. Penn currently serves as a research fellow at the Center for International Environmental Law—U.S. (CIEL) in Washington, D.C.

Letty Cottin Pogrebin's articles on feminism, Jewish-American experience, friendship, and child-rearing have appeared in many periodicals, including *Ms.* and the *New York Times Magazine*. Her books include *Getting Yours: How to Make the System Work for the Working Woman* (1975), *Growing Up Free: Raising Your Child in the 80's* (1980), *Antisemitism in the Women's Movement* (1982), *Family Politics: Love and Power on an Intimate Frontier* (1983), and *Deborah, Golda, and Me: Being Female and Jewish in America* (1991).

Adrienne Rich has published numerous volumes of poetry and essays and has contributed to many periodicals. Her books of verse include *The Fact of a Doorframe* (1984), *Time's Power: Poems 1985–1988* (1989), and *An Atlas of the Difficult World* (1991). Her essays on women's experience appear in *Of Woman Born: Motherhood as Experience and Institution* (1986), *On Lies, Secrets, and Silence: Selected Prose, 1966–1978* (1979), and *Blood, Bread, and Poetry: Selected Prose, 1979–1985* (1986). Rich currently teaches at Stanford University.

May Sarton's writings range from novels and autobiographical memoirs to children's books and scripts. Collections of Sarton's poetry include *Encounter in April* (1937), *A Durable Fire* (1972), *Halfway to Silence* (1980), and *Letters from Maine*

(1984). Sarton's nonfictional reflections on her life and work include *I Knew a Phoenix: Sketches for an Autobiography* (1959), *Plant Dreaming Deep* (1968), *Journal of a Solitude* (1973), and *At Seventy* (1984).

Dani Shapiro has published two works of fiction: *Playing with Fire* (1989) and *Fugitive Blue* (1993). Her articles have appeared in *Glamour, New Woman,* and *New York Times Magazine.*

Jane Shapiro has contributed to the *Village Voice.* Her novel, *After Moondog,* was published in 1992.

Jane Slaughter is a staff writer for *Labor Notes* and has written and co-authored several books on aspects of business and labor negotiations, including *Concessions, and How to Beat Them* (1983) and *Choosing Sides: Unions and the Team Concept* (1988).

Gloria Steinem's work as a feminist is well-known and her influence widespread. She founded *Ms.* magazine and continues to speak and write on feminism and issues concerning women. A collection of her essays, *Outrageous Acts and Everyday Rebellions,* was published in 1983. Her biography of Marilyn Monroe, *Marilyn: Norma Jean* (1986), examines the exploitation of women's sexuality. She has recently published *Revolution from Within: A Book of Self-Esteem* (1992).

Amy Tan was born in Oakland, California, in 1952. She is a contributor to the *Atlantic Monthly, Grand Street, Lear's, McCall's,* and the *Threepenny Review,* among other periodicals. Her novel *The Joy Luck Club* (1989), which was translated into sixteen languages and made into a film in 1993, won the Commonwealth Club Gold Award for Best Fiction and the Bay Area Book Reviewers Award for Best Fiction, and was nominated for the National Book Critics Circle Award. Tan's *The Moon Lady* (1992) won the American Library Association's award for best book for young adults. Her other novels are *The Kitchen God's Wife* (1991) and *The Chinese Siamese Cat* (1994).

Alice Walker, a prolific writer of fiction, poetry, and social commentary, resides in the San Francisco Bay area. Among her best known works are the novels *Meridian* (1976) and *The Color Purple* (1982), the latter of which earned awards both as a novel, including the Pulitzer Prize, and as a film. Her most recent novel is *Possessing the Secret of Joy* (1992).

Patricia J. Williams is Professor of Law at Columbia University. Her book, *The Alchemy of Race and Rights* (1991), concerns the relationships between African Americans, civil rights, feminist criticism, and teaching the law. Williams is a regular contributor to *Ms.* and the *Village Voice.*

Terry Tempest Williams is the author of *Pieces of White Shell: A Journey to Navajoland* (1984), which received the 1984 Southwest Book Award, *The Secret Language of Snow* (1984), *Between Cattails* (1985), *Coyote's Canyon* (1990), *Refuge: An Unnatural History of Family and Place* (1991), and *An Unspoken Hunger: Stories from the Field* (1994). She has also written "Earthly Messengers," a collection of poems. Her prose has appeared in the *New Yorker, Outside Magazine, Audubon, North American Review, Northern Lights,* and other journals. Williams was one of ten recipients of a 1993 Lannan Literary Award. She is currently Naturalist-in-Residence at the Utah Museum of Natural History in Salt Lake City.

CREDITS

Grateful acknowledgment is made to the following for permission to reprint previously published material:

Marcia Aldrich: "Hair" by Marcia Aldrich. Originally published in *Northwest Review*. Copyright © 1992 by Marcia Aldrich. Reprinted by permission of the author.

Beacon Press: "An American in New York" by LeAnne Howe. From *Spiderwoman's Granddaughters* by Paula Gunn Allen. Copyright © 1986 by Paula Gunn Allen. Reprinted by permission of Beacon Press.

Beacon Press and Nancy Mairs: "Here: Grace" by Nancy Mairs. From *Ordinary Time* by Nancy Mairs. Copyright © 1993 by Nancy Mairs. Reprinted by permission of Beacon Press and Nancy Mairs.

Broadside Press and Gwendolyn Brooks: "Dreams of a Black Christmas" by Gwendolyn Brooks. From *Report from Part One: An Autobiography*. Copyright © 1972 by Gwendolyn Brooks Blakely. Reprinted by permission of Broadside Press and the author.

The Conde Nast Publications, Inc.: "Only Daughter" by Sandra Cisneros. Copyright © 1990 by The Conde Nast Publications, Inc. Reprinted by the courtesy of *Glamour*.

Curtis Brown, Ltd.: "Thoughts on Becoming a Grandmother" by Betty Friedan. Originally appearing in *Ladies' Home Journal*. Copyright © 1983 by Betty Friedan. Reprinted by permission of Curtis Brown, Ltd.

Farrar, Straus & Giroux, Inc., and Joan Didion: "On Going Home" from *Slouch-*

ing Towards Bethlehem by Joan Didion. Copyright © 1968 by Joan Didion. Reprinted by permission of Farrar, Straus & Giroux, Inc., and the author.

Anne Taylor Fleming: "Sperm in a Jar" by Anne Taylor Fleming. Originally published in the *New York Times Magazine*. Copyright © 1994 by Anne Taylor Fleming. Reprinted by permission of the author.

Mary Gordon: "A Moral Choice" by Mary Gordon. Originally appearing in *The Atlantic Monthly*. Copyright © 1990 by Mary Gordon. Reprinted by permission of Mary Gordon.

Harcourt Brace & Company and David Higham Associates, Ltd.: "Brothers and Sisters" from *In Search of Our Mothers' Gardens: Womanist Prose*. Copyright © 1975 by Alice Walker. Published by Harcourt Brace in the U.S. and The Women's Press in the British Empire. Reprinted by permission of Harcourt Brace & Company and David Higham Associates, Ltd., as agents for the author.

Harcourt Brace & Company and A. M. Heath: "Names" from *Memories of a Catholic Girlhood*. Copyright © 1951 and renewed 1979 by Mary McCarthy. Reprinted by permission of Harcourt Brace & Company and A. M. Heath, as agents for the estate of Mary McCarthy.

Harper's Magazine: "A Rape"—Anonymous. Copyright © 1986 by *Harper's Magazine*. All rights reserved. Reprinted from the February issue by special permission.

Linda Hogan: "Walking" and "Waking Up the Rake" by Linda Hogan. Reprinted from *Parabola, The Magazine of Myth and Tradition*, vol. 15.2 (Summer, 1990) and vol. 13.2 (Summer, 1988). Copyright © 1988 and 1990 by Linda Hogan. Reprinted by permission of the author.

bell hooks: "Writing from the Darkness" by bell hooks. Originally appearing in *TriQuarterly* 75 (Spring/Summer 1989): 71–77, a publication of Northwestern University. Copyright © 1989 by bell hooks. Reprinted by permission of the author.

International Creative Management, Inc.: "A Knowing So Deep" by Toni Morrison. Copyright © 1985 by Toni Morrison. Reprinted by permission of International Creative Management, Inc.

Virginia Kidd and Ursula K. Le Guin: "A Very Warm Mountain" by Ursula K. Le Guin. Copyright © 1980 by Ursula K. Le Guin. Originally appearing in *Parabola*. Reprinted by permission of the author and the author's agent, Virginia Kidd.

Kitchen Table: Women of Color Press and Cherríe Moraga: "La Güera" by Cherríe Moraga from *This Bridge Called My Back: Writings by Radical Women of Color*. Copyright © 1983 by Cherríe Moraga and Gloria Anzaldua. Used with permission of the author and Kitchen Table: Women of Color Press, P.O. Box 908, Latham, NY 12110.

Nancy K. Miller: "My Father's Penis" from *Getting Personal*. Copyright © 1991 by Nancy K. Miller. Reprinted by permission of the author.

Monthly Review Foundation: "I Just Came Out Pregnant" by Felicita Garcia. Originally published in *Powers of Desire*. Copyright © 1983 by Snitow, Stansell, and Thompson. Reprinted by permission of Monthly Review Foundation.

William Morrow and Company, Inc.: "On Having a Baby" from *Blackberry Winter* by Margaret Mead. Copyright © 1972 by Margaret Mead. Reprinted by permission of William Morrow and Company, Inc.

Ms.: "Amazing Rage" by Barbara Mor. Reprinted by permission of *Ms*. Copyright © 1990. "Trying (and Trying and Trying) to Get Pregnant" by Carolyn Coman. Reprinted by permission of *Ms*. Copyright © 1983. "Standard Operating Procedure" by Jane Shapiro. Reprinted by permission of *Ms*. Copyright © 1975.

New York Times Company: "Consequences" by Letty Cottin Pogrebin. Copyright © 1991 by the New York Times Company. Reprinted by permission. "Hers: Balancing Act" by Dani Shapiro. Copyright © 1994 by the New York Times Company. Reprinted by permission.

New York Times Company and Sally R. Brady: "Give and Take" by Linda Katherine Cutting. Copyright © 1993 by the New York Times Company and Linda Katherine Cutting. Reprinted by permission of the New York Times Company and Sally R. Brady, Brady Literary Management, as agent for the author.

New York Times Company, Susan Faludi, and the Sandra Dijkstra Literary Agency: "Speak for Yourself" by Susan Faludi, as first appeared in *The New York Times Magazine*. Copyright © 1992 by Susan Faludi. Reprinted by permission of the author, the Sandra Dijkstra Literary Agency, and the New York Times Company.

W. W. Norton & Company, Inc., and A. M. Heath, Ltd.: "May 3rd" by May Sarton. Reprinted from *At Seventy: A Journal* by May Sarton. Copyright © 1984 by May Sarton. Reprinted by permission of W. W. Norton & Company, Inc., and A. M. Heath, Ltd., as agents for the author.

W. W. Norton & Company, Inc., and Virago Press: "Split at the Root: An Essay on Jewish Identity" is reprinted from *Blood, Bread, and Poetry, Selected Prose 1979–1985* by Adrienne Rich. Copyright © 1986 by Adrienne Rich. Reprinted by permission of W. W. Norton & Company, Inc., and Virago Press.

Pacific News Service: "A Friendship Forged in Concrete" by Kathy Dobie. Copyright © 1991 by Pacific News Service. Reprinted by permission of Pacific News Service.

The Progressive: "A Beaut of a Shiner" by Jane Slaughter. Copyright © 1987 by Jane Slaughter. Reprinted by permission from *The Progressive*, 409 East Main Street, Madison, WI 53703.

Random House, Inc.: "The Deterioration of My Marriage" by Maya Angelou from *Singin' and Swingin' and Gettin' Merry Like Christmas* by Maya Angelou. Copyright © 1976 by Maya Angelou. Reprinted by permission of Random House, Inc.

Gibbs Smith Publishing: "The Bowl" and "A Woman's Dance" by Terry Tempest Williams. Reprinted from *Coyote's Canyon*, by Terry Tempest Williams. Copyright © 1989 by Gibbs Smith Publishing, Layton, UT. Reprinted by permission of Gibbs Smith Publishing.

Gloria Steinem: "Ruth's Song" by Gloria Steinem. First appearing in *Ms.* Copyright © 1983 by Gloria Steinem. Reprinted by permission of the author.

Russell & Volkening: "Sight into Insight" by Annie Dillard. Copyright © 1974 by Annie Dillard. Reprinted by permission of Russell & Volkening, as agents for the author.

Amy Tan: "Mother Tongue" by Amy Tan. Copyright © 1989 by Amy Tan. Reprinted by permission of the author.

Tikkun: "Death of Popeye" by Shana Penn. Copyright © 1989 by Tikkun. Reprinted by permission of *Tikkun*, a bimonthly Jewish critique of politics, culture, and society, based in Oakland, CA.

University of Chicago Press: Excerpts from "On Being the Object of Property" by Patricia J. Williams. Originally appearing in *Signs*, a publication of the University of Chicago Press. Copyright © 1988. Reprinted by permission.

NATIONAL UNIVERSITY
LIBRARY   SACRAMENTO